The Revolt of 1857
Saugor and Nerbudda Territories

The Revolt of 1857

Saugor and Nerbudda Territories

DR. P.S. Mukharya

Foreword

DR. J.P. MISHRA

SHARADA

Sharada Publishing House
Delhi-110 035
2001

First Published : 2001

ISBN : 81-85616-02-7

Published under the Publication Grant of UGC provided by Rani Durgawati Vishwavidyalaya, Jabalpur

Published by :
B.L. Bansal
SHARADA PUBLISHING HOUSE
(Publishers on India's Past & Present)
40, Anand Nagar, Inderlok,
Delhi - 110035. Tel. : 5117390

Laser Typesetting by :
Sri Balaji Computers
4615/13, Tri Nagar, Delhi-35
Ph. : 7108270

Printed at :
Santosh Offset
Delhi-110 035

To

The loving memories of my parents,

Late Shri Durga Prasad Mukharya

and

Late Smt. Parvati Devi Mukharya

Foreword

The concept of rebellion underwent a phenomenal transformation after our independence although it had taken quite sometime for the students of history to mark the difference between 'mutiny' and 'revolt'. In the growing literature on the Revolt of 1857, one finds no mention of the contribution of obscure topographical areas which were the intense battle-areas of organised revolts against the British rule. The revolt in the Saugor and Nerbudda territories in 1857 was not a localised sporadic incident but was an event which depicted wider awakening of a unified determination and valour to oust the foreign rule from our country.

This is an admirable attempt by the author of this book Dr. P.S. Mukharya to document this epic struggle with an unbiased approach. Unfortunately this area had been ignored by the historians and consequently, this area of research had been shrouded in mystery. The Revolt in the Saugor and Nerbudda territories had all the similarities and pecularities that characterised the 'Revolt of 1857' elsewhere. It underwent the phases of sepoy revolt, feudal resistance, popular outbreaks and sporadic attacks from outside the state. The activities of the rebels had instilled in the people a sense of pride and kindled the desire of freedom amongst the nationalists.

The author has vividly drawn his facts from the available variety of archival material and after careful shifting of evidences has provided insight in the neglected segment of this aspect of study. This is an account of rebellious activities of rebels under the leadership of the discontented and dispossessed feudal chiefs who faced the British with courage and determination. The causes of discontent have been analysed giving practical illustrations. The suppression of the revolt has been described in great detail. The scholar has also assessed the effects of the widespread movement.

It is indeed a matter of pride and pleasure that a comprehensive history of the Revolt of 1857 in the Saugor and Nerbudda territories is being published. This is a story of absorbing interest, well-documented and authoritative research. This documentation will be as much of abiding interest to the common reader as it will be a valuable addition to the growing literature on regional and micro-studies in history.

Since the subject has been dealt with almost entirely on the basis of primary and unpublished sources, the authenticity of the whole story and the conclusions drawn by the scholar from this study may be taken to be worthy of credence as they are free from bias.

JABALPUR :
26 January, 2000

JAI PRAKASH MISHRA
Professor and Head,
Department of Postgraduate Studies
& Research in History,
Rani Durgavati Vishwavidyalaya,
Jabalpur (M.P.)

Preface

The revolt of 1857 in the Saugor and Nerbudda Territories against the British rule was but a part of the countrywide movement to destroy the British dominion in India. The historians have paid scant attention to the revolt of 1857 in these territories. We find only the scattered references of it in the History books and, therefore, its picture does not emerge in entirety. An important and vital gap has thus been created in the nationalist movement of India in general and these territories in particular. The object of this research-project is to fill this gap. I am grateful to the Indian Council of Historical Research, New Delhi, for providing me this opportunity by awarding the Senior Research Fellowship after my retirement.

These territories played an important role in the revolt of 1857. The disaffection among the military and civil classes in the North-Western Provinces found its way across the Yamuna to Bundelkhand and these territories also. Like other parts of the Northern India, these territories were one of the major theatres of the rebellious activities. They were swept by the waves of the revolt of 1857 only a month after it had flooded the Meerut-Delhi area in May 1857. First of all, it had touched the Sagar district in June and then it spread to the other parts and the disturbances became general.

The important role played by these territories can be gleaned by these references, some contemporary and some modern. In the "Revolt in Central India, 1857-59"[1] compiled in the Intelligence Branch, Army Head Quarters, India in 1908, it was pointed out[1] that "proximity of the Saugor and Nerbudda districts to other areas of disturbances in 1857 naturally rendered them liable to infection with the spirit of revolt that was spreading from northern India." According to G.B.Malleson[2] "in four northern provinces - Oudh, Rohilkhand, Bundelkhand and the Saugar and Narbada the great bulk of the people rose against the British rule." In the opinion[3] of Dr. R.C. Majumdar "the mutiny of the sepoys outside Delhi, North-Western Provinces and Awadh did not lead to the revolt of the civil people on a large scale, except in a small part of Bihar, particularly the Shahabad district and the Santhal Parganas, Bundelkhand and the Saugar and Narmada districts and the eastern fringe of Punjab. These formed an outer circle to Awadh and Rohilkhand which constituted the central zone of the civil rebellion." In the same manner Dr. Har Prasad Chattopadhyay has expressed[4] that "in almost the whole of the North-Western Provinces, in Bundelkhand, Oudh, the Saugor and Nerbudda Territories, in West Bihar and Chhota Nagpur, the mutiny wore the appearance of a popular revolt. Those areas had been scenes of risings of the sepoys and people alike."

These territories were acquired by the East India Company in 1818 from the Marathas and comprised of the districts of Sagar and Damoh obtained from the Peshwa Baji Rao II and the districts of Mandla, Seoni, Betul and the districts of the Narmada valley, namely, Jabalpur, Narsinghpur and Hoshangabad, from Appa Sahib Bhonsla of Nagpur. They were formed what was called the "Saugor and Nerbudda Territories" in 1820 and placed under an Agent to the Governor General posted at Jabalpur. After the suppression of the revolt of 1857, these territories were merged in the Nagpur territory in 1861 to form the Central Provinces. Thus, these territories came into existence in 1820 and had a span of nearly 40 years till merged in 1861 in a newly-created Central Provinces. Another object of this research-project is to delineate the nature and consequences of the British rule in these territories which led to the Bundela rebellion of 1842 and the revolt of 1857 in them.

It may, however, be added that the spelling of persons and places have been modernised in the text but the old spelling of the Saugor and Nerbudda Territories, frequently used by the British officials, has been retained in order to maintain its old identity.

REFERENCES

1. *The Revolt in Central India, 1857-59* : Compiled in the Intelligence Branch, Army Head Quarters, India (1908), p. 33.
2. G.B. Malleson, *History of the Indian Mutiny*, Vol. III (1880), p. 487.
3. R.C. Majumdar, *British Paramouncy and Indian Renaissance*, Vol.IX (1963), p. 548.
4. Har Prasad Chattopadhyay, *The Sepoy Mutiny : A Social Study and Analysis* (1957), p. 189.

Acknowledgements

I take this opportunity of expressing my obligations to those who have helped me in the preparation of this work.

I am grateful to the Indian Council of Historical Research, New Delhi, for the award of a Senior Research Fellowship to me after my retirement to work on this research-project.

I have no words to express my gratitude to Dr. J.P. Mishra, Head of the History Department, Rani Durgavati Vishwavidyalaya, Jabalpur, who was helpful to me from the inception of my research-project. He had provided me all the facilities of research in his department. He also gave me important suggestions in times of need and was always helpful in its successful completion. I thought it befitting that he should write the foreword of my book. It is a matter of great pleasure that he had acceded to my request.

I am thankful to Dr. Raj Kumar, Deputy Director, Indian Council of Historical Research, New Delhi, who was a constant source of inspiration to me during my Senior Research Fellowship.

I am also thankful to the staff of the National Archives of India, New Delhi; the Record Room of the Madhya Pradesh Government, Nagpur and the District Gazetteers Library, Bhopal for their help in the collection of the material of this research-project.

Dr. S.K. Tiwari, Head of the Department of Tribal Studies, Rani Durgavati Vishwavidyalaya, Jabalpur, deserves my grateful thanks for the preparation of the map of the Saugor and Nerbudda Territories in 1857.

I express my heartfelt thanks to Prof. Raj Kumari Pande, Head of the Department of English, Mankunwar Bai Govt.

Arts and Commerce College for Women, Jabalpur, my former colleague, for reading through the manuscript with care and interest to make helpful suggestions in regard to the drafting.

A word of special thanks is due to all the staff members of Balaji Computers for typing this manuscript in time with excellence..

I am very indebted to my University, Rani Durgavati Vishwavidyalaya, Jabalpur for sanctioning its publication-grant of the U.G.C. without which it would not have been published.

A word of special thank is due to my friend, Dr. R.K. Sharma, retired Professor, Department of Ancient Indian History, Culture and Archaeology in the R.D. Vishwavidyalaya, for making valuable suggestions in its publication.

I cannot express in words my thanks to my wife, Asha Mukharya, for silently bearing with me in the preparation and publication of this book.

I am also thankful to Mr. B.L. Bansal, Proprietor of Sharada Publishing House, New Delhi, for the excellent and early publication of my book.

JABALPUR : **P.S. MUKHARYA**

10 October 1999

Contents

Key to Abbreviations

Cons.	...	Original Consultations
Court	...	Court of Directors
C.P.A.R.	...	Central Provinces Administrative Report
C.P.D.G.	...	Central Provinces District Gazetteers
F.P.P.	...	Further Parliamentary Papers relative to the Mutinies in the East Indies presented to both Houses of Parliament by command of Her Majesty in 1857
J.D., B.C.	...	Jubbulpore Division, Bundle Correspondence
M.P.D.G.	...	Madhya Pradesh District Gazetteers
N.E.	...	Major W.C. Erskine : Narrative of Events attending the Outbreak of Disturbances and the Restoration of Authority in the Saugor and Nerbudda Territories in 1857-58
Progs.	...	Proceedings

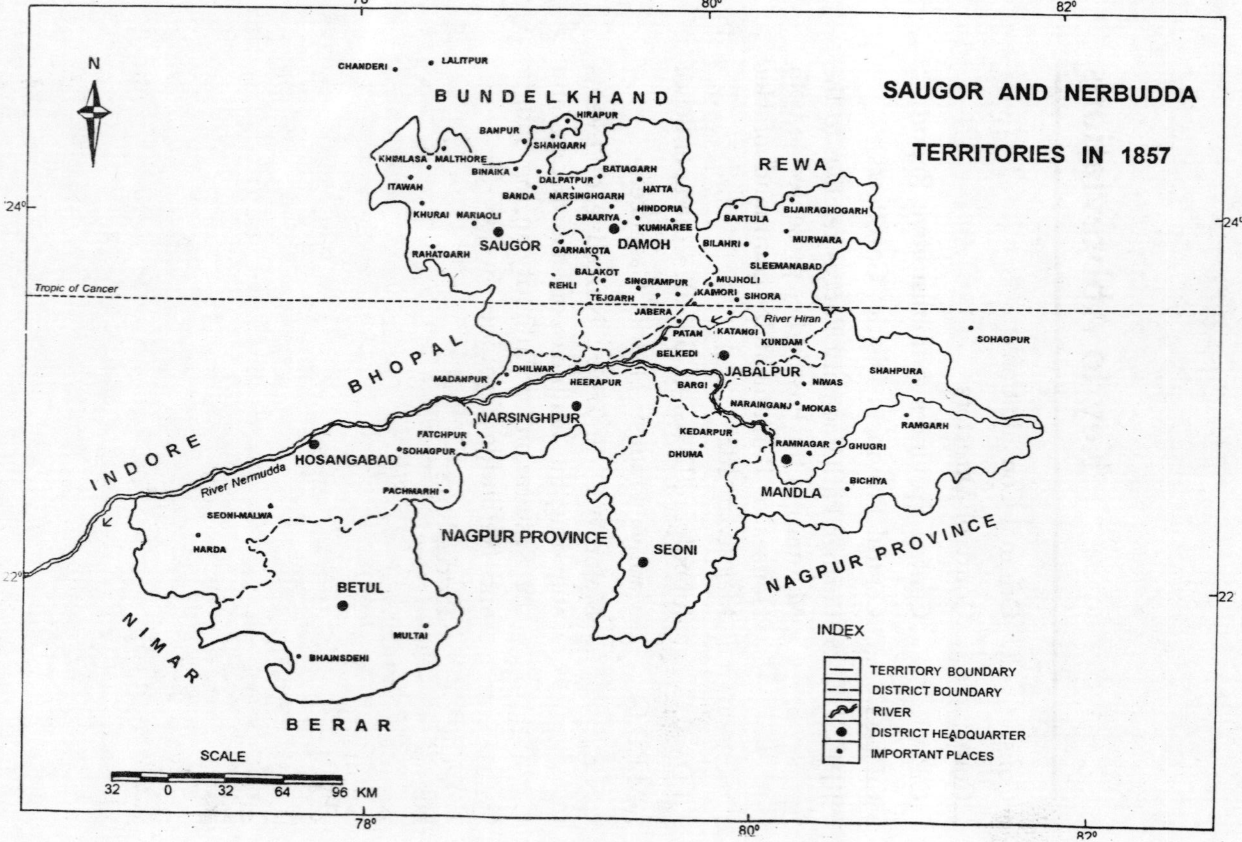

SAUGOR AND NERBUDDA
TERRITORIES IN 1857
N
BUNDELKHAND
REWA
BHOPAL
INDORE
NIMAR
BERAR
NAGPUR PROVINCE
NAGPUR PROVINCE
SAUGOR
DAMOH
JABALPUR
NARSINGHPUR
HOSANGABAD
BETUL
SEONI
MANDLA
CHANDERI
LALITPUR
HIRAPUR
BANPUR
SHAHGARH
KHIMLASA
MALTHORE
BINAIKA
DALPATPUR
BATIAGARH
HATTA
ITAWAH
BANDA
NARSINGHGARH
HINDORIA
KHURAI
NARIAOLI
SIMARIYA
KUMHAREE
RAHATGARH
GARHAKOTA
BALAKOT
REHLI
SINGRAMPUR
TEJGARH
JABERA
KAIMORI
MUJHOLI
SIHORA
BARTULA
BIJAIRAGHOGARH
BILAHRI
MURWARA
SLEEMANABAD
River Hiran
PATAN
KATANGI
KUNDAM
BELKEDI
SOHAGPUR
SHAHPURA
NIWAS
MADANPUR
DHILWAR
HEERAPUR
BARGI
NARAINGANJ
MOKAS
RAMGARH
KEDARPUR
RAMNAGAR
GHUGRI
DHUMA
BICHIYA
FATCHPUR
SOHAGPUR
River Nermudda
PACHMARHI
SEONI-MALWA
HARDA
MULTAI
BHAJNSDEHI
Tropic of Cancer
78°
80°
82°
24°
22°
INDEX
TERRITORY BOUNDARY
DISTRICT BOUNDARY
RIVER
DISTRICT HEADQUARTER
IMPORTANT PLACES
SCALE
32 0 32 64 96 KM

CHAPTER 1

History and Administration of the Saugor and Nerbudda Territories

For the proper evaluation of the revolt of 1857 in the Saugor and Nerbudda Territories, it may be worthwhile to know about the broad outline of its history and administration. We will examine that part of it which is relevant to the subject. Alongwith the British occupation of these territories in 1818, the British administrative system which was developing here will also be examined, the evils of which led to the Bundela rebellion of 1842 and the revolt of 1857.

These territories contained the highest part of the tableland of Central India and had towards its south Hyderabad and Berar dominions; in the north and west were lying the territories of Bhopal, Gwalior, Bundelkhand, Baghelkhand and Rewa.[1] The Narmada Valley, which constitutes the heart of the region, "lies between two mountain ranges, namely the Vindhyas in the north and the Satpuras in the south. The width of the valley varies at different places as two ranges come closer or drift away. The length of the valley, taking into consideration, the greater and important part of it, had been accepted to be about 200 miles from Jabalpur to Harda."[2]

In the "Revolt in Central India, 1857-59" compiled in the Intelligence Branch, Army Head Quarters, India in 1908, the physical features of the Saugor and Nerbudda Territories are described[3] as follows : "On the north the districts of Saugor and Damoh form part of the Vindhyan plateau, while to the south, in the valley of the Narbada river, are Jubbulpore, Narsinghpur, Hoshangabad, and Nimar, the latter extending to the Tapti river. Like the rest of the central portion of the Indian peninsula, the level of this country is broken by frequent hill ranges and a very large portion of these territories is covered with forests, through which pour the Narbada and Tapti rivers and their tributaries." It may, however, be noted that in 1864, Nimar district was ceded to the British for the payment of the Gwalior contingent.

These territories were "interspersed by hills and valleys, largely covered by jungles, except in the uplands of Sagar and in the valley of Narsimhapur, Hoshangabad and Jabalpur. The tract possessed natural fertility and great productive capabilities which under proper management, could be made to yield rich results."[4] But under the British administration "the result perhaps inevitably, was to impoverish the land and create a large influential class of dispossessed persons who bore a grudge against the foreign rulers and would, therefore, willingly lend their ears to any scheme calculated to subvert authority."[5]

Maratha rule

Prior to the British occupation, these territories were under the Maratha rule. The Marathas had overthrown the Gond Rajas who ruled this area for centuries which was formerly known as Gondwana or the country of Gonds. The country of Gondwana properly "included the Satpura plateau and a section of the Nagpur plain and Nerbudda valley to the south and west."[6]

Before the occupation of these territories by the Marathas, its two districts of Sagar and Damoh were acquired from the Gond aborigines by Maharaja Chhatrasal of Bundelkhand which formed the integral part of his kingdom. In 1728, Muhammad Khan Bangash, the Pathan chief of Farrukhabad, attacked Chhatrasal. When the situation became grim, the latter requisitioned the assistance of Peshwa Baji Rao I in quelling the invasion.[7] The latter was not slow to provide it and thereby acquired a footing in Bundelkhand. He came forward to help Chhatrasal and the combination of the two armies succeeded in suppressing the war-like activities of Muhammad Khan Bangash. Chhatrasal was so grateful to Peshwa that he reciprocated by adopting him as his own son, and also bestowed one-third of his kingdom on him. Hence, Baji Rao became the legitimate possessor of a far-flung area of Bundelkhand which was the earliest acquisition of the Marathas in Northern India and was considerably extended by subsequent conquests.[8]

The districts of Sagar and Damoh formed part of the share given by Maharaja Chhatrasal to Peshwa Baji Rao I which was managed by his Subedar, Govind Rao Kher later on known as Govind Rao Bundele. He and his descendants further extended the dominion of the Sagar *Subedari*. In 1781 when the last Gond ruling chief of Garha-Mandla was deposed, Mandla and Jabalpur were brought under the control of the Raja of Sagar. But they remained under Sagar only for a period of eighteen years. In 1798, Peshwa gave away both Jabalpur and Mandla to Raghuji II of Nagpur better known as Appa Sahib Bhonsla and they continued to remain under Bhonsla's rule till its occupation by the British in 1817. The Bhonsla administration proved to be arbitrary and corrupt in every branch of administration.[9]

After dislodging mainly the Gond rule from a major portion of the region, the Marathas gradually organised their administration in the far-flung areas which suited both to the genius of the people and their traditional social and economic structure. However, since the early part of the nineteenth century, the Marathas were involved in continuous warfare with the British and the neighbouring Indian powers. The Maratha Confederacy was also weakened due to the frictions among the different Maratha rulers. This paved the way for the British to exploit their obvious disunited power hierarchy. In order to fight the British, the Marathas had enlisted the support of the free-booters, who were popularly known as the Pindaris. The latter launched a movement of loot and plunder and created an atmosphere of fear and insecurity among the people. This very fact undermined the efficiency of the Maratha rule.[10]

British occupation

In the Third Anglo-Maratha War of 1817-18, the Marathas were finally defeated as they failed to undertake a co-ordinated action against the British and consequently a major portion of the Central India was occupied by them. The Peshwa Baji Rao II and Appa Sahib Bhonsla hoped that they would be able to overwhelm the small British forces stationed at their capitals. However, this was not to be. After the deposition of the last Peshwa Baji Rao II by Lord Hastings, by Article XIII of the Treaty of Poona concluded on 13 June 1817 between them, the Peshwa ceded to the British the districts of Sagar and Damoh, amongst other territories in Bundelkhand.[11] These districts were annexed by the British in 1817. But not until March 1818 these were brought under actual control by General Marshall after subduing the resistance offered by Vinayak Rao, who administered the Sagar kingdom on behalf of the widow of its Subedar under the Peshwa.[12]

The rest of the area of the Saugar and Nerbudda Territories came under the British control as a result of the defeat of Appa Sahib of Nagpur in the war of 1817-18. Appa Sahib after his defeat in the Sitabaldi on 27 November 1817, ceded the districts of Mandla, Seoni and Betul and the Narmada valley (namely, the districts of Jabalpur, Narsinghpur and Hoshangabad) to the British and in the midst of stiff resistance General Marshall occupied all these territories. However, Appa Sahib continued to challenge the British occupation for a long time. He raised the banner of revolt and sought refuge in the Mahadev hills of Pachmari where he received assistance from a number of Gond chiefs including the Pindari leader, Chitu. The British Government was forced to proclaim a reward of Rs. 1 lac for his capture but he successfully escaped to Punjab.[13]

With regard to the Peshwa, Lord Hastings decided in favour of his perpetual exclusion alongwith his family from any share of influence or dominion, and the annihilation of the Peshwa's name and authority forever. No symbol of Maratha unity was to be left; no further opportunity was to be given to the Marathas to rally round their traditional chief. Baji Rao was granted a generous pension of eight lacs and sent to Bithur (near Kanpur). There he lived in confinement till his death in 1851. As mentioned earlier, Appa Sahib fled to Punjab. He was then formally deposed and Raghuji Bhonsla III, his minor grandson by his daughter was recognised on 26 June 1818 as the ruler of the Bhonsla territories except the above-mentioned area which was annexed by the Company. He eventually died in Rajasthan when he ended his life at the age of 44 in Jodhpur in 1840.[14]

While the third Maratha War was in progress, Lord Hastings had also undertaken the task of annihilating the Pindaris and was successful in disbanding their organised free-booter gangs. However, he did not pay any attention towards the *Thug* gangs who were operating not only in Central India but also in other parts of the country. The Narmada Valley was the original home of *Thuggee*. The first band of *Thugs* was discovered here and these tracts were mostly frequented by them that wandered about to loot the travellers after strangling them to death. Apart from *Thuggee*, these territories were also infested with the dacoity menace. On the Sagar frontier, the dacoity occurred in a very aggravated form as the robbers were coming from the wild and hilly country belonging to Bhopal and also from the Sindhia's dominions.[15]

After the occupation of Sagar, the British Government issued a Proclamation[16] on 10 March 1818 assuring the people of Sagar an efficient administration : "To all the Chaudharies, Kanungoes, Zamindars and other inhabitants of the country of Saugor"

"Whereas the country of Saugor having come into the possession of the British, the Superintendent of the Political Affairs hereby proclaims to the inhabitants of all classes that they will hereafter be governed by those established principles of Justice, and indulgence whichever regulate the conduct of the British Government towards its subjects. They will be effectively protected against those merciless cruelities and depredations of foreign plunderers to which they have hitherto been exposed. The rights and property of all will be secured and protected and their religious temples and worship will be scrupulously preserved and protected."

The Assistant to the Superintendent of Political Affairs, T.H. Maddock reached Sagar on 7 April 1818 with detachment and was satisfied with the control of the British over the territory. He remarked,[17] "The inhabitants of the town are perfectly quiet and well pleased with the prospects of being placed under the authority of the British Government."

There was no opposition on the part of the people of Sagar to these foreign rulers, "partly because the real nature of British control and its consequences were not fully realised at the beginning and partly because they were accustomed to such change of rulers and were indifferent to it. As a matter of fact they even welcomed the British rule due to the misgovernment of the decaying Maratha rulers and consequent depredations of the Pindaris. They hoped their property and lives would be protected under the British who successfully suppressed the Pindari raids."[18] Thus, the people of these territories in general did not protest against the British occupation because at the outset they could not realise the real nature of the British rule and its consequences towards their socio-economic life. In the past also the people had witnessed the change of rulers and hence they did not offer resistance. But "gradually there grew a feeling of aversion against them, not so much on the ground that they were foreigners, as on account of the evils of their administration."[19]

The territories ceded by the Nagpur Raja and the Peshwa were joined together in 1820 and called the "Saugor and Nerbudda Territories" and placed under an Agent to the Governor-General residing at Jabalpur who was directly responsible to the Supreme Government at Calcutta.[20]

After the constitution of the North-Western Provinces in 1835, the administration of these territories was placed under the general supervision of the Lieutenant-Governor of these provinces with an Agent to the Lieutenant-Governor posted at Jabalpur. After the suppression of the Bundela rebellion of 1842, the administration of these territories was invested in a Commissioner in direct communication with the Government, while the supervision of fiscal and judicial reforms remained with the Sadar Revenue Board and the Sadar Court of the North-Western Provinces. In 1852, the administrative supervision of these territories was again given to the Government of the North-Western Provinces till its merger with Central Provinces in 1861.[21] Thus, "due to these frequent changes, the administration could not acquire stability and lacked a continuation of policy in the spheres of revenue assessment and matters of general policy towards the chiefs and common people."[22]

Introduction of the British administration

After dislodging the Marathas, the British established a new pattern of administration in these territories. We will examine it and its consequences in detail, the evils of which led to the Bundela rebellion of 1842 and the revolt of 1857.

These territories were divided into eight districts for an effective judicial and revenue administration. In 1835, the number of districts were reduced on the recommendation of R.M. Bird, a member of the Sadar Board of Revenue, North-Western Provinces, deputed to examine the conditions of these territories. The districts of Narsinghpur, Hoshangabad and Betul were merged into one with district headquarters at Hoshangabad and Assistants at outstations.

Similarly Seoni was amalgamated with Jabalpur. Initially, the district officer was designated Superintendent and later re-designated as Principal Assistant Commissioner and again as Deputy Commissioner. The district officer was also given the responsibility of performing police functions to maintain law and order in which he was assisted by Tehsildar, village Patels and watchmen. The police of the town was managed by a Kotwal and police *chowkies* were also established at strategic places to exercise effective control over the unlawful elements. The district officer was also given magisterial powers of inflicting punishment for two years. The population was peaceful and easily manageable and surprisingly people did not carry arms habitually as was seen elsewhere in the country that travellers generally possessed arms for their security.[23]

The judicial administration of the region was invested in a Commissioner who was assisted by the Principal and Junior Assistants. The civil administration was also conducted by these officers under instructions issued for their guidance from the Supreme Government and the final court of the appeal was the Sadar Diwani Adalat. In criminal matters they were subjected to the Sadar Nizamat Adalat. In the opinion[24] of R.M. Bird there was no general uniformity in administration in these territories, "each district being managed according to the particular fancy of the officer in charge and the whole territory at the mere discretion of the Commissioner."

For the purpose of efficient administration, the districts were sub-divided into tehsils. Jabalpur, besides being a chief town of the region, was also the headquarters of the Commissioner and Divisional Civil Sessions Judge. The Commissioner was the chief executive officer who supervised the revenue jurisdiction and general political and administrative control over the region.[25] For the purpose of revenue administration the district was sub-divided into four tehsils, viz., Jabalpur, Sihora, Murwara and Patan.[26]

Sagar was having its four tehsils, Khurai lying to the north-west, Banda north-east, Sagar in the centre and Rehli in the south.[27] Damoh was having two tehsils which were Hatta (North) and Damoh (South).[28] Narsinghpur was also divided into two tehsils namely, Narsinghpur (East) and Chhindwara (West). The parganas of Chawarpatha and Tendukhera were added to the district in 1825. Nearly two decades after the British take-over, Narsinghpur was annexed to the Hoshangabad district in pursuance of a plan drawn up for the dimunition of the number of districts, but the plan having proved to be of "doubtful expediency" had to be scrapped in 1843. The Bundela rising of 1842 led to the revival of the district into which Taluq of Hirapur was added.[29] Hoshangabad district was comprised of Hoshangabad, Harda, Sohagpur and Pachmari tehsils.[30] The adjoining district, Betul was having two tehsils i.e. Betul and Multai, each having a Tehsildar and Naib-Tehsildar with executive powers.[31] Like Narsinghpur district this district was also annexed to the Hoshangabad district but after the Bundela rising, this district was revived in 1843. From 1818 to 1835 Mandla district was a part of the Seoni district and was administered as a tehsil of Seoni. In 1835, Mandla was made into a Munsiffi and in 1849 was promoted to the status of a district; six months later it was reverted to its old position, and finally in 1851 it became a district consisting of Mandla, Ramgarh and Sohagpur tehsils. A Tehsildar was also stationed at Shahpura. After the revolt of 1857, Sohagpur was transferred to the Rewa state and the Raja of Ramgarh was deposed by the British Government.[32]

The higher posts in the administration were reserved for the Europeans and the Indians were given the insignificant executive jobs only in the judicial and police administration. In the other areas of administration, the services of the Indians were utilised in the lower category. It was evident that the British did not trust the Indians for the higher responsible posts. Naturally, the Indians developed a feeling of being ignored, which was not the case during the Gond and Maratha rule. Thus, the higher class which enjoyed considerable influence during the previous regimes was deprived of the places of honour, which was one of the causes of the resentment against the British and which was openly expressed during the Bundela rebellion of 1842 and the revolt of 1857.[33]

Judicial administration

The judicial system of this region under Company's rule was full of defects. The absence of a complete set of laws, civil and criminal, might have been one of the major defects of the system. The same dispute or crime could be decided differently by two judges in the absence of a written and fixed principles of law. They were also not acquainted with the law of land and the customs and manners of the people of the country and consequently could not pay much attention to the proper dispensation of justice. For removing these defects, in 1831 the pargana courts were established which resulted in the decrease of suits in the courts of the district officers. The system proved acceptable to the people but only for a few years because in practice a good deal of difficulties were being experienced as these courts were placed under the superintendence of the Tehsildars who were not empowered to execute their own decrees.[34]

For a speedy deliverance of justice, R.M. Bird had recommended in 1834, that in each district Sadar Ameens might be appointed for hearing appeals from the pargana courts and might also be empowered to receive, hold trial and decide all original cases from Rs. 1,000.00 to Rs. 2,500.00. He further suggested for hearing appeals from Sadar Ameens, a Principal Sadar Ameen or a native judge might be appointed to hold the Appealate Court at the station of the Commissioner. Appeals should be made from the Principal Sadar Ameen to the Commissioner alone.[35] These proposals of Bird were implemented and the civil judicial system was reorganised on the lines of the North-Western Provinces. A.A. Roberts was appointed judge to exercise effective control over the civil and judicial courts. An Indian judicial staff comprising of a Principal Sadar Ameen, Sadar Ameen and Munsiffs were also appointed to discharge the civil and judicial duties under a procedure code drafted by A.A. Roberts himself.[36] These reforms brought some relief to the people. Thus, the separation of judiciary from the executive was limited to the administration of civil justice only, whereas the administration of criminal justice was still in the hands of executive officers. This modified system of justice continued to function till 1861, when these territories were finally amalgamated in the Central Provinces.

Law and order : suppression of Thuggee and dacoity

During this period the British Governor Generals were fully aware of the atrocities of the *Thugs*, but they deliberately ignored organised operations against them because all their attention was centered on defeating the Marathas and other Indian rulers to acquire new territories under their direct rule. It was only when the *Thugs* became more active in the territories under their direct rule and the miseries of the people were increased considerably, that the eyes of the British rulers were opened against the evil.

The word *'Thuggee'* means 'cheating' and 'deceiving'. The *Thugs* infested the high roads and committed widespread murders without actually spilling blood and used a scarf or handkerchief to strangle travellers for their belongings. The *modus operandi* of the *Thugs* was based on their mythological belief in the devotion of the Goddess Kali. Majority of the *Thugs* were either low-caste Hindus or Muslims.[37] It is ironic to point out that the *Thugs* considered themselves to be merely agents of God and were carrying out their murderous activities at the behest of Goddess Kali.

The suppression of *Thugs* was seriously taken in hand by the *Thuggee* and Dacoity department under the direction of Sir William Sleeman, who was Superintendent of the operations in 1835 at Sagar and subsequently Commissioner for the suppression of *Thuggee* and Dacoity in 1839. A large number of British officers were also deputed for the work of hunting down the *Thugs*. During this period about 14,000 *Thugs* were arrested, some of them were either hanged or transported or kept under restraint, one of them had committed 700 murders. By 1848, this form of crime was completely eliminated. For the support of the approver *Thugs* and their families and others, a labour colony was established at Jabalpur which subsequently developed into the school of Industry and was the parent of the existing Reformatory School. Here these criminals were taught tent and carpet-making and other trades, and gradually grew to be ashamed of the murderous calling in which they had once taken pride.[38]

The administration spent twenty five long years not only in eradicating the *Thuggee* but also dacoity which had spread along the Sagar frontier. In order to stamp out dacoity, the Government had reorganised the entire police system of the Sagar district.[39] Thus, despite the drawbacks of the British rule, there were a few measures which brought a great relief to the people. The Pindaris were suppressed by Lord Hastings and during the Governor Generalship of Lord William Bentinck, *Thuggee* was totally stamped out under the able direction of W.H. Sleeman. He also succeeded in putting a check to the spread of dacoity which was more prevalent in the Sagar territory.[40]

Revenue administration

Before dealing with the revenue administration of the British, we will examine the land revenue policy of the Marathas who were the immediate predecessors of the British in these territories. During the early days of the Maratha rule, the land revenue assessment was reasonable and considerate.[41] The villages were kept under *khalsa* (state) management or they were farmed out to the highest bidder. In *khalsa* villages the assessment was made annually; its amount was fixed in the first place by the *Kamvisdar* (Pargana Officer). The village headman or *Patel* was also consulted during revenue assessment because both were equally responsible for apportioning the village demand among the cultivators whose share was based on a rough estimate of the capacity of their holdings. The revenue collections were made direct from the cultivators. It left an adequate margin to the cultivators for their own living and agricultural operations.[42]

In the later days of the Maratha rule, however, there were of course years of stress and emergency arising out of bad seasons or the ravages of the Pindaris which led to the increase of the state demand. The power of the Marathas was also weakened due to the frequent conflicts with the British and among the various rulers of the Maratha Confederacy. This gravely affected the prospects of agriculture as the cultivators were scared of the unlawful elements and the danger of war. Hence, the policy of farming out the villages to the highest bidder was extended to the *khalsa* villages also. The village headmen or *Patels* were deprived of the power of revenue assessment and the Government officials were entrusted with the task of collecting revenue from the tenants who oppressed them.[43]

In the villages which were farmed out, leases were given for short terms from one to three years which left a very small margin to the lessee, seldom more than one-tenth of the rent assets. The lessee's profit was called *'dupasi'* (corruption of *do-biswa*) i.e. two-twentieth of an acre, one-tenth of the income. The remaining nine-tenths constituted the State's share. But the lessees were squeezed by the revenue officials in many ways and, therefore, compelled in self-defence to meet out similar treatment to his cultivators.[44]

It is, however, to be noted that under the Marathas, the tenants or cultivators had no secured rights[45] but the assessment of the land revenue was light and variable according to the nature of the harvest. The revenue collections were made direct from the cultivators who were permitted to pay both in cash and kind. Consequently, the Maratha revenue did not cause any indignation to the people and the country had prospered and the peasantry was satisfied.[46]

The British were to a great extent dependent on the land revenue for their exchequer to carry on the administration and the empire-building activities. It was because of the revenue collection that the British came in close contact with the subjects, specially the peasants. But as is only to be expected, the change from one system to another created a number of problems and gave a death-blow to the already existing institutions apart from giving rise to a sense of insecurity. The revenue administration of the British was full of defects. Here the British committed the same blunder as in other parts of the country like Madras and elsewhere. The excessive assessment of revenue was not commensurate with the paying capacity of the peasants. Consequently, the economic development of the region was brought to a halt and impoverished the people. J.W.Kaye had rightly remarked,[47] "We began to regard our dusky subjects as many millions of revenue payers, people from whom it is our bounden duty to extract so much in the shape of rent or taxes in recognition of their subjection."

At the commencement of the British rule, the land revenue system rested on the same lines adopted by their predecessors in these territories. Leases were still given for short-terms but certain changes were effected. To begin with, the British unlike the Marathas fixed the revenue for one year which was to remain unchanged for five years. The Marathas before them, however, used to modify their demand from year to year in consideration of the nature of harvests and other unforeseen exigencies. Another very important modification made by the British was that now the lessee could not distribute the yearly demand among the peasants which enabled them easily to tide over difficult times. The British discontinued this practice and thus placed a heavy demand on the lessee.[48] In the matter of recovery also, there was a difference between the Maratha and the British system. Under the British the recovery was a rigid affair whereas under the Marathas the revenue was adjusted from year to year in accordance with the nature of harvest as they seldom expected to recover their demands in full. However, the British expected to recover full amount ignoring the deteriorating condition of the peasants.[49] The British believed that a peaceful atmosphere was necessarily the only ingredient required for revenue payment in full and hence extracted whatever they could from the peasants and left them with just bare minimum to subsist on.[50]

The cultivators suffered greatly from the revenue demands of the state between 1818-34. Raised assessments left most cultivators with little beyond the necessities of life and forced peasants in Sagar, Damoh, Seoni, Narsinghpur, Hoshangabad and Betul into poverty and debt by the early thirties.[51] The excessive assessment of revenue and the rigidity in its recovery led to disastrous results. The land revenue was assessed so high and the levy demanded was so exhorbitant that they led to the rapid impoverishment of the people, and retarded the progress of the country.[52]

Twenty years settlement

This sorry state of affairs attracted the attention of the Government of North-Western Provinces under which these territories were subjected in 1835. Hence, R.M. Bird, a member of the Sadar Board of Revenue, North-Western Provinces, who was known as the father of the land settlements in India, was entrusted the task of undertaking a rapid survey of the Saugor and Nerbudda Territories to study the prevailing unsettled conditions. He submitted a detailed report on the unhappy state of these territories. He roundly condemned the revenue system then prevalent and proposed among other things, a reduction of the revenue and long-term settlement. He observed[53] in his famous report that "the system which has hitherto been permitted is no other than an attempt to prop up by temporary expedients a revenue confessedly excessive. ... This system combined with that of short leases and no security for renewal, is of itself sufficient to account for the unimproved and exhausted state of the lands which are ruined by over-cropping and want of culture." He further observed[54] that "the nominal demand is too high for the present condition of the country. ... The reduction of the present high nominal *jamma* to an amount which can, on an average of years, be collected is an indispensable preliminary to the introduction of a successful system of administration." He also furnished a vivid account of the British administrative structure and offered various suggestions for its improvement.

He recommended that a settlement should be made for a period of twenty years on lenient terms and all the unnecessary interference between headmen and tenants, to which government officials had been so prone, should be strictly prohibited. In accordance with his suggestions, orders were issued for a twenty years settlement at a reasonable assessment, on which no remission would be allowed except in extraordinary circumstances. The headmen were to be left to fix the rents of the tenants and alter them at their pleasure, provided that they filed annual rent-rolls showing the changes effected. The headmen were allowed to distrain the standing crops and the personal property of the cultivators other than cattle, grain and implements of husbandry; and for arrears of rent and in pursuance of unsatisfied decrees for arrears, to eject the defaulters. Moreover, all interference with the internal management of the village on the part of the Government officers was prohibited.[55]

On the basis of Bird's recommendation, the twenty years settlement was made in this region between 1834 and 1838. But the method of assessment in this settlement was again summary without any proper survey. The principal guide of the settlement officer was only his personal observation of the tracts, their crops, prices etc.[56] The rates were fixed as high as 66% which proved to be a huge burden on the peasant who could not pay his land revenue easily. Thus, it gave a serious setback to the village economy. Although, the settlement was made at reduced rates with the Patels, yet it did not confer any proprietary rights in lands which had already been granted in 1833 in the North-Western Provinces.[57] It was in vogue though to a limited extent, during the Gond and Maratha rule.

During the Maratha rule revenues were paid in cash but the poor cultivators also paid in kind. The grain was the medium of exchange in village. But the British demanded land revenue only in coin without enquiring their sufficient availability in circulation to allow for such a sudden change. Consequently, the value of the agricultural produce in terms of money swiftly dwindled. "The ryot was forced to dispose of part of his produce to meet a cash demand and had only one channel through which to sell. He had to think of wealth in terms of money instead of as cattle or grain; money was a medium of which he knew little."[58] Hence, cultivators could not meet the revenue demand in full and also their own requirements. Due to revenue arrears, they were also harassed in the civil courts. The personnel who were entrusted with the responsibility of maintaining the records of tenures and rights further harassed the cultivators by demanding bribes.[59] Thus, the agricultural community became a prey to the corrupt British administrative machinery.

Implementation of the twenty years settlement

After discussing the main features of the Maratha and British land revenue administration, prior to the twenty years settlement, we will now examine the revenue assessments under the new settlement and their results in the various districts of these territories prior to the Bundela

Rebellion of 1842. It is, however, to be noted that the British land revenue policy proved to be the backbone of the insurrectionary movement which emerged against them in the Bundela rebellion.

In the Sagar district

In the early decades of the British rule in the Sagar district, three five year settlements were made in 1819, 1824 and 1829, but in their zeal for increasing the revenue, the Settlement Officers assessed the land so high that they not only maintained the previous Maratha assessments but also enhanced them and realised the amount which was not commensurate with the paying capacity of the peasantry. The table below shows the amount of the demand fixed at these settlements[60] :

Year	Amount (Rs.)
1819-1823	5,88,104
1824-1828	6,49,701
1829-1833	6,27,598

These settlements were of a summary character and the revenue demand was fixed on general considerations. Apart from the heavy assessments and the manner of their realisation, the closing years of the third settlement left the lessees in arrears due to a succession of droughts. This forced the government to offer heavy reductions, resulting in considerable fall of revenue collections. But these remissions proved advantageous to the Patels and cultivators derived no relief.[61] The long term settlement of 1834 lowered the demand from Rs. 6,27,598 to Rs. 6.27 lacs which did not work well and failed to offer any relief.[62]

In the Damoh district

In the Damoh district, the earliest British settlements were made with the village headmen or farmers usually for triennial periods. The first settlement entailed a demand of Rs. 3.54 lacs which was 2 per cent higher than the land revenue of the district as it stood before the settlement of 1893-94. During these three years, half a lac of rupees fell into recoverable arrears. The demand was then lowered to Rs. 3.04 lacs which was collected with less difficulty. At the third settlement, it was again raised to Rs. 3.24 lacs, and large remissions had to be made, partly owing to the bad seasons. The revenue dwindled through successive reductions till 1835 when the first long term settlement was made, the period being twenty years and revenue fixed at Rs. 3.05 lacs.[63] The assessment again proved too high for a district broken down by an excessive taxation. The landed property entirely lost its value and the landholders were forced in distress to surrender their leases and leave large number of villages to be managed direct or farmed to money lenders.[64]

In the Jabalpur district

In the Jabalpur district, the early British rule witnessed a series of summary and short-term settlements which followed the Maratha precedent of high demands and short collections. The first settlement was made in 1818 for a year when the demand of the district was fixed at Rs. 4,17,375. This was followed by three quinquennial settlements, their periods and demand being as follows :

Year	Amount (Rs.)
1820-1824	4,48,169
1825-1829	6,41,007
1830-1834	6,05,014

These settlements were made with the Patels or managing farmers, the chief test of their continuance being the payment of the revenue demand. The first settlement of 1820-24 worked satisfactorily. But under the latter two settlements those of 1825-29 and 1830-34, the land revenue fixed pressed heavily and remissions had to be made in both the cases. In fact, there was no fixed principle of measurement nor any fixed system of survey in these settlements.[65]

On Bird's recommendation, the twenty years settlement became operative in 1835-36, when the rental estimates were estimated at Rs.10,58,492, out of which the demand was fixed at 4.76 lacs. The settlement was made with the Patels who were in possession of villages and which were not to be displaced without the sanction of the Revenue Board, a step which was taken to protect them against the cancellation of their leases. Even at this settlement, there was no fixed system of survey but it worked well during the full period of its term and was described as the best settlement of those days under which the district gradually recovered its prosperity.[66]

In the Narsinghpur district

In the Narsinghpur district, the earlier British settlements were also carried on the same lines as in the other districts. They were of a summary nature and the demand was fixed on the general considerations. The first formal five years settlement was made in 1820, under which the total demand was fixed at Rs. 5.56 lacs which proved disastrous and the malguzars or revenue payers were ruined. The reason for this was that after the overthrow of the Marathas, the Narmada Field Force was removed and in the absence of communications, the district was at once deprived of its market. Moreover, the object of the English officers was to extort maximum possible revenue without considering the paying capacity of the people. Hence, considerable reductions had to be made at successive settlements. In 1825, in the second settlement, the total demand was reduced to Rs. 4.39 lacs; while in the two settlements which followed, it was gradually brought down to Rs. 4 lacs. During the first five years the remission averaged Rs. 66,000 per year, the second five years proved disastrous and heavy reductions had to be effected and considerable reductions were made at the triennial settlements of 1830 and 1833.[67]

On Bird's recommendation in the twenty years settlement, the demand was reduced from Rs. 4 lacs to Rs. 3.47

lacs. It enabled the district to recover itself completely.[68] This was the first long term settlement and was simple in procedure. During this settlement the district continued to enjoy the advantages of the lenient assessment of the twenty years settlement. Proof of prosperity may be drawn from one single fact that the gross rental increased from Rs. 6,69,667 to Rs. 8,26,924 or at the rate of 24 per cent.[69]

In the Hoshangabad district

During the early period of British rule, several short-term settlements in the Hoshangabad district were characterized by the mistake of over-assessment. The outstanding feature of the early settlement of the area ceded in 1818 was the exhorbitant demand of the Government. As a result, the peasantry became impoverished and the country became depopulated. In 1820 after the formation of the Saugor and Nerbudda Territories, Major Macpherson's first five year settlement was considered the worst settlement ever made. The Government's demand, therefore, had to be reduced in the subsequent settlements which brought some relief.[70]

At last in 1836, a twenty years settlement was made by Captain Ouseley and a moderate demand of 66% of the total assets was fixed, which was still considered nearly three times of the old Maratha demand.[71]

In the Seoni district

In the earlier short-term settlements in the Seoni district, an excessive land revenue was imposed. In 1818 on the cession of this district, land revenue stood at Rs. 51,805. Three years later the demand rose to Rs. 1.76 lacs in a quinquennial settlement following on two annual ones. This was succeeded by a decennial settlement on a slightly reduced demand. In 1835, a settlement of twenty years was made by Major Low which lowered the revenue to Rs. 1.34 lacs. The demands of the previous six settlements were at Rs. 1,56,520 under first years settlement, Rs. 1,56,889 under second years settlement, Rs. 1,75,986 under first five years settlement, Rs. 1,74,114 under second five years settlement, Rs. 1,67,892 under ten years settlement and Rs. 1,33,504 under twenty years settlement.[72] Even under the reduced demand of Rs. 1.34 lacs fixed in 1835, some areas of the district suffered and further remissions had to be allowed.[73]

In the Betul district

In the Betul district, the first British settlement was made for a period of five years in 1818 and a demand was fixed at Rs. 2.78 lacs which was 16 per cent more than the average demand in the Nagpur kingdom. In fact, the district was too far removed from important markets to permit of any influx of external capital, while the restoration of tranquillity had the effect of producing an enormous decline in the prices of agricultural produce. The people, therefore, were unable to pay the enhanced land revenue and remissions had to be granted. The average annual collections during the period did not amount to more than Rs. 2.56 lacs.

The next assessment was made in 1823 for three years by Captain Low. The revenue was reduced to Rs. 2.03 lacs. But even so, considerable remissions had to be granted mainly owing to the failure of the crops of 1824-25. In the year 1826, another quinquennial settlement was made by Captain Low in which the demand was further slightly reduced to Rs. 2 lacs. The settlement was carried on with large remissions. All the reports speak of the poverty both of the Patels and cultivatoRs. [74]

In the fourth settlement of 1831 by Smith for a period of three years, the demand was fixed at Rs. 1.61 lacs. At this time, a number of cultivators had left the district particularly from the Atner pargana for Berar, which was in a much better state than Betul. Several Malguzars too had thrown up their villages and there was difficulty in finding anyone to take their place. It was intended to leave the Malguzars 25 per cent on the gross collections and to give abandoned lands on three years lease free of rent to encourage cultivation with the result that the new men came forward to take up the village which had been thrown up by the former MalguzaRs.

The triennial assessment expired in 1834 and it was decided in accordance with the Bird's recommendations to have a twenty years settlement on liberal terms. The amount of the new assessment was about Rs. 1.40 lacs, a reduction of Rs. 21,000 or more than 12 per cent upon the preceding settlement.

From all these settlements in the Betul district, it is evident that the settlements upto 1834 were excessive, balances accrued from year to year and the people were reduced to a state of actual poverty and destitution, while from 1834 the district enjoyed the moderate assessment and as such it prospered and there was an addition to the wealth and general resources of the community.[75]

As Mandla district was a part of the Seoni district upto 1851, its study has been taken up with the Seoni district. From the study of the land revenue settlements prior to and after the twenty years settlements in all these districts, it can be seen that these districts suffered from the over-assessment of the land revenue demand which the cultivators could not pay. Consequently, it led to the dispossession of the lands and the poverty of both the local chiefs and the cultivatoRs. Even the Bird's settlement was not found to work well. It brought relief to some districts like Jabalpur, Narsinghpur and Betul where the assessment was reduced, while in other districts it brought none, because the method of assessment was again summary without any proper survey. The demand based on the then usual percentage of 66 per cent of the assets was too high. It had damaged the village economy and proved to be a huge burden on the peasant who could not pay his land revenue easily.[76] The owners of land in these territories were thus in distress. The course of law was so mercilessly pursued against the numerous Taluqdars, Thakurs and Zamindars that they were dispossessed of their holdings during the British rule.[77]

The twenty years settlement gave relief to the hard-pressed tenants to a certain extent but it had no such effect on the local landowners, who were exploited and stripped to their skin. The British Government devoid of any social philosophy, excercised all its skill and energy for economic exploitation when the Indian society itself was burdened with the most reactionary forces of feudalism and individualism.[78]

Social condition

The society in India as well as in these territories was more or less orthodox due to the prevalence of illiteracy. Prior to the British rule, the orthodox customs and superstitions amongst the various tribes and castes were strictly followed. Despite their different customs, a feeling of fellowship created a harmonious society. It is a strange but true fact. However, the division between the upper and lower classes was quite evident. The upper class followed the practice of *Sati* but widow-marriage was not prevalent among them. Whereas several tribes did not believe in *Sati* but widow-marriages were permitted.

When the British established their rule in India, they were so much involved in the management of land revenue and general administration and also in dealing with the unlawful elements like *Thugs* and dacoits, they did not try to reform the society by eradicating social evils. Moreover, the British were unwilling to disturb the prevalent social structure out of fear as it would have antagonised a large section of the people resulting in widerspread discontment. They, therefore, pursued a very cautious policy towards the Indian society.

However, when Lord William Bentinck became the Governor-General, he enlisted the support of the Indian social reformers like Raja Ram Mohan Roy and others to do away with the social evil of *Sati*. During his visit to this region in 1832-33, he saw a large number of memorials erected in the honour of those women who had committed *Sati* on the funeral pyres of their husbands. This social evil made a deep impact on his mind. His predecessor, Lord Amherst, had consulted the views of seven district officers of these territories for the elimination of this custom. It is to be noted that the Mandla district came into existence in 1851. All these district officers had expressed themselves against this reform. However, Bentinck defied their views and enforced the regulation XVII of 1829 to stamp out the practice of *Sati*.[79] In some quarters of these territories slavery was also found but it did not spread to a great extent and was exterminated in a very short period.[80]

Disruption of the local self-government

A form of the local self-government existed throughout the length and breadth of these territories. The village *Panchayat* or little village commune functioned with its own organisation and government and its little staff of functionaries, artisans and traders:

"Under the ancient system of the country, each village managed its own affairs, and although there is little trace in the Central Provinces of those complicated village committees which still thrive in Northern India, yet the system of village management was, until comparative recent date, complete. Every village had its headmen or 'Patel' who acted as the guide, agent and leader of the village. By the Maratha revenue system, under which the village community was jointly responsible for the whole revenue, and all details of assessment were left to the villagers themselves, the people were forced to act together under their headmen, and to arrange their own affaiRs. "[81]

The system of village self-government tnus gave to the whole social structure a firm foundation based on mutual obligation and trust. As long as the state got its share of the produce from the village, it was content to leave the allocation of each villager's share to the village panchayati. One of the consequences of this system was that the people rarely fell into the arrears of revenue, and the State was saved from all the protracted legal processes of collection and the intricacies of land revenues.[82]

With the introduction of the British rule in this region, this ancient system was destroyed. The system of excessive centralisation of executive and judicial powers in the hands of the Government officials, deprived the village functionaries of their age - old power and influence. The *Patel* soon came to be practically deposed from his position as the head of the community. He was shorn of his powers and relieved of his duties. Under the British rule, he was merely a farmer of government revenue, liable to be summarily ejected on the expiry of the period for which the village might have been settled with him, and generally, such period was very short. Moreover, the deliberate introduction of landlordism or malguzari system and ryotwari system as against the mauzavari or village system dealt almost a death-blow to the corporate life of the village communities. It was widely believed that the maintenance of native institutions was against the spirit of British rule.[83]

What the British did not, or could not understand was that "the foundations of the people's lives in our country were thousands of years older, and therefore stronger, than anything they had known. They did not realize that these were the product of the genius and character of the people, possessing the resilience and adaptability of natural growth. To the British, convinced of their superior civilization, all this appeared primitive and barbarous. What they could not understand they considered contemptible. Thus began a silent but determined conflict between the indigenous social order and the alien administrative system, which could never be reconciled. Now and then this conflict erupted into violent outbreak and resulted in widespread loss of life and property. Superior force, supported by the might of a nation thousands of miles away, succeeded in putting down such outbreaks everytime at an increasing cost. But, though the eruption was, for a time, subdued, the smouldering fires burnt in undying embers, and burst into flames whenever circumstances provided combustible material."[84]

Thus, the establishment of the British rule and administration was followed by the political, social and economic unsettlement in the Saugor and Nerbudda Territories. On the economic front, the foreign rule failed miserably and brought havoc for the agricultural community. It can be said that the greatest evil consequence of the British rule was its land revenue policy. Its drawbacks were the principal cause of disaffection which resulted in the outbreak of the Bundela Rebellion of 1842 in these territories.

REFERENCES

1. J.D., B.C., Political Case File No. 56 of 1854, p. 1.
2. C.P. A.R., 1862-63, p. 3 and *Imperial Gazetteers of India*, Vol. X (1908), p. 4.
3. *The Revolt in Central India, 1857-59* : Compiled in the Intelligence Branch, Army Head Quarters, India (1908), p. 33.
4. D.P. Mishra, ed., *History of the Freedom Movement in Madhya Pradesh* (1956), p. 29.
5. *Ibid*.
6. R.V. Russell and Rai Bahadur Hira Lal, *The Tribes and Castes of the Central Provinces of India*, Vol. III (1916), p. 41.
7. Chhatrasal's appeal to Baji Rao was said to have been couched in a Bundeli verse recalling a mythological story :

   'Jo biti gaj-grah par, so gati bhai hai aaj
   Baji jat Bundel ki, rakho Baji laj.'

   (What befell the famous elephant when caught by the crocodile has come to pass now, the Bundela's honour is being lost, save him O, Baji Rao). There is a pun in the word 'Baji'. It means a stake, meaning that the Bundelas are loosing their stake. O Baji Rao save their honour. Bhagwan Das Gupta, Maharaja Chhatrasal (Hindi edition, 1958), p. 91.
8. C.U. Aitchison, *A Collection of Treaties, Engagements and Sanads*, Vol. V (1933), pp. 1-2; V.G. Dighe, *Peshwa Baji Rao I and Maratha Expansion* (1944), pp. 106-8.

9. C.P. D.G., Jubbulpore (1909), p. 54 and Mandla (1912), pp. 35-6.
10. D.E. Chowfin, *Society and Economy in the Sagar-Narmada Territories, 1818-61*, unpublished thesis, University of Jabalpur (1991), p. 249.
11. Aitchison, *op. cit.*, Vol. III (1909), p. 84.
12. C.P. D.G., Saugor (1905), p. 23; Damoh (1906), p. 21, M.P. D.G., Sagar (1967), p. 62.
13. R.M. Sinha, *Bhonslas of Nagpur* (1967), pp. 28-9; M.P. D.G., Hoshangabad (1979), p. 64 and C.P. D.G. Betul (1906), pp. 38-40.
14. G.S. Sardesai, *The New History of the Marathas*, Vol. III (1948), p. 472.
15. C.P. A.R., 1862-63, p. 41.
16. Jubbulpore Divisional Records, 1818, Vol.104, pp. 31-2, quoted in the M.P. D.G., Sagar, *op. cit.*, p. 62.
17. *Ibid.*, Ref. CXXVI-I(3).
18. J.P. Mishra, *The Bundela Rebellion* (1982), p. 4.
19. *Ibid.*
20. C.P. D.G., Hoshangabad (1908), p. 36 and M.P. D.G. Narsinghpur (1971), p. 57.
21. Report on the Administration of the Central Provinces, 1892-93, p. 16; J.F. Dyer, *Introduction to the Land Revenue System of the Central Provinces* (1924), p. 3.
22. J.P. Mishra, *op. cit.*, p. 245.
23. R.M. Bird, *Note on the Saugor and Nerbudda Territories* (1834), pp. 6 and 10.
24. *Ibid.*, p. 5.
25. C.P. D.G., Jubbulpore (1909), p. 312.
26. M.P. D.G., Jabalpur (1968), p. 401.
27. C.P. D.G., Saugor (1905), p. 191.
28. *Ibid.*, Damoh (1906), p. 172.
29. *Ibid.*, Narsinghpur (1906), p. 191.
30. *Ibid.*, Hohangabad (1908), p. 266.
31. *Ibid.*, Betul (1906), p. 217.
32. *Ibid.*, Mandla (1912), pp. 36-7 and 211.
33. D.E. Chowfin, *op. cit.*, p. 75.
34. R.M. Bird, *op. cit.*, p. 17.
35. *Ibid.*, pp. 19-20.
36. C.P. A.R., 1862-63, p. 29.

37. A.J. Weighman, *No Friend for Travellers* (1956), pp. 13-15.
38. J.P. Mishra, *op. cit.*, p. 12.
39. J.D.,B.C., Judicial Case File No. 2 of 1827 and Case File No. 4 of 1829, quoted in D.E.Chowfin, *op. cit.*, p. 61.
40. D.E. Chowfin, *op. cit.*, p. 258.
41. Report on the Land Revenue Settlement of Saugor District, 1889-97, p. 44.
42. J.F. Dyer, *op. cit.*, pp. 101-3.
43. Report on the Land Revenue Settlement of Saugor, *op. cit.*, pp. 44-5.
44. *Ibid.*, p. 45.
45. B.H. Baden Powell, *The Land Revenue Systems of British India*, Vol. II (1974), p. 373.
46. J.P. Mishra, *op. cit.*, p. 29.
47. J.W. Kaye, *The Administration of the East India Company*, (Reprint 1966), p. iii.
48. J.F. Dyer, *op. cit.*, pp. 22-5.
49. Report on the Land Revenue Settlement of Saugor, *op. cit.*, p. 45.
50. Baden Powell, *op. cit.*, p. 374 and *Imperial Gazetteersof India*, Vol. X, *op. cit.*, p. 76.
51. D.P. Mishra, *op. cit.*, p. 139.
52. J.F. Dyer, *op. cit.*, pp. 101-3.
53. R. M.Bird, *op. cit.*, pp. 3-4.
54. *Ibid.*
55. Report on the Land Revenue Settlement of Saugor, *op. cit.*, p. 47 and J.F. Dyer, *op. cit.*, pp. 101-3.
56. J.F. Dyer, *op. cit.*, p. 103.
57. Baden Powell, *op. cit.*, p. 374.
58. Edward Thompson and G.T. Garrat, *British Rule in India* (1935), p. 428.
59. *Ibid.*
60. Report on the Land Revenue Settlement of Saugor District, (1911), p. 29.
61. J.F. Dyer, *op. cit.*, pp. 22-5 and C.P. D.G., Saugor, *op. cit.*, p. 184.
62. *Imperial Gazetteers of India*, Vol. XXII (1908), p. 145.
63. M.P. D.G., Damoh (1974), pp. 319-20.
64. *Ibid.*, and C.P. D.G., Damoh (1906), p. 156.
65. M.P. D.G., Jabalpur (1968), p. 415.

66. *Ibid.*, p. 416.
67. Report on the Land Revenue Settlement of Jabbalpore District, 1886-94, pp. 26-7.
68. Report on the Land Revenue Settlement of Narsinghpur District, 1885-94, p. 31.
69. M.P. D.G., Narsinghpur, *op. cit.*, p. 270.
70. M.P. D.G., Hoshangabad (1979), p. 261.
71. J.P. Mishra, *op. cit.*, p. 21; *Imperial Gazetteersof India*, Vol. XIII (1908), p. 189.
72. Land Revenue Settlement of Seoni District, 1867, p. 59, quoted in M.P. D.G., Seoni (1989), pp. 146-47.
73. *Imperial Gazetteers of India*, Vol. XXII (1908), pp. 173-74.
74. M.P. D.G., Betul (1971), p. 256.
75. *Ibid.*, p. 257.
76. Baden Powell, *op. cit.*, p. 374.
77. J.P. Mishra, *op. cit.*, p. 30.
78. M.P. D.G., Narsimhapur (1971), p. 59.
79. M.P. D.G., Sagar, *op. cit.*, pp. 64-5.
80. Parliamentary Papers, House of Commons, No. 319 of 1842, quoted in J.P. Mishra, *op. cit.*, p. 12.
81. Speech of Crosthwaite on introducing the C.P. Local Self-Government Bill before the Governor General's Council of 12 January 1883, quoted in M.P. D.G., Jabalpur, *op. cit.*, p. 499.
82. D.P. Mishra, *op. cit.*, p. 30.
83. Speech of Crosthwaite, *op. cit.*
84. D.P. Mishra, *op. cit.*, pp. 31-2.

CHAPTER 2

The Bundela Rebellion of 1842 and Its Aftermath

Outbreak of the rebellion

The first eruption, caused by the political, social and economic unsettlement that had taken place among the dispossessed landlords and chieftains of the Saugor and Nerbudda Territories, known as the Bundela rebellion, occurred in 1842. As discussed in the preceding chapter, the process of settlement of these territories was accompanied by large-scale dispossession of long-standing Malguzars, some of whom were suspected of hostile intent, while some others had defaulted in their payments. Against those who had fallen in arrears, action was taken and, after much harassment were deprived of their lands and property. Partly for this reason, and partly from an awareness of the British disaster in Afghanistan, the Bundelas broke out in open rebellion.

Early in 1842 two influential Bundela Thakurs in the north of the Sagar district, Jawahar Singh of Chandrapur and Madhukar Shah of Narhat were served with decrees of Civil Court of Sagar to pay an excessive amount of revenue, and were threatened with attachment of property. Both of them defied the Government order and the insurrection began by an attack on the police at Narhat on 8 April 1842, some of whom they killed and rose in open rebellion against the Government. This was just the opportunity that the other landlords were waiting for and now all of them joined this rebellion with the aim of overthrowing the oppressive British rule[1].

Since it was started by the prominent Bundela chiefs of this region in 1842, it has been described as the Bundela rebellion. The causes of this rebellion were varied and deep-rooted. The rugged and independent chieftains of this area had never really got reconciled to the British rule. The land and legal administration of the British Government enraged the people, particularly the independent chiefs of the region. It is noteworthy that the districts of Mandla, Seoni and Betul were unaffected by it. A few dispossessed rulers of Bundelkhand also joined it. The major centres of resistance in these territories were precisely those places which took a leading part in the Great Revolt of 1857.[2]

During the Maratha rule, the local chiefs, Thakurs and Malguzars wielded considerable power and influence. They also had been accustomed to a considerable freedom provided they paid the annual revenue assessed on them. They belonged mainly to the Gond, Lodhi and Bundela Rajput clans. They also had access to the higher echelons of the administration and people held them in high esteem as they were helpful to them in time of grave necessity. They were the natural leaders of the common people who looked at them for leadership and guidance.

With the advent of the British rule in this region, all this was changed. These big landlords and Malguzars were deprived of their rights and privileges. The early British administrators were fore-sighted enough to realize that the existence of the landed aristocracy could be a source of danger to the Company. Accordingly, they used every possible plea to dispossess these nobles and landlords of their property, and bring the tenants directly under them.[3] They were forced to pay an amount of land revenue which was not commensurate with their produce. When they failed to do so, the process of law was forced against them relentlessly. They were harassed in the civil courts and ultimately deprived of their land holdings. When they were suppressed, it was more easy for the British to subdue peasantry and instil loyalty and obedience in them.[4]

Consequently, the early period of the British rule brought substantial changes in the rural society. Many of the great landlords lost both revenue and higher status and became disaffected and dangerous. They were also deprived of the authority and power as the hereditary village headmen in consequence of the administrative measures of the British Government. This attempt of obliterating the landed aristocracy was a great political blunder.[5] This cruel, wrong and grievous error converted into bitter enemies those whom sound policy would have made friends and supporters of the state.[6]

In the opinion[7] of Dr. J.P. Mishra, who has done a pioneer-work on the Bundela rebellion, "the Bundela Rebellion was a feudal revolt against the British rule in the Saugor and Nerbudda Territories. The British annexation of the region in 1818 after dislodging the Marathas had undermined the power and influence of local chiefs and the imposition of an excessive land revenue had brought about economic ruin of the peasantry."He further observed[8] that "it was a feudal resistance against the British power as a result of the loss of political power by the local chiefs who were looked upon as the traditional centres of authority by the general masses."

The time of the revolt was cleverly chosen. Its outbreak coincided with the British disaster in Afghanistan which had greatly undermined the strength and prestige of the British armed forces. The rebels were encouraged to challenge the British authority in view of the reduced strength of the British army in the region. Captain W.H. Boland, who was the Principal Assistant at Hoshangabad, in his letter to C. Fraser, the Agent to the Lieutenant-Governor, Saugor and Nerbudda Territories, dated 5 January 1843, writes[9] : "They were impressed with a conviction that it was in their power to assert independence, and the exaggerated accounts of our Kabul disasters and the extremely reduced state of the military forces in the Division led them to think that the Government could not coerce them."

Causes of discontent

For a time the British were unable to understand the real cause of this widespread and successful revolt. M.C. Ommanney, Principal Assistant Commissioner of Sagar wrote[10] to the Governor-General in April 1842, "It is probable they (the Boondelas) have been excited by the arrest, during the past and preceding year, of a number of their relatives for acts of rebellion committed in Scindhia's territory."

After the suppression of this rebellion, the British Government appointed Major W.H. Sleeman, Commissioner of the Saugor and Nerbudda Territories to enquire into the causes of the disaffection. In his opinion[11], the leaders of insurrection were the petty chiefs of the Sagar district who held their estates in quit rent tenure along the northern border of the Vindhya range. The other leaders of the same class though not of the same clan were residing along the southern border of the Vindhya range. "Those along the northern border were Boondelas, related to or connected by marriage with the chiefs of Bundelkhand and everywhere assisted by them either openly or clandestinely. Those along the southern border were Gonds and Lodhis related to or connected by marriage with the petty chiefs of the same clans scattered over the whole region of the Saugor and Nerbudda Territories."

With regard to the British land revenue policy which proved to be the backbone of this insurrectionary movement, Sleeman observed[12] that the assessments had been high from two causes. Firstly, the British administration had not sufficiently taken into consideration the dimunition in the demand for agricultural produce caused by the great reductions which were continuously taking place in the local defensive establishments. The value of lands in these territories gradually went down and more than one-third of the revenue fell off. With the restoration of order, the British officials concluded that the capability of the cultivators to pay rents must have increased but this was not the case.

Secondly, it was assumed that "fifteen percent of the gross rents of an estate would be sufficient to cover all the costs and risks of management, and the Government required to leave not more than this rate to landholders. More just and liberal views have since prevailed and thirty six per cent of the gross rents have been considered as no more than sufficient to cover the costs and risk of management. Assessments were revised and reduced and where not revised in time, they reduced themselves through long periods of much suffering."

In his reports Sleeman delineated the causes of the discontent in these territories. He also threw light on how he remedied these evils of the British administration. It will be better if we examine both these together.

The misinterpretation of certain orders issued from the Sadar Board of Revenue had produced a great deal of dissatisfaction among the people. In 1836, the restriction imposed by the Sadar Board of Revenue on the heirs to obtain the shares in farms without the consent of the alive shareholders deprived several hereditary proprietors of their estates. The partners of the farms never gave their consent without receiving large amount from heirs. This produced a great deal of dissatisfaction among the hereditary proprietors.[13] The Board had also imposed restrictions on subletting the Government farms without prior consent of the Collector. The lease was liable to be cancelled on the breach of this condition. By subletting their estates, the landholders used to obtain credit to overcome difficulties.[14] In both these orders the Board of Revenue meant by the word "farm" only "such estates as have no proprietors or no proprietors willing to engage on the terms proposed by the Collector for the time being and which are held by temporary lessees." But the Commissioner and his Assistants understood the orders as applicable to all estates held under *Pattas* and not under *Sanads*. They applied these orders to all estates except such as were held as rent free or quit rent tenure. This lamentable error led to an extensive transfer of proprietary rights from lawful owners to others. Sleeman exerted himself to remove the evils which flowed from the erroneous interpretation of Board's directives.[15]

The heads of the aristocratic families of these territories had traditionally enjoyed an exemption from the process of civil courts. But in 1836, Shore, the Commissioner, brought them on equal footing with the common people. The civil courts were presided over by a class of persons who did not use their power discreetly. They did not always vindicate the character of the Government by their own dignity. This had produced a great deal of dissatisfaction among the landed gentry.[16] Sleeman took special care to appoint a better class of native officers to preside over these courts. Some measures were also taken to exempt a certain number of heads of these families from the processes of the civil courts.

The petty chiefs or owners of estates of more than one village had been left to make their own arrangements with the tenants but several complaints of oppression were made against them. For removing this evil, the government officers were empowered to make the settlement with the tenants to realize the land revenue from them. After the assessment, a deduction of twenty per cent was to be made for the risk, cost and management to the village holder and eighteen per cent to the landholders. The landed aristocracy of these territories was dissatisfied with this arrangement to a great extent as they realised that they had been deprived of a major portion of their income. Sleeman took necessary steps to remove the evils of this arrangement and mitigated the discontentment of big landholders.[17]

The behaviour of the European officers with the general public was not satisfactory. This rendered intercourse between the members of middle and higher classes of the native community and their European superiors less easy. The people could not communicate their wants and wishes freely to the government. Such atmosphere had alienated the masses from the government. Sleeman realised the evil effect of this policy of the European officers and took several measures to remove this cause of discontent including a short circular letter to the European officers to show courtesy to the native gentry.[18] Thus, the growing estrangement between the British officers and the Indian people caused bitter resentment among the people of India towards the British rule. This feeling reached the highest pitch during the revolt of 1857 and afterwards.

In the opinion[19] of Sleeman the complaints against the administration of civil justice were general, loud and just. The European officers did not have time, though they had the ability and inclination, to supervise efficiently the proceedings of the Indian officers, who looked after the local administration. The whole machinery was disrupted due to the vast number of pending cases of appeal before C. Fraser, Commissioner, from the districts and Sadar Ameen Courts. Many of the Indian judges had become careless, some of them being corrupt and others altogether incompetent. For removing this evil,[20] the want of efficient supervision over the administration of civil justice, the appropriate remedy was the separation of the judicial administration of these territories from the office of Commissioner. Accordingly, this had been achieved by the appointment of C.M. Caldecott, Civil and Sessions Judge of these territories and great changes in and additions to the subordinate Indian judges and the best effects might be expected from this new system.[21] As already referred, the separation of judiciary from the executive was limited to the administration of the civil justice only, whereas the administration of the criminal justice was still in the hands of the executive officers.

Sleeman also pointed out one more cause of this rebellion. He observed[22] that the landholders and peasantry of the country complained that they were not permitted to carry arms and knew not how to use them. In some districts the sale of arms was prohibited without the previous sanction of the police and the people thought that the restriction had been imposed by the British Government.

Spread of the rebellion

As already mentioned, the rebellion started with two Bundela Thakurs in the north of the Sagar district, Jawahar Singh of Chandrapur and Madhukar Shah of Narhat, who were served with the decrees of the Civil Court of Sagar early in 1842 to pay excessive amount of revenue with a threat of attachment of property.[23] In retaliation, both of them defied the Government order and attacked the police, some of them they killed. They then raided the police outposts and plundered towns of Khimlasa, Khurai, Narioli, Dhamoni and Sagar.[24]

The rebellion spread like a wild fire over a vast area of the northern region which for about a year was in turmoil. The timing of the rebellion was cleverly chosen just after the British army had a crushing defeat in Afghanistan. This depletion threw them in an inferior position against these insurgents, who kept a guerilla warfare and rose simultaneously at a number of places. It is not very easy to establish the duration of the disturbances nor the sequence in which one act of revolt followed another.

The rebellion was quite a success in the Narsinghpur district, specially in the Chawarpatha pargana, where every landlord except Dewan Prithvi Singh of Bamhni, either openly or secretly rallied under the leadership of Raja Delun Shah, the Gond chief of Madanpur and captured Deori and Chawarpatha. The other prominent leader of this district was the Gond Raja Narwar Singh of Dhilwar. At the Chawarpatta fort, they worshipped its presiding deities and fed the Brahmans. At Barman they fired upon the Naib-Tehsildar and appointed Trimbak Rao as *Amil* of Chawarpatha and Barman. From there they proceeded to Suatala and Maharajpur and captured these places easily. In order to safeguard their position and to consolidate their possession, the insurgents posted their trusted guards at all important *ghats* of the Narmada. They also appointed their own Patwari, *Nazir* and *Seristhadar* in the captured area, free of rent on the condition that they would be loyal to them against the British. After Chawarpatha, Tendukhera was captured without a single shot. The Tehsildar of Narsinghpur fled at the sight of their approach. Both the Gond Thakurs of Madanpur and Dhilwar had also commenced an open and undisguised activity of plunder and rapine in the Narsinghpur and Hoshangabad districts.[25]

The spirit of revolt had spread rapidly. With Narsinghpur and Sagar up in arms, the next to rise was Jabalpur. The swell of the rebellion was felt in the Jabalpur district early in April 1842. The Junior Assistant at this town observed[26] that "the consternation to be naturally expected as the result of this successful inroad (by the insurgents) is spreading throughout these territories on account of eruption reaching the ears of the people, and the alarm at Jubbulpore has been so great as to render it necessary to postpone the departure to Sagar until the confidence of Jubbulpore restored. Instructions have been sent to the district officers at Hoshangabad, Seoni, Betul and Damoh to increase their police, and I propose to superintend the execution of the orders, as far as possible, in person."

The leading spirit of the Jabalpur revolt was Raja Hirde Shah of Heerapur *Taluq* then included in the Jabalpur district (now in the Narsinghpur district). He had been in correspondence for some time with the other Thakurs, sounding them about a joint rising against the British. Captain Brown writing to Major Sleeman on 20 November 1842, explained[27] how from the intercepted letters he had come to know that the time fixed for the outbreak was the *Dussehra* festival : "As in former times it was usual for all persons of rank to assemble at this season at the residence of the chief local authority, advantage was taken of the custom to invite the suspected parties to visit me at Jubbulpore. Some came, others did not, and amongst the latter was Hirde Shah." Hirde Shah's followers attacked the police post at Gajpura under the leadership of Raja Gajraj Singh. The Jabalpur detachment was sent to Heerapur to have an encounter with these rebels but they were delayed at the Narmada for want of conveyance. When they ultimately reached Heerapur, the insurgents had already marched to Tejgarh on their way to Chawarpatha so as to effect a junction with the forces of Raja Delun Shah who had captured it.

The British officers found it extremely difficult to track down and tackle these insurgent leaders, because they could not get any reliable information about them. Captain Boland rather ruefully admitted,[28] "I have been disappointed in my expectation that the malguzars who attended me would cause the surrender of the rebels still in arms against us, and I regret to state that some of them while professing the strongest fidelity to Government were affording supplies and protection to the insurgents." It is obvious that the success of the Bundela insurgents was largely due to the support which they received from the people of the area that the insurgents moved without fear of betrayal. They moved in a mass in a broad daylight and were unmolested by the large and powerful Taluqdars through whose lands they passed, and in the vicinity of whose towns they encamped.[29]

Observing the movements of Raja Hirde Shah, General Tombs ordered Col. Watson to Tejgarh. In the meantime Hirde Shah had doubled back with the intention of getting into Bundelkhand, and on his way a British detachment fell upon him, not far from Tejgarh. Although Raja Hirde Shah escaped, several of his party were captured or killed, and some property was also seized. He made his way to Jaitpur in Bundelkhand where the ex-Raja Parichhat had invited him.[30] Thus, the exertions of Hirde Shah and his associates succeeded in eliminating, though temporarily, the

British power from a large part of the trans-Narmada portion of Narsinghpur, Sagar and Jabalpur districts.[31] Major Sleeman stressed the need of crushing Raja Hirde Shah for the restoration of peace and order in the region as he was a principal leader of rebels who had been instigated by others to rebel against the government. He believed that the destruction of Hirde Shah would give a decisive blow to the rebels.[32]

Another rebel chief was Thakur Hindupat of Katra-Belkhera, who mounted a gun, collected arms and ammunitions, and started raising armed followers at the very commencement of the revolt. He was, however, forced into submission, and he surrendered himself before the Principal Assistant Commissioner at Jabalpur on 19 September 1842.[33]

In April 1842 the impact of the revolt was so great that the authorities in Betul were directed to be vigilant and ascertain whether insurgents had assembled anywhere on the banks of Tapti. They were also instructed to increase the police force to be strong enough to face any danger. Thereupon several *chowkies* were established at different *ghats* leading into Berar to ward off any danger from that direction. A line of patrol was established near Tapti to report about anv movement of insurgents.[34]

Suppression of the rebellion

The British suppressed the rebellion of 1842 with relentless fury. The district officers were armed with summary powers to deal with the alarming situation caused by the widespread insurrection. A large number of troops were summoned from all directions to hunt down the rebel leaders and their followers.[35]

As the revolt had spread like wild fire enveloping the entire region, the fighting went on till the end of 1842 at a number of places. None of these engagements was of a decisive nature, because the Bundelas kept up a guerilla warfare in the mountains and jungles of their country. It was felt that the rebels could never be wiped out, nor could they be captured in substantial numbers. The wild countryside of Bundelkhand and the Narmada valley provided them excellent places of refuge whenever they were overpowered by superior force. Partly for this reason, and partly from an awareness of their own depleted position after the disasters of the retreat from Kabul, the British were inclined to come to terms with the insurgents. Captain Boland, writing from Hoshangabad to the Agent at Sagar on 5 January 1843, suggested[36] a prudent way of settling the trouble : "As it would be impossible and impolitic to punish so large a body of influential people, I would suggest that the principal Jagirdars, Taluqdars and Gond Rajas be summoned in and promised forgiveness for the past, if they take an active part against the insurgents. Until some such measure be adopted, I anticipate no decided results and an indefinite prolongation of the existing state of disturbance."

In the meantime, some success was achieved by the government against the rebels, but it was not satisfactory. On 17 November 1842, C. Fraser, Agent in the Saugor and Nerbudda Territories, issued a Proclamation[37] calling upon all chieftains to lay down arms. The Proclamation was as follows :

> "Whereas the Raja Hirde Shah had been foolish enough to follow the example of insurgents and the plunderers, and whereas the said Raja having opposed the Government troops had fled, the Agent to the Lieutenant Governor is desirous of his apprehension."
>
> "But in order to comfort and assure all landholders, possessors of Estates and property, this proclamation is issued to impress upon all, that the British Government is not desirous of punishing any but the leaders of the insurgents. Therefore, all those who may have induced to do so through intimidation or

ignorance or inability to resist them are called upon to dismiss their fears, and are invited to wait upon either the District Officer or the Agent and explain their reasons for having joined the insurgents. The Agent may himself minutely enquire into their cases and guarantee their lives. All persons who may have any plundered property in their possession are requested to bring it to the Agent as the best proof of their innocence. The Agent is bent on the apprehension and punishment of the ring-leaders only."

The British Government issued another Proclamation[38] on 24 November 1842, offering a series of rewards for the arrest, dead or alive, of the prominent ring-leaders. They issued another Proclamation[39] on 19 December 1842, offering fresh rewards for the apprehension of the prominent rebel leaders. Since the rewards already announced did not prove effective, the Government raised the amount in case of important leaders.

A notable success was achieved by the British when Bakhat Bali, the Raja of Shahgarh, captured the prominent rebel leader, Raja Hirde Shah of Heerapur with the whole of his family on 22 December 1842. The latter was coming from Jaitpur and going towards Sagar with his family and other members of the rebel party.[40] In consideration of the service rendered by the Shahgarh Raja to the British Government, Sleeman was induced to help the former that he would solicit the pardon of his illegitimate brother, Lachman Singh, who had joined the rebels in plundering the British territory.[41] The capture of Raja Hirde Shah and his party was a major setback for the insurgents. The captured prisoners were sent to Chunar *via* Damoh under a strong police escort. Some indication of the anxiety which the British authorities had regarding the influence which Raja Hirde Shah exercised over the minds of the people in these territories, is provided by the fact that while they were conducting him and his family under a strong police guard to Chunar, Major Sleeman, Agent in Bundelkhand, wrote to Captain Brown informing him that while Hirde Shah and other persons were taken through the town of Damoh, the people of the place, who knew him, should be asked to confront him, so that no doubt might be left among the people of the capture of their leaders. The former believed that the arrest of Raja Hirde Shah would induce other rebel leaders to surrender one by one.[42]

In the meantime, Sleeman recommended to the Governor General of India that Raja Hirde Shah be given pardon and restored to his estate and some of his associates might be put on trial. He was of the view that Raja Hirde Shah never had any intention to rebel against the government but had been induced to take up arms by Raja of Jaitpur and his own close relatives. Accordingly, Mirbhan Singh, the son of Hirde Shah, alongwith two others, Eshree Singh and Rao Aman Singh, were committed for trial in the Sessions Court.[43] Mirbhan Singh later on played an important role in the revolt of 1857. As recommended by Sleeman, Lord Ellenborough, the Governor General, ordered the release of Raja Hirde Shah and restored his estate on the terms which existed before the outbreak. He was hopeful of their future good behaviour and zealous service in preserving the peace of the country.[44] This step was, apparently, recommended to divide the rebels and win the confidence of some prominent leaders for the British government.

It may be worthwhile to discuss how these rebels were captured and the rebellion suppressed. Only the capture of some prominent leaders have been taken into account. Some of them later on played an important role in the revolt of 1857. Due to the difficulties in prolonging the revolt in February 1843, the rebel Thakurs of Madanpur and Dhilwar, Delun Shah and Narwar Singh, in the Narsinghpur district, surrendered themselves alongwith their followers before Ramcharan, the Tehsildar of Chawarpatha. In order to effect their surrender, Ramcharan had promised these Thakurs to secure full pardon for them. Sleeman submitted this proposal to the Governor General and the latter agreed so the government might not be charged with the breach of faith.[45] The Governor General further decided to restore their estates with the intimation that any new crime would be punished by complete forfeiture and extreme penalties.[46] Both these Thakurs later on played an important role during the revolt of 1857 in their region.

Dewan Jawahar Singh of Chandrapur, who alongwith Madhukar Shah of Narhat had started the rebellion in the Sagar district, for whom a reward of Rs. 10,000 was offered, surrendered himself to the government in June 1843. He was by far the most formidable leader in the Sagar district. He was induced to surrender by his cousin, Raja Khet Singh, the new Raja of Jaitpur. However, Sleeman recommended[47] to the Governor General to grant pardon to him as the British had little or no chance of taking him prisoner with his extensive connections and high personal character. Consequently, the Governor General granted him full pardon. His small estate was given in lease to others and he was ordered to reside in Jaitpur. The reward of Rs.10,000 for his arrest was also paid to him as the foundation of a future provision for support.[48]

Another prominent leader, Madhukar Shah of Narhat was captured by Captain Hamilton in February 1844. In his capture Thakur Mardan Singh of Banpur had co-operated with the British. A reward of Rs.5,000 had been offered for the apprehension or destruction of Madhukar Shah. Thakur Mardan Singh refused to accept the proposed award. Since the number of persons, who were engaged in his seizure was small, the amount was distributed liberally among them[49]. After his trial, Madhukar Shah was publicly executed and his body burnt behind the Sagar jail.[50] He, however, became a popular hero and the subject of folk-songs and folk-lore which are widely current in this area. At the place where his body was cremated, a *chabutra* has been raised and the people who live in Gopalganj (a part of the Sagar town) still look upon this monument with great reverance.

After the seizure of Madhukar Shah, his younger brother, Ganeshjoo, intimated his desire to surrender. He was a young man of 19 years of age and was deeply implicated in all of the disturbances from April 1842 to December 1843. He was induced to take to plundering activities by his elder brother, Madhukar Shah, to whom he was very much attached. After the capture of Madhukar Shah, he surrendered himself on the sole guarantee that his life would be spared.[51] He was put on trial and subsequently sentenced to transportation.[52]

A prominent leader of Bundelkhand who was intimately connected with these territories, Parichhat Singh, the deposed Raja of Jaitpur, alongwith his relatives and followers, decided to give up plundering activities. They surrendered themselves in October 1844 on the sole guarantee of being pardoned by the British Government. After his surrender, he was given a pension of Rs. One Thousand and Two Hundred per month from the government but he did not live long.[53] During the revolt of 1857, his widow Rani made heroic exertions for the recovery of his lost principality and occupied Simariyain Hatta Tehsil of Damoh district in the Saugor and Nerbudda Territories.

A large number of rebel leaders and their followers were, however, induced to surrender to the government. Gradually many of them were allowed to return to their peaceful occupations. Sleeman believed that these leaders would not again disturb the peace of the country. The district of Chanderi in which these rebels had taken shelter was placed under strong police guard by the government.[54]

Thus, the proclamations offering rewards of big amounts for the apprehension of the prominent ring leaders worked and many of them were either captured or surrendered themselves voluntarily.[55] In order to strike terror among the people, some estates of the small proprietors were confiscated and men of affluence and position suddenly found themselves turned into paupers. The white terror that followed was mainly political, meant to strike fear in the heart of Indians, so another such rising might not take place.[56] We also find that the British Government adopted dual policy towards the rebels. Several leaders who had taken prominent part in the disturbances were pardoned and restored to their estates. However, a few of them received high-handed treatment. Perhaps this was to divide the rebels and win the confidence of some important leaders for the British Government.[57]

By the end of August 1845, all the leaders and their followers had been either punished or pardoned.[58] In this way by a policy of judicious combination of punishment and clemency, the British Government ultimately succeeded in suppressing the rebellion.[59]

Although the leaders of the rebellion came from the disaffected and dispossessed classes but all were united in the objective they had in view, the expulsion of the British from this region. The movement failed to gather any momentum because there was no co-ordinated plan and an over-all leadership among the insurgents. Moreover, "they were opposed by the well-equipped and ably-led British army who, when the first shock of surprise was overcome, were able to round them up in isolated groups and thus suppress the revolt effectively."[60] Thus, after eighteen months of struggle, the Bundela rebellion was suppressed and it "met with utter failure due to the lack of a cementing factor, efficient leadership, paucity of resources and inferior equipment of arms."[61]

Aftermath of Rebellion

As already referred to, the early administration of the British in these territories was defective and weighed heavily upon the people. The authorities had already realised that the true causes of the rebellion lay in the acts of misgovernment committed by the British officers. They assessed the lands too high, impoverished the people and retarded the progress of the region.[62] It attracted the anxious attention of Lord Ellenborough, the Governor General of India. He was convinced that the misgovernment in this part of country was forcing the landlords and the people to resort to arms against the British Government. He believed that the real cause of the outbreak was the administration of the Government in a "spirit of harshness and repulsiveness towards the people."[63] He, therefore, ordered the adoption of far-reaching measures to rectify the evils which disturbed the peace of the region.

In consequence of the supposed discredit thrown by this rebellion on the British administration, Lord Ellenborough inaugurated the newly gained peace by making a clean sweep of the British officials in these territories. In February-March 1843 he literally remodelled the administration of the territory. He separated this region from the North-Western Provinces as this system did not prove successful. The orders flowed from Agra regarding land revenue, farm leases, and other administrative decisions were misinterpreted by the authorities in these territories which was one of the major causes of the Bundela rising of 1842. Hence, after the suppression of the Bundela rebellion, these territories were placed under a Commissioner in direct communication with the Government. However, the fiscal and judicial administration remained under the Sadar Revenue Board and Sadar Court of the North-Western Provinces. He placed this region under an Agent to the Governor General in Bundelkhand. Major W.H. Sleeman, Agent in Bundelkhand, was also given the charge of Commissioner in the Saugor and Nerbudda Territories in place of C. Fraser.[64] Several appointments of Principal Assistants, First Junior Assistants and Junior Assistants to the Commissioner were abolished. A new set of officers was appointed to improve the image of the administration. The establishment under the Commissioner was composed of twelve Deputy

Commissioners in three classes and each class comprised of four officers.[65] The Deputy Commissioners were given only revenue and criminal powers of a Collector and Magistrate of the Regulation Provinces.[66]

On the suggestion of R.M. Bird, the number of the districts in these territories were reduced and the Narsinghpur and Betul districts were annexed to the neighbouring district of Hoshangabad in 1836. This step had caused great inconvenience and dissatisfaction among the people due to the long distance between their residence and the headquarters of the district administration. The people were subjected to unnecessary expense and great hardships. After the suppression of the rebellion, Narsinghpur and Betul were again made full-fledged districts in 1843.[67]

Before the outbreak of the rebellion, there were several complaints against the admininstration of the civil justice in these territories. During the Bundela rebellion, the whole machinery of the judicial administration was disrupted. There had been a very great accumulation of undecided cases of appeal before C. Fraser from the districts and Sadar Ameen Courts. No civil business was attended to during the disturbances. To remedy these evils, the judicial duties were placed under the sole control of a separate officer styled Civil and Sessions Judge.[68] Mr. Caldecott was appointed to this post with the powers which were exercised by the Commissioner in the civil cases. He was authorised to supervise over the Courts of Principal Sadar Ameen, Sadar Ameens and Munsiffs, all purely civil judicial functionaries, but were in no manner made subordinate to the district officers who thus ceased to excercise any civil judicial functions.[69] As far as criminal matters were concerned, the Civil and Sessions Judge was made subordinate to the Nizamat Adalat in the North-Western Provinces.[70] C.M. Caldecott exerted himself to overcome the initial difficulties and made important improvements in the administration of the courts.[71]

We have already discussed how the implementation of the twenty years settlement in this region proved disastrous for the agrarian economy. It was concluded without any proper survey. The Settlement Officers had fixed the land revenue on the basis of their own observations regarding the tracts, their crops and prices etc. This settlement assessed the revenue demand to the extent of 66% of the total assets which was confessedly excessive and retarded the progress of the village economy. Another lacuna in this settlement was that it did not recommend the conferment of proprietary rights to the actual cultivators which was in vogue, though to a limited extent, during the Gond and Maratha rule.[72]

However, it seems that by the end of twenty years settlement in 1853, the British were fully aware of the discontentment both among the land holding classes and other cultivators. By the time the term of the twenty years settlement (1834-54) expired, the land revenue policy of the Government of the North-Western Provinces had undergone a change in respect of these territories. While issuing instructions in 1853 for a resettlement of these territories, the Government had directed, among other things, that proprietary rights should be conferred on lessees with whom settlements had been made in the past as farmers. In 1855 the Saharanpur Settlement Rules were also extended to these territories. Under these rules, the demand of the State upon the new proprietors was limited to one-half of the average net assets instead of two-thirds as before.[73]

Hence, the British Government decided to confer the proprietary rights with the hope that it might encourage the cultivators to invest their capital for the development of agricultural farms and thereby acquiring more land revenue for the British treasury. But, this was interrupted due to the outbreak of the revolt of 1857 and it was only in mid-sixties that another long term settlement was concluded and the proprietary rights were given to the cultivators.

The administration of Sleeman, the Commissioner of the

Saugor and Nerbudda Territories, was characterized by ability and good judgement. As already referred to, he introduced new policies in the administration and fairly succeeded in pacifying the discontented people and chiefs alike.[74]

The proximity and connection of the Saugor and Nerbudda Territories with the Maratha kingdoms of Central India i.e. Gwalior and Indore always kept it see thing with discontent. When in 1843 "the Gwalior Durbar commenced those hostilities against the British which culminated in the battle of Maharajpur, the chiefs and people of Saugor and Narbada territories broke out into open rebellion. This rebellion was partly to the great dislike felt by the people to the civil courts, and more particularly to the mode in which they were administered and partly to the propaganda of the Gwalior Durbar."[75] However, the British suppressed the rebellion both in the Gwalior and in this region.

After a tenure of three years, Sleeman was promoted to be a Resident at Lucknow. He handed over the administration of this region to his successor, Bushley, in perfect order. Bushley carried on the administration of this region for five or six years with ability and good judgement. However, this arrangement was not found to work well and these territories were again attached to the North-Western Provinces in 1852[76].

It is, however, to be noted that ever since these territories were taken over from the Marathas, their administrative arrangements had been frequently changing, shifting back and forth between the North-Western Provinces and direct administration under the Supreme Government. Hence, the British could not adopt a consistent policy in the spheres of revenue assessment and matters of general policy towards the chiefs and the common people.

It is also to be noted that by the suppression of the Bundela rebellion of 1842, the spirit of rebellion was simply scotched and not killed in these territories as is evident fifteen years later when the smouldering discontent ultimately burst into the flames of 1857.

REFERENCES

1. D.P. Mishra, ed., *History of the Freedom Movement in Madhya Pradesh* (1956), p. 33.
2. *Ibid.*, p. 82.
3. M.P. D.G., Narsimhapur (1971), p. 59.
4. J.P. Mishra, *The Bundela Rebellion* (1982), p. 248
5. J.W. Kaye, *A History of the Sepoy War in India* Vol.I (1870), p. 165.
6. M.P. D.G., Narsimhapur, *op. cit.*, p. 62.
7. J.P. Mishra, *op. cit.*, inner flap of the book.
8. *Ibid.*, preface, p. xii.
9. Quoted in the *History of Freedom Movement in Madhya Pradesh*, *op. cit.*, p. 34.
10. J.D.,B.C., Political Case File No. 22 of 1842, pp. 101,109-10.
11. Jubbulpore Divisional Records, Ref. CLII-151 of 1843, para 4.
12. *Ibid.*, para 33.
13. *Ibid.*, para 35.
14. *Ibid.*, para 39.
15. *Ibid.*, paras 38 and 40.
16. *Ibid.*
17. J.P. Mishra, *op. cit.*, p. 238.
18. *Ibid.*
19. Jubbulpore Divisional Records, *op. cit.*, para 46.
20. *Ibid.*
21. Foreign, Political, Letter from the Secretary of State, 1 November 1843, No. 34.
22. Jubbulpore Divisional Records, *op. cit.*, pp. 173-74. This statement surprisingly contradicts Bird's opinion that people were not habitual of carrying arms for their security (*vide* footnote No. 23, Chapter I).
23. Jubbulpore Divisional Records, 1842-44, Vol.152, p. 1. quoted in M.P. D.G., Narsimhapur (1971), p. 60.
24. M.P. D.G., Sagar (1967), p. 66.
25. M.P. D.G., Narsimhapur, *op. cit.*, p. 60.
26. J.D., B.C., Political case File No. 12 of 1842, p. 86, quoted in J.P. Mishra, *op. cit.*, p. 121.
27. D.P. Mishra, *op. cit.*, p. 35.
28. *Ibid.*, pp. 35-6.

29. J.D., B.C., Political Case File No. 20 of 1842, pp. 236-38, quoted in J.P. Mishra, *op. cit.*, p. 110.
30. *Ibid.*
31. Foreign, Political, Cons. 14 June 1843, No. 740, Quoted in M.P. D.G. Narsimhapur, *op. cit.*, p. 33.
32. J.D., B.C., Political Case File No. 1 of 1842, p. 139, quoted in J.P. Mishra, *op. cit.*, p. 191.
33. J.D., B.C., Political Case File No. 1 and 56 of 1842, quoted in M.P. D.G., Jabalpur (1968), p. 100.
34. M.P. D.G., Betul (1971), p. 52.
35. J.P. Mishra, *op. cit.*, p. 183.
36. Quoted in D.P. Mishra, *op. cit.*, p. 37.
37. *Ibid.*, pp. 37-8.
38. J.D., B.C., Political Case File No. 50 of 1842, quoted in J.P. Mishra, *op. cit.*, p. 195.
39. Jubbulpore Divisional Records, Ref. CLII-I, p. 1, quoted in J.P. Mishra, *op. cit.*, p. 195.
40. J.P. Mishra, *op. cit.*, p. 196.
41. Jubbulpore Divisional Records, Ref. CLII-11.
42. J.D., B.C., Political Case File No. 1 of 1842, p. 232, quoted in J.P. Mishra, *op. cit.*, p. 197.
43. Foreign, Political, Cons. dated 15 July 1843, No. 119.
44. *Ibid.*, Nos.120-21.
45. J.P. Mishra, *op. cit.*, pp. 202-3.
46. J.D., B.C., Political Case File No. 25 of 1842 to 1844, pp. 191-95.
47. Jubbulpore Divisional Records, Ref.CLII-110, p. 111.
48. J.D., B.C., Political Case File No. 40 of 1843, p. 1.
49. Jubbulpore Divisional Records, Ref.CLII-322 and Foreign Political, Cons. 17 February 1844, No. 90.
50. *Ibid.*, CLII-384.
51. J.D., B.C., Judicial Case File No. 13 of 1844, p. 2.
52. J.P. Mishra, *op. cit.*, p. 213.
53. *Ibid.*, p. 215.
54. Jubbulpore Divisional Records, Ref. CLII-384 (90), quoted in J.P. Mishra, *op. cit.*, p. 215.
55. *Ibid.*, p. 250.
56. *Ibid.*
57. *Ibid.*
58. J.P. Mishra, *op. cit.*, p. 216.

59. *Ibid.*, p. 217.
60. D.P. Mishra, *op. cit.*, p. 39.
61. J.P. Mishra, *op. cit.*, p. 252.
62. *Ibid.*, p. 232.
63. Hoshangabad District Records, Case File No. 25 of 1842-44, p. 192, quoted in J.P. Mishra, *op. cit.*, p. 232.
64. J.D., B.C., Revenue Case File No. 19 of 1843, p. 14.
65. *Ibid.*, p. 7.
66. M.P. D.G., Jabalpur (1968), p. 449.
67. Jubbulpore Divisional Records, Ref. CLII-151, pp. 175-76, M.P. D.G., Narsinghpur, *op. cit.*, p. 3, Betul, *op. cit.*, p. 3.
68. J.D., B.C., Political Case File No. 19 of 1843, pp. 11-12.
69. M.P. D.G., Jabalpur, *op. cit.*, p. 449.
70. J.D., B.C., Political Case File No. 19 of 1843, pp. 1 and 11.
71. Foreign, Political, Despatch from the Secretary of State, dated 2 October 1844, No. 33.
72. D.E. Chowfin, *Society and Economy in Sagar-Narmada Territories, 1818-61*, unpublished thesis, University of Jabalpur, 1991, pp. 251-52.
73. J.F. Dyer, *Introduction to Land Revenue System of the Central Provinces* (1924), pp. 33-5 and 37-8.
74. J.P. Mishra, *op. cit.*, p. 241.
75. J.W. Kaye and G.B. Malleson, *History of Indian Mutiny*, Vol. V (1897), p. 60.
76. M.P. D.G., Jabalpur, *op. cit.*, p. 101.

CHAPTER 3

Causes of the Revolt of 1857 in the Saugor and Nerbudda Territories

In the preceding two chapters, we have discussed the history and administration of the Saugor and Nerbudda Territories and the Bundela rebellion of 1842 in them. We have seen how the British revenue settlement in this region was the backbone of this insurrectionary movement. More or less this was a feudal revolt against the British rule. These two chapters form the background of the revolt of 1857 in these territories. It can, however, be said that the Bundela rebellion was a prelude to that of 1857 in this region "as the major centres of resistance were precisely those places which had risen against the British during the Bundela rebellion of 1842. Sagar itself, Damoh, Narsinghpur, Chawarpatha, Tendukhera, Heerapur were the places where the Thakurs and Malguzars refused to reconcile themselves to subordination and dependence fifteen years ago."[1]

The years that followed the suppression of the Bundela rebellion were years of smouldering discontent which ultimately burst into the flames of 1857. The history of the causes of the revolt, its outbreak, its progress, its ruthless suppression and its effects here is not different from the other parts of the country. In this chapter we will discuss the causes of the discontent in detail which led to the revolt of 1857 in India in general and these territories in particular.

In the revolt of 1857, millions of soldiers, people, dispossessed rulers and feudal lords made a combined effort to overthrow the British rule in India. The revolt was, however, no sudden occurrence. It was the culmination of nearly a century of old discontent against the British rule and its imperialist policies since the battle of Plassey which exploited the country to the extreme. The British had conquered India and colonised its society and economy through a long-drawn process which led to the continuous resistance by the people. A series of civil rebellions led by the deposed rulers and impoverished landlords, assisted by the people in general, posed a threat to the British empire in India. From 1765 to 1857, there were forty six rebellions as enumerated by Dr. S.B. Choudhuri in his book, 'Civil Disturbances during the British Rule in India (1765-1857)' against the British rule including the Bundela rebellion discussed earlier. These rebellions though massive in their totality, were, however, wholly local in character and effects and were isolated from each other. The nature of the revolt of 1857 was more widespread which involved millions of people in various parts of the country and shook the British rule to its very roots.[2]

The revolt of 1857 was the outcome of the changing conditions which disturbed the placid currents of life in all its aspects and produced widespread discontent against the British rule. It was liable to flare up at any moment. The sepoys broke out into open revolt at Meerut on 10 May 1857. The next morning they galloped to Delhi where they proclaimed the aged titutar king, Bahadur Shah II, as emperor of Hindustan. It brought the latent spirit of revolt in action and the whole country from the Sutlej to the Narmada was ablaze.

The disaffection among the military and civil classes in the North-Western Provinces found its way across the Yamuna to Bundelkhand and these territories also.[3] Like other parts of the Northern India, these territories were one of the major theatres of the rebellious activities. They were swept by the waves of the revolt of 1857 only a month after it had flooded the Meerut-Delhi area in May 1857.

Causes of discontent

The causes of the discontent in these territories may

properly be studied in the background of the general causes of the revolt of 1857 in India. As already referred to, the evils of the British administration led to the Bundela rebellion of 1842 in them. The aftermath of the Bundela rebellion and the policies adopted thereafter by the British further aggravated the discontent which added fuel to the fire of the revolt of 1857 in this region. In the background of the general discontent that prevailed in the entire country, the causes of the revolt in this region can be broadly divided into three major heads, *viz.*, (1) grievances of the feudal class; (2) discontent of the people and (3) grievances of the sepoys.

I. Grievances of the feudal class

As Lord Dalhousie had left behind him the legacy of unrest on completing his term as the Governor General of India in 1856, one of the major causes of the unrest was the 'Doctrine of Lapse' or 'escheat', pursued by him which centered round the policy of annexation for extending the limits of the British dominion in India. It meant[4] that "in dependent states or those that owed their very existence to the British power, the sovereignty, when the natural heirs of the royal line came to an end, passed back or lapsed to the supreme power." The states that were thus absorbed by him into the British empire were Satara in 1848, Jaitpur and Sambalpur in 1849, Baghat in 1850, Udaipur in 1852, Jhansi in 1853 and Nagpur in 1854. The prospects of losing their ancestral possessions were, therefore, upsetting the mind of the local rulers. This policy had far-reaching effects in the discontent of the employees including the army thrown out of service consequent upon the assumption of possessions of their masters.

As the British occupied the Saugor and Nerbudda Territories from the Marathas in 1818, there were no ruling chiefs in this region. Hence, the problem of the Doctrine of Lapse did not arise here but it did arise in other form of the feudal lords and chieftains whose grievances contributed immensely to the revolt of 1857 in this region. They spearheaded the revolt of 1857 like the Bundela rebellion of 1842 in it.

We have discussed earlier in detail the position of the feudal lords in the society and their rights and privileges during the Maratha and the British rule. The British conquest "resulted in the debasement of the local Jagirdars, Thakurs and chiefs who enjoyed considerable autonomy under the Maratha rule. They also had a high place in administration and the people in this area looked upon them as leaders of society in times of necessity. All this was changed with the assumption of power by the British. The importance of the local chiefs, Rajas etc. became a thing of the past[5]." It was "the deliberate policy of the British rulers to cut down the tall poppies in the Indian society and thus undermine the traditional organisation of the society."[6] The social structure in the country was so organised that the initiative for leadership and the responsibility for any movement of resistance had to come from the feudal leaders. The people looked upon them for guidance and were traditionally habituated to following their lead. The first phase of India's movement for assering her freedom, therefore, had necessarily to be a struggle under feudal leadership, a struggle by the great dispossessed.[7] Thus, under the prevailing circumstances, it was the feudal chiefs who were in a position to take up arms. Hence, they spearheaded the rebellion and the common peasantry gradually rallied round them.

Another source of discontenment amongst the feudal class was that they were deprived of a role in the administration. During the Maratha rule, the feudal class of the society had enjoyed considerable influence both in the government and society. But the British did not bestow the same powers to them as the whole administration was in the hands of the British.

It must be kept in mind that the British land revenue policy was very unpopular. The classes most hit by it were those who had much to lose - the ruling and proprietary classes. The dispossessed landlords and chieftains had become disaffected and a source of danger to the British rule.

II Discontent of the people

(i) Land revenue settlements : Overassessment and sale

The land revenue imposed during the Maratha rule was light and variable according to the circumstances. The new land revenue system established by the British was oppressive to the peasants. We have discussed earlier in detail how the British land revenue settlements made before and after the twenty years settlement in this region were unpopular and fraught with widespread discontent amongst both the feudal class and the people. The vast masses began to feel the burden of foreign rule especially as the land revenue demands began to increase five-fold and eight-fold which caused great difficulties to the people.[8] In can be said that the greatest evil consequence of the British rule was its land revenue policy which resulted in the economic exploitation of the region.

The main drawbacks of the British revenue policy were that the twenty years settlement was made without proper survey and the proprietary rights were not given to the cultivators. The lands were overassessed and in the collection of land revenue extortions were made and sale of the lands for the non-payment of revenue were the salient features of the British land revenue policy. The rigidity in the recovery of the land revenue resulted in the deprivation of the large number of cultivators of their rights and privileges and thus they lost their means of livelihood. The greater landlords and many chiefs had their lands expropriated leading to growing unemployment among their followers. All these led to the disastrous results. The British administrators made the same mistake here which they had made in Madras and elsewhere by imposing assessments which were too high and demanding an impossible revenue. Such a policy was found to impoverish the people and retard the progress of the country. A wave of anti-British feeling consequently swept the whole area from end to end.[9] It happened before the Bundela rebellion of 1842 and again before the revolt of 1857.

It seems by the end of twenty years settlement in 1853, the British were fully aware of the prevailing discontentment both among the land holding classes and the cultivators. The new settlement was, therefore, to be made for which preparations began. Measures were taken for the proper survey of the land and for conferring the proprietary rights on the actual cultivators and owners in order to rally round the support of the agriculturist with the hope that it would encourage the cultivators to invest their capital for the development of their agricultural farms and thereby acquiring more land revenue for the British treasury. However, this was interrupted due to the outbreak of the revolt of 1857 in this region and the old settlement continued upon the mid-sixties when the new thirty years settlement was made and the proprietary rights were given to the cultivators.

(ii) Evils of the British administration

After occupying these territories in 1818 from the Marathas, a new administration was introduced here which created widespread discontent among the people. Under the impact of the British system of administration, "the time-honoured and outmoded system of the Marathas crumbled, while the people could not be acclimatised with the new that was taking its place."[10]

The administration of these territories had passed through several vicissitudes. On the formation of the Saugor and Nerbudda Territories in 1820, it was placed under an Agent directly responsible to the Supreme Government at Calcutta.

In 1835, on the formation of the North-Western Provinces, it was tagged on to the administrative control of the Lieutenant Governor of it. In 1843, after the suppression of the Bundela rebellion, once again it was taken under the control of the Supreme Government. When this arrangement was not found to work well in 1852, the administrative supervision of these territories was again given to the Government of the North-Western Provinces. Thus, "due to these frequent changes, the administration could not acquire stability and lacked a continuity of policy in the spheres of revenue assessment and matters of general policy towards the chiefs and the common people."[11]

As pointed out earlier, while enumerating the causes of the Bundela rebellion of 1842, that the British had deliberately pursued a policy of eliminating the Indians from any administrative key-posts. The beaurocratic set-up established by them was purely Europeanized. The Indians were associated only with the judicial and police administration, that too in the middle and lower category. The same policy continued upto the revolt of 1857 which was one of the important causes of the discontent against the British rule.

During the preceding years of the revolt of 1857, the British had been involved in continuous external wars, such as, the Crimean War of 1855, the Chinese War of 1854-56 and the Persian War of 1856, for the imperial purposes. Due to the involvement in the foreign wars, the internal administration of India was neglected and the welfare of the people undermined[12] as India had to bear the expenses of these wars in sending out its armies to those countries.

(iii) Defective judicial system

The people were also dissatisfied with the British judicial system. It was complicated and expensive. It did not offer relief to the people as the courts were situated in the district headquarters and the people were required to travel long for the weary court proceedings. However, on Bird's recommendations a few reforms discussed earlier, were introduced in the judiciary which brought some relief to the people but the separation of judiciary from executive was limited to the administration of the civil justice only, whereas the administration of the criminal justice was still in the hands of the executive officers.

Another cause of discontent was the imposition of a foreign jurisprudence which was wholly unfamiliar with the people. It was also not properly implemented. It seems that the British officials charged with the administration did not perform their duties honestly. Some of them were not competent enough to dispense justice. The people did not receive fair treatment at their hands as well as from the officers of the inferior ranks subordinate to them. Hence, this system also added to the unpopularity of the British rule.[13]

(iv) Economic exploitation of the region

This region was lying in the geographical heart of the country. It was a rural and agricultural region marked by severe poverty and under-development. After occupying these territories from the Marathas in 1818, the British did not pay any attention for the development of this region. The development of the various areas like agriculture, industries, trade and commerce, transport and communications and others were neglected by them. Instead they exploited this region to the full in their own interests which contributed immensely to the widespread discontentment among the people.

(a) Agriculture

These territories covered a wide area of the Narmada valley which was very fertile. Moreover, the hilly tracts were also suitable for the cultivation of various crops. The various soils present in the region had a vast potential to enhance the agricultural produce. It is evident that there was a wide fertile tract in the region for the cultivation of various crops including cotton and sugarcane. Despite the geographical features favourable for agriculture, the pace of the growth in the cultivated area was not sufficient. This was due to the poverty of the people in general and the policy of the over-assessment of land revenue which left a very limited amount to them for the development of their fields.[14] Moreover, the system of leases, whether short term or long term did not encourage the cultivators to invest as they were not sure of the continuance of their leases. Hence, due to limited investment in agriculture, it did not develop into a considerable extent despite the availability of the fertile soil, ample water for irrigation and a great number of farm labourers.[15]

The primitive methods of cultivation further impeded its progress. The British could have provided them better agricultural implements which were prevalent in England due to the Industrial and Agricultural Revolutions. But their objective was not the progress of the economy of the region but to exploit the natural and other resources for the consolidation of their empire in other parts of the country.[16]

(b) Industries

The British rule ignored the growth of the urban economy by not paying any attention to the establishment of various industries despite the availability of superior quality of minerals in abundant quantity alongwith other natural resources. They were more particular in acquiring raw materials specially cotton for the progress of their own textile industry in England. Consequently, only a few cottage industries could develop in this region and the indigenous industries already established here declined due to the lack of patronage.[17]

(c) Transport and Communications

These territories were isolated from the other parts of country before the construction of railways in 1870, and the internal traffic was scarce except along a few main roads. As the large tracts of the territories were covered by impenetrable forests, the state of communication was backward.[18] The roads were also ill-managed, unsafe and infested with various unlawful elements. Due to the paucity of the means of communications, the agricultural produce could not be transported to various places easily. The procurement of essential commodities for livelihood was also not easy on account of the non-availability of the roads for the movement of bullock carts and other primitive vehicles. It was only after 1830, that some efforts were made to link Jabalpur with Nagpur and Mirzapur by a metalled road for the speedy movement of troops and to carry essential items useful for the British. After the Bundela rebellion of 1842, the British realised the necessity of good roads in the interior of territories, so that the troops could be sent immediately to suppress the insurrectionary movements.[19]

The postal system was also in its infancy and it was developed in 1850's when the British themselves experienced great difficulty in transporting the essential Government *dak*. However, due to the construction of a few good roads, and the development of postal system, the people were also benefitted to some extent.[20]

(d) Trade and Commerce

Due to the lack of transport in many parts of the region, even after a good harvest, there was no possibility of handsome profits to the cultivators and actually the grain rotted in the country side. It was only in the 1850's that a considerable trade had sprung up between Nagpur, the Narmada valley and Bombay. The staple articles like grain, oilseeds, raw cotton etc. were exported outside the territories in the country-carts or pack-bullocks. The imports consisted of all kinds of manufactures and fabrics, piece-goods, cutlery, hardware, brass-pots, wrought iron, salt, coconuts, etc.[21] All these factors were responsible for the very slow growth of the economy of the region. The British did not take any interest in developing it.

Another result of the economic exploitation of this region was the increase in the rural indebtedness. Due to the undeveloped trade, the pressure of the population was increased on land. The British revenue policy, uneconomic land holdings, poor means of irrigation and primitive methods of cultivation resulted in low production. Moreover, the social and religious customs of the people involved extra expenditure which further aggravated the problem of rural indebtedness. The money lenders not only charged heavy interest but also took advantage of ignorance and illiteracy of the peasants and resorted to deceitful measures such as false accounting, forged signatures, making the debtor sign for larger amounts than the latter had borrowed, etc.[22]

(v) Duty on salt

The other important tax levied on the people besides land revenue was duty on salt. In the Saugor and Nerbudda Territories salt from the salt lakes of Rajputana was consumed. A duty was levied on it for the first time by a notification, dated 9 May 1855, of the Lt. Governor, North-Western Provinces. A regular line was drawn from Agra *via* Jhansi to the Sagar frontier and thence across the Narmada to Seoni (in the Satpura range) and then turning eastward and north-eastward, so as to guard the access to Mirzapur. Thus, no salt could enter these districts from Rajputana in the West without crossing this line. On the Sagar and Seoni line, the duty was first raised in 1855-56 to Re. 1 and 8 annas per maund of 80 lbs., it was raised to Rs. 2 and 8 annas in 1859-60 and in 1862-63 to Rs. 3 to make it uniform with the duty in the North-Western Provinces. The duty was considered to be too high and a few complaints were also filed against its levy. However, the above duty was not levied in Hoshangabad, Betul and some parts of the Narsinghpur district which were exempted from any duty on salt.[23] The imposition of the tax on salt had been intensely disliked by the people everywhere. It was highly obnoxious to them and created great discontentment among both the rich and poor classes. Captain Gordon, Collector of Chanderi, who was imprisoned at Lalitpur during the movement of 1857, also complained about it. When he was rescued and sent to Sagar, he observed[24] that "all through the Banpur, Tehri and Shahgarh states, the people were bitterly hostile to salt department." Thus, it prove to be the greatest calamity inflicted on the poor and became a potent cause of resentment against the British rule.

(vi) Dread of conversion

(a) Christian missionaries and their activities

With the establishment of British rule in India, the activities of the Christian missionaries also increased and the Christianity gained converts. They were in the habit of giving their discourses in the public places where they not only preached their doctrines but also ridiculed the rites and practices of other religions. As they were often accompanied by the police, the people considered them as the henchmen of Christian Government. Sir Syed Ahmad Khan observed[25] that it was commonly believed that the missionaries were appointed and maintained by the Government. In their institutions also, the missionaries did not confine themselves to the work of teaching alone. To them the proselytism was the inevitable corollary of western education. Christian religion formed one of the subjects of the examination. Besides, the missionary propaganda within the military cantonments hurt the religious feelings of the sepoys and aroused suspicion among them regarding the real motive of the government.[26]

(b) Social legislation

To remove the prevalent evils in the Indian society, the British Government introduced social legislation without appreciating how much they were ingrained in the very texture of their lives and were having the religious sanctity behind themselves since a long time. The prohibition of the inhuman practice of infanticide by the Regulations of 1795 and 1802, and the abolition of *Sati* by the Regulation XVII of 1829 during the Governor Generalship of Lord William Bentinck, created apprehension in the minds of the people. They feared that the foreign rule would soon undermine the religious and social institutions in the country. They were not received with general approval of the people who considered as a deliberate and studied onslaught on the Hindu religion.[27] The result was that a feeling of bitterness was created everywhere.

During the Governor Generalship of Lord Dalhousie, 'the Caste Disabilities Removal Act' of 1850 was passed. It rescinded "all laws and usages throughout India which inflicted upon any person forfeiture of rights and property by reason of renunciation of or exclusion from the communion of any religion."[28] The Act enabled the converts to inherit their ancestral property. Both the Hindus and Mohammedans considered it as concession to Christian converts. The Act evoked loud complaints from Hindus, as under Hindu Law, inheritance of property was associated with the religious and ceremonial obligations.[29]

'The Hindu Widows Remarriage Act' of 1856 legalised the marriage of Hindu widows in India.[30] Although this was a good measure, the orthodox people interpreted it as unwarranted interference in their social and religious practices. 'Religion is in danger' became the common cry of the people.

(c) Western education

For the promotion of English education in India, Lord William Bentinck had passed a Resolution[31] on 7 March 1835 which declared that "the great object of the British Government ought to be the promotion of European literature and science among the natives of India; and that all the funds appropriated to education would best be employed on English education alone."

During the period of Lord Dalhousie, Sir Charles Wood's despatch[32] of 19 July 1854 although considered the English and Vernacular languages of India "together as the media for the diffusion of European knowledge" but priority was in fact given to English as medium of education and it remained a passport for government service. The whole scheme of education was looked upon with suspicion and aversion. It was deemed as an inroad on the caste prejudices and the religion of the people. Besides, the attempts made by the missionaries and by the government afterwards to introduce female education was not favoured by the conservative section of the people.[33]

(d) Innovations

The introduction of railways and telegraphs created a ferment in the public mind. They considered travelling by railways as defilement of caste and telegraphs as a bit of legerdemain.[34] These innovations aroused suspicion in the minds of the masses and they considered them as instruments of conversion.

When the activities of the missionaries, social legislation relating to abolition of infanticide and *sati*, widow remarriage, inheritance of converts, expansion of western education and the introduction of railways and telegraphs were creating alarm among the people of the entire country, the Saugor and Nerbudda Territories could not remain unaffected and both the Hindus and Mohammadans there became panicky about their religion.

(vii) Rumours

The general public also felt panicky by the rumours that were spreading during these days. The mysterious role of '*Chapaties*', 'Lotus' and the 'Bone-Dust Story' went a long way in spreading the feeling of revolt in the country as well as in these territories.

(a) Chapaties

Before the outbreak of the revolt of 1857, *chapaties* or small wheaten cakes were circulated in a mysterious manner in many rural villages throughout the country. The bearer knew apparently no more than those from whom they last received the cakes and what the purpose of injunction was which directed the preparations of five cakes to be carried on to the villages in advance. "They would be called for", it was stated, and in this way *chapaties* travelled often over 160 or 200 miles in a night.[35] The object of its distribution was interpreted in different ways; as a warning of impending calamity and an invitation to the people to unite for some secret subject to be disclosed afterwards.[36]

All endeavours by the Government failed to discover any explanation of this mysterious movement. It was generally acknowledged to be the Hindu origin and believed to have some bearing upon the prophecy limiting British rule to a Hundred years.[37] Its starting point was probably in Bundelkhand or Nagpur. Whatsoever the real nature of the *chapaties* might have been, it kept the minds of the people agitated and excited.[38]

Like the rest of the country, the people of the Saugor and Nerbudda Territories were also excited by the circulation of the *chapaties*. It stirred up the rural population of the region for participating in the revolt in the early parts of the year 1857. Major Erskine, the Commissioner of these territories, described[39] how "so far back as January 1857 small wheaten cakes (*chapaties*) were passed in a most mysterious manner from village to village in most of the districts, and although all took it as a signal that something was coming, nobody in the division I believe, knew what it protended, or whence it came, and it appeared to have been little thought about except that in the money market of Saugor it is said to have had some slight effect in bill transactions." At that time he reported this matter to the Government but "even now it is a matter of doubt if the signal was understood by any one, or it referred to the coming rebellion, though such is now the general opinion."

Captain Ternan, the Deputy Commissioner of Narsinghpur, was first to inform[40] Major Erskine on 18 March 1857 about the circulation of *chapaties* in his district that "on 24 January 1857, when encamped at village Nerwerah, a village Kotwar came with five small cakes about an inch in diameter saying that he had distributed fifteen giving each village Kotwar five where he had been five, and wanted to know what he was to do with the remaining five." On enquiry he could not get any explanation of it. The cakes as the Kotwar said to Captain Ternan, were received by him in the morning with instructions to leave them with the watchmen of every village *to be kept till called for* and that he had so distributed them in the neighbouring villages. Ternan who had passed through the experience of the Bundela rebellion saw[41] in those unleavened cakes "the fiery cross sent through the land to unsettle the minds of the great mass of people" and distributed broadcast indicated "a sudden danger that might come at any moment upon the people, threatening their caste and undermining their religion."

Lieutenant J.C.Wood, the Deputy Commissioner of Hoshangabad informed[42] Major Erskine on 19 March 1857 that "small baked *atta* cakes have also been distributed throughout the Hoshangabad district. The signal came from the Bhopal direction and passed rapidly through my district to Baitool and the Chhindwara district." Similarly, the Deputy Commissioner of Betul[43] informed the Commissioner on 27 March 1857 about the distribution and circulation of cakes from village to village through the Kotwars. Lieutenant Edward Clerk, the Deputy Commissioner of Seoni also informed[44] the Commissioner on 20 March 1857 that "cakes have lately been distributed by Kotwars throughout the district." Captain Pinkney, the Deputy Commissioner of Sagar informed[45] the Commissioner on 19 March 1857 that "the

Kotwars of the different villages in this district had messages accompanied by a small cake passed to them from the Kotwars of the neighbouring villages. Cakes were transmitted to this district both from the Narsinghpur and Damoh districts." Thus, in these territories the *chapaties* were circulated in all the districts which intended to be a message and a warning of the uprising so that the people might be prepared for it.

(b) Lotus

Besides *chapaties*, the lotus was another symbol of mystery. It was a common occurrence for a man to come to a cantonment with a lotus flower, and give it to the chief native officer of a regiment. The flower was circulated from hand to hand in a regiment. "Each man took it, looked at it and passed on saying nothing." When the lotus came to the last man in the regiment, he disappeared and took it to the next military station. This mysterious process occurred in almost all the military stations where the regiments of the Bengal army were cantoned.[46] It may however be noted that the reference of the circulation of the lotus flower is not found in the records of these territories.

(c) Bone-dust story

Before the outbreak of the revolt of 1857, there grew a strong belief that all the flour sold in the market was mixed with the finely ground bones of cows and pigs.[47] Such reports strengthened the conviction of the people that the Government was bent upon destroying their castes "by fraudulently bringing in one way or the other, the unclean things to their lips."[48]

The rumours that the flour sold in the market was mixed with finely ground bones of cows and pigs further agitated the minds of the people of these territories. Early in May 1857, stories were current in Sagar, Damoh and Jabalpur districts that *ghee*, *atta* and sugar had been adulterated by the Government orders with cow's and pig's blood and bone-dust to defile the religions of both the Hindus and Mohammadans. Major Erskine confirmed[42] it that "stories were current in Saugor, Dumoh and Jubbulpore to the effect that the *ghee*, *atta* and sugar had been adulterated by order of Government with pig's and cow's blood and bone-dust, in order that all Hindoos and Mahomedans partaking of them might lose their caste or religion." He then issued a proclamation that all reports of the kind were false. He also recommended to the Commanding Officers to have their men's provisions purchased and examined by the Committees of Indian Officers and the *atta* to be grounded in their presence. This had a good effect and two or three persons having been caught spreading false reports were well flogged.[50]

Major W.C. Western, the Deputy Commissioner of Sagar informed[51] Major Erskine, the Commissioner, that since the beginning of May considerable excitement prevailed in the city and Sadar Bazar, "it appears that some evil disposed persons had circulated a report that from the 1st of June the Government would sell *Atta* and sugar at absolutely cheap rates and that pigs blood and cows bone would be mixed with those articles, that any person refusing to purchase from the Government store which was said to be in the Fort and Commissariat godowns, would be punished." He deemed it necessary to issue a proclamation pointing out the absurdity of such a rumour and called upon good men to assist the Government in seizing the originators of these false reports. Such rumours that were current in Sagar seemed to have caused considerable excitement amongst the people.

III Grievances of the sepoys

(i) Conditions of service

The sepoys were discontented and disaffected due to their grievances relating to the conditions of their service. Army service offered little prospect to the Indians as compared to their British counterparts. T.R. Holmes was of the opinion[52] that "though he might give signs of the military genius of a Hyder, he knew that he could never attain the pay of an English subaltern, and the rank to which he might attain, after same thirty years of service, would not protect him from the insolent dictation of an ensign fresh from England."

The sepoys, therefore, smarted under a sense of unjustified inferiority, for there was immeasurable gulf between the seniormost Indian officers and the youngest British officer. In these circumstances, "it did not seem altogether reasonable to expect from the sepoy any strong affection for the alien officer who had usurped all the high places of Army and who had kept him down in the dead level of the dust."[53]

(ii) General Service Enlistment Act of 1856

The feeling of discontent was intensified further by Lord Canning's 'General Service Enlistment Act' of 1856 which decreed that no recruit should in future be accepted who would not undertake to march wheresoever his services might be required.[54] The new Act was viewed with great alarm by the sepoys. They felt that the avenues of military service were now indirectly closed to their sons.[55] It was interpreted by the Hindu sepoys as an insidious attempt to destroy their caste, by forcing them to cross the sea.[56]

(iii) Dread of losing faith : Greased cartridges

In 1856 a new type of rifle, commonly called 'Enfield Rifle' was introduced in India which involved the use of greased cartridges. For the use of the new cartridges, the sepoys had to bite off the greased portion with their mouth instead of tearing with their hands.[57] Soon the suspicion grew that the greased cartridges were smeared with the fat of cows and pigs to destroy the religions of both the Hindus and Mohammedans. The suspicion of the sepoys was not without foundation.[58] Although the Government tried to remove the suspicion of the sepoys by issuing a circular[59] on 29 January 1857 which directed that "when applying tallow to articles which Native soldiers are required to handle, only the tallow of sheep or goat is to be employed, that of swine or cow being most carefully excluded." Yet the disaffection caused by it continued unabated.

The greased cartridge was the lever used in many instances to excite the sepoys but it was not the only factor responsible for the outbreak. It no doubt brought the latent spirit of revolt into action.[60] Sir John Lawrence was of the opinion[61] that the mutiny had its origin in the army itself and its "proximate cause was the cartridge affair, and nothing else." But as we have seen the sepoys were smarting under many other grievances of their own.

In April 1857 excited letters from the Bengal army reached the Bengal regiments at Sagar, Damoh and Jabalpur alleging that the new greased cartridges were designed to offend their religion. Major Erskine also confirmed it[62] that in April 1857 there was some excitement amongst the Bengal troops regarding the introduction of the new cartridges at certain stations in the Presidency; "but none of these cartridges reached my division and the agitation was confined to the soldiers to whom many false reports came by dak that the Government had a design on their religion, &c., and there can be no doubt that emissaries were going about and letters passing between regiments, boding no good."

The Deputy Commissioner of Sagar reported[63] to Major Erskine that "the sepoys spoke strongly on the subject of the cartridges and threatened to refuse to receive any fresh ones that might be served out. Nightly meetings were held in both in and out of cantonments in which the destruction of Europeans was contemplated but it was decided to postpone their designs until they saw what befell the Delhi mutineers." On 23 May 1857 the Brigadier commanding this division issued an order on the subject of the cartridges that the Government would do nothing to injure their caste. It had good affect in allaying the complaints about the cartridges. On the same day the Irregular Cavalry accepted these cartridges and fired them.

Thus, the grievances of the sepoys were many. They were alarmed with the activities of the military Generals who preached Christianity in the cantonments. The 'General Service Enlistment Act' was interpreted by the Hindu sepoys as an attempt to destroy their caste. The introduction of the greased cartridges for their use further confirmed their suspicion about the Government's attempt to infringe their faith and thus prepare the way for their conversion to Christianity.

It is noteworthy that the aggrieved ruling chiefs and the discontented civil society bore with the situation sullenly. It was the sepoys who took the initiative of giving lead to the revolt. In the Saugor and Nerbudda Territories, in the Sagar district the 3rd Irregular Cavalry and 42nd Regiment of Bengal Native Infantry; in the Damoh district, two Companies of the 42nd Bengal Native Infantry and in the Jabalpur district the 52nd Regiment of the Bengal Native Infantry broke out during the course of revolt. They shared in common the grievances of the rest of the sepoys of the Bengal army and consequently, they moved in its wake. The official records corroborate that the greased cartridge had been the constant subject of discussion among the sepoys in these territories.

It can, however, be concluded that the above-mentioned causes of the discontent were responsible for the explosive situation in India in general and in the Saugor and Nerbudda Territories in particular. It was like a ripe volcano and only a spark was needed which was supplied by the greased cartridges. As referred to earlier, these territories were swept by the waves of revolt of 1857 only a month after it had flooded the Meerut-Delhi area in May 1857. First of all, it touched the Sagar district in June and then it spread to the other parts and the disturbances became general.

REFERENCES

1. D.P. Mishra, ed., *History of Freedom Movement in Madhya Pradesh* (1956), p. 82.
2. D.E. Chowfin, *Society and Economy in Sagar-Narmada Territories, 1818-1861*, unpublished thesis, University of Jabalpur, 1991, pp. 28-9.
3. H.P. Chattopadhyay, *The Sepoy Mutiny : A Social Study and Analysis* (1957), p. 180.
4. P. E. Roberts, *History of British India under the Company and the Crown* (Reprint,1945), p. 350.
5. R.M. Sinha, foreword, J.P. Mishra, *The Bundela Rebellion*, (1982), p. v.
6. J.P. Mishra, *op. cit.*, p. 34.
7. D.P. Mishra, *op. cit.*, p. 60.
8. M.P. D.G., Betul (1971), p. 59.
9. J.P. Mishra, *op. cit.*, p. 246.
10. R.M. Sinha, foreword, J.P. Mishra, *op. cit.*, p. vi.
11. J.P. Mishra, *op. cit.*, p. 245.
12. *Ibid.*, p. 247.
13. *Ibid.*
14. D.E. Chowfin, *op. cit.*, pp. 253-54.
15. *Ibid.*, p. 158.
16. *Ibid.*, p. 254.
17. *Ibid.*, p. 258.
18. C.P. A.R., 1862-63, p. 25.
19. D.E. Chowfin, *op. cit.*, p. 259.
20. *Ibid.*, p. 260.
21. C.P. A.R., *op. cit.*, pp. 25-7.
22. D.E. Chowfin, *op. cit.*, pp. 259-60.
23. C.P. A.R., 1861-62, pp. 209-11.
24. *The Revolt in Central India, 1857-59*; compiled in the Intelligence Branch, Army Head Quarters, India (1908), p. 24.
25. Syed Ahmad Khan, *Asbab-e-Sarkashi-e-Hind*, p. 15, quoted in S.N. Sinha, *The Revolt of 1857 in Bundelkhand* (1982), p. 40.
26. S.N. Sinha, *op. cit.*, p. 40.
27. J.P. Mishra, *op. cit.*, p. 40.
28. *Cambridge History of India*, Vol.VI (1932), p. 125.
29. J.W. Kaye, *A History of the Sepoy War in India*, Vol. I (1870), p. 189.
30. Lee Warner, *Life of the Marquis of Dalhousie*, Vol. II, (1904), p. 189.

31. *Selections from Educational Records* (1781-1839), Vol. I (1920), Document No. 32, p. 130.
32. *Ibid.*, (1840-59), Vol. II (1920), Document No. 126, p. 368.
33. J.W. Kaye, *op. cit.*, Vol. I (1870), p. 187.
34. Lee Warner, *op. cit.*, Vol.II (1904), p. 363.
35. *Narrative of Events*, Agra Division, p. 4, quoted in S.N. Sinha, *op. cit.*, p. 45.
36. Kaye and Malleson, *History of the Indian Mutiny*, Vol. V (1897), p. 80.
37. Kaye, *History of the Indian Mutiny*, Vol. V (1897), p. 485.
38. *Ibid.*, p. 572.
39. N.E., para 5.
40. J.D., B.C., Political Case File No. 4 of 1858 (No paging).
41. Kaye and Malleson, *op. cit.*, p. 62.
42. J.D., B.C., Political Case File No. 4 of 1858, *op. cit.*, (No paging).
43. *Ibid*.
44. *Ibid*.
45. *Ibid*.
46. G.D. Dodd, *The History of the Indian Revolt and the expedition to Persia, China and Japan*, p. 36, quoted in S.N. Sinha, *op. cit.*, p. 46.
47. Kaye, *op. cit.*, Vol.I (1870), p. 568.
48. *Ibid.*, p. 570.
49. N.E., para 8.
50. *Ibid.*, para 9.
51. Foreign, Secret, Cons., dated 30 October 1857, No. 560, para 6.
52. T.R. Holmes, *History of the Indian Mutiny* (1885), p. 50.
53. Kaye, *op. cit.*, Vol. I (1870), pp. 327-28.
54. *Ibid.*, p. 467 and T.R. Holmes, *op. cit.*, p. 76.
55. Kaye, *op. cit.*, pp. 469-70.
56. Field Marshal Roberts, *Forty One Years in India* (1914), p. 243.
57. Gautam Sharma, *Indian Army through the Ages* (1966), p. 238.
58. T.R.Holems, *op. cit.*, p. 79.
59. Kaye, *op. cit.*, p. 519.
60. Kaye and Malleson, *History of the Indian Mutiny of 1857-58*, Vol. V (1897), p. 280.
61. C.U. Aitchison, *Lord Lawrence* (1916), p. 74.
62. N.E., para 6.
63. Foreign, Secret, Cons., dated 30 October 1857, No. 560, paras 3-4.

CHAPTER 4

Outbreak of the Revolt in the Sagar District

The outbreak of the revolt of 1857 in the Sagar district in the Saugor and Nerbudda Territories, like the outbreak of the Bundela rebellion of 1842 in it, can be said a remarkable coincidence of its own kind. This district gave the lead both in 1842 and 1857 and other districts followed.

Narrative of Events by Major W.C. Erskine

Before discussing the outbreak of the revolt in the Sagar district, it may be worthwhile to know about the 'Narrative of Events' by Major W.C. Erskine, the Commissioner of these territories during the revolt of 1857. He was asked by the Secretary to the North-Western Provinces on 30 April 1858 to submit an historical narrative of the events attending the mutinies and rebellion in 1857-58 in his division until the final restoration of peace. Accordingly, he submitted[1] on 10 August 1858 'the narrative of events attending the outbreak of the disturbances and the restoration of authority in the Saugor and Nerbudda Territories in 1857-58.' This can be said the first-person account of this important event in this region. It contains almost a month to month account of the incidents that happened under his eyes. He was a witness to it or he got information from men who witnessed them. In the absence of other accounts left over by the residents of these territories, about how the sepoys and civilians confronted the situation brought about by the outbreak, this narrative of events forms the primary source of this research project. The author has liberally drawn from it in discussing the main events of the revolt in this region. The other primary sources are the original records in the record-room of the Madhya Pradesh Government, Nagpur, in the National Archives of India, New Delhi and the Further Parliamentary Papers relative to the mutinies in the East India presented to both Houses of Parliament by command of Her Majesty in 1857. These primary sources are discussed in detail under Bibliography alongwith the secondary sources.

Before preparing his narrative of events, Major Erskine had directed[2] the Deputy Commissioners of all the districts under him to submit the district reports as "they should carefully specify the dates on which disturbances broke out, and on which such leading events as the withdrawal of officers, the overthrow of authority and its restoration took place." He had compiled his narrative from the returns of the district officers and from his own private notes and official documents. He stated that it was truthful but long containing thirty eight manuscript sheets.[3] Thus, his narrative is a trustworthy document. At times it tells more of the British point of view of the event. We have to study it carefully and impartially.

He stated[4] in his narrative that when the mutinies broke out, he was a Commissioner and Agent to the Lieutenant Governor in the Division, then known as the Saugor and Nerbudda Territories consisting of eight districts namely, Sagar, Damoh, Jabalpur, Mandla, Seoni, Narsinghpur, Hoshangabad and Betul, with an area of 33,000 square miles. The following troops garrisoned the head-quarter stations of his districts when the mutinies broke out at Meerut :

Sagar	: 1 Company of European Battalion Artillery 3rd Irregular Cavalry 31st Regiment of Bengal Native Infantry 42nd Regiment of Bengal Native Infantry
Damoh	: 2 Companies of 31st Regiment of Bengal Native Infantry
Jabalpur	: 52nd Regiment of Bengal Native Infantry

Mandla	: No troops except a Havildar's guard of 52nd Native Infantry
Seoni	: 1 Company of Madras Native Infantry
Narsinghpur	: 4 Companies of 28th Madras Native Infantry
Hoshangabad	: 4 Companies of 28th Madras Native Infantry
Betul	: 2 Companies of 28th Madras Native Infantry

Later on in June 1857, the two Companies of the 31st Bengal Native Infantry at Damoh were replaced by the two companies of the 42nd Bengal Native Infantry.[5]

He further stated[6] that "till the mutinies at Delhi and Meerut occurred in May 1857, no country could have been in more profound peace than my division (now officially styled the Jubbulpore Division) was. The whole was under survey, and everything was progressing for a new and light settlement of the land revenue, which was promised to the people." As referred to earlier, after the completion of the twenty years settlement in 1853, measures were taken for the new land revenue settlement in these territories which were however not completed due to the outbreak of the revolt of 1857.

As all communications had ceased with the North-Western Provinces during the revolt, the Governor General invested Major Erskine with the powers of a Chief Commissioner in the end of June 1857. He then took measures by himself without reference to any authority.[7]

The Government of India also asked[8] him on 22 June 1857 to submit immediately a connected Narrative of Events which had taken place in the Saugor and Nerbudda Territories and in future submit weekly narratives. He had duly submitted the weekly narratives till the final submission of his narrative of events on 10 August 1858. It may, however, be added that these weekly narratives formed the bulk of the Further Parliamentary Papers presented to both Houses of Parliament by command of Her Majesty in 1857.

As Major Erskine was of the opinion[9] that the authority over the chiefs in Bundelkhand existed in the Agent to the Governor-General at Indore and to his Assistant at Nagod, was injurious to the public service, he was temporarily granted[10] authority over them by the Government of India with the provision that he should keep inform the Agent to the Governor-General in Central India everything he did.

The Government of India had also passed a Resolution[11] on 11 August 1857 "constituting as a temporary measure a Lt. Governorship for the Central Provinces of the Presidency of Fort William in Bengal. The territorial jurisdiction of the Lt. Governor will, for the present, extend to the Allahabad and Benaras Divisions, and to the Saugor and Nerbudda Territories." Benaras was made its headquarters. Thus, Major Erskine was empowered with the powers of a Chief Commissioner and the authority over Bundelkhand and Rewa. He was directed to submit his proceedings to the Lt. Governor of the Central Provinces of Fort William in Bengal with headquarters at Benaras.

Sagar district in 1857

Before describing the outbreak in the Sagar district in 1857, two important aspects of the revolt of 1857 in these territories are noteworthy. Firstly, "the major centres of resistance were precisely those places which had risen against the British during the Bundela rebellion of 1842. Sagar itself, and Damoh, Narsinghpur, Chawarpatha, Tendukhera, Heerapur were the places where the Thakurs and Malguzars refused to reconcile themselves to subordination and dependence fifteen years ago."[12] Secondly, the revolt came to a climax more slowly in this region but in the long run, proved far more troublesome.

After the suppression of the Bundela rebellion of 1842, the Saugor and Nerbudda Territories were in a state of restless dependence. Since then there had been only a kind of uneasy peace, but no tranquillity in them. While dealing with the aftermath of the Bundela rebellion, we have discussed in detail the changes made in the general, judicial and revenue administration. These changes further aggravated the discontent of the people as we witness the revolt of 1857 in these territories only fifteen years after the Bundela rebellion, as a part of the all-India movement to oust the Britishers from India.

In the Sagar district, one of the important consequences that flowed from the Bundela rebellion, led to the agricultural depression. In 1845 it was found necessary to give a general reduction of ten percent of the revenue throughout the district.[13] Before the revolt of 1857, this district had been suffering from bad harvests for a succession of years. The wheat harvests failed in 1854, 1855 and 1856.[14] Scarcity of food, high prices, acute suffering and inadequate and discriminating relief measures by the British Government earned them a great deal of unpopularity.

While discussing the causes of the revolt, we have discussed in detail the role of the *chapaties*, bone-dust story and the greased cartridges in these territories in general and the Sagar district in particular. Signs of the approaching storm had begun to appear at least six months before it actually burst. Major Erskine had described[15] how as early as in January 1857 small *chapaties* were sent round in a mysterious way from village to village in Sagar and other districts. They were intended to be a message and a warning of the impending rising so that the people might be prepared for it. In April excited letters from the regiments in Bengal reached the Sagar regiment alleging that the new greased cartridges were designed to offend their religion. Early in May stories were current in Sagar that *ghee*, *atta* and sugar had been adulterated by the Government orders with pig's and cow's blood and bone-dust to defile the religions of both the Hindus and Muslims.

In spite of the inadequate means of communication, the news of the events at Delhi and Meerut reached Sagar and Jabalpur on 17 May 1857 and the next day at Damoh, a week after they had occurred. Major Erskine stated[16] that "it did not appear to create any great excitement amongst the natives but a good deal of horror at the cruelties was expressed by the sepoys and the towns people, and much alarm was felt by many of the Europeans at all the stations." Nothing however occurred till the end of May 1857 except the *Mahajans* of Sagar immediately ceased to transact any business in *Hoondies*, exchange etc.[17]

Rebellious activities of Raja Mardan Singh of Banpur and Raja Bakhat Bali of Shahgarh in the Sagar district

With the news of the stirring events in Jhansi on 8 June 1857 in which all the seventy six Europeans were murdered, came the report that Raja Mardan Singh of Banpur, a neighbouring state, had gathered a large body of men at Lalitpur, the headquarters of the Chanderi district. These news "caused much excitement amongst the sepoys and the Thakoors near Saugor and at Jubbulpore the sepoys were very uneasy, not apparently inclined to mutiny, but expressed a fear of being disarmed."[18]

On 9 June Major Erskine in a letter to Mr. Plowden, the Commissioner of Nagpur, had observed[19] : "I greatly fear, when the Saugor troops hear of the Jhansi affair, that they will rise and seize the treasury and magazine at Saugor and if so, I can hardly expect the 52nd to stand quiet here. There is great alarm here amongst many of the Europeans, and I rather think that some of them have resolved to send their families towards Seonee, but I hope all the civil officers will stand fast, and I can answer for myself and the Deputy Commissioner."

Regarding the conduct of the Raja of Banpur, Captain A.C. Gordon, the Deputy Commissioner of Chanderi, had reported[20] to Major Erskine that the wing of the Gwalior contingent stationed at Lalitpur were not to be dependend on, and that he doubted the loyalty of the Raja of Banpur, who had been called to assist him, but had surrounded the station with his followers. Consequently, he had requested Brigadier Sage, Commander at Sagar, to send him troops.

At this time Raja Bakhat Bali of Shahgarh, whose principality situated within the Sagar and Damoh districts, had started raising soldiers with the intention of making war on the British.[21] It is, however, to be noted that both these Rajas of Banpur and Shahgarh had co-operated with the British in suppressing the Bundela rebellion of 1842, but in the revolt of 1857, both of them changed their sides and fought with the rebels.

Grievances of Raja Mardan Singh of Banpur

We will now discuss the situation of the states of Banpur and Shahgarh which were in close proximity of the Sagar district. The disturbed state of the Chanderi State, situated in the Gwalior territory, was always a source of anxiety and there was danger of trouble spilling over into the British territory. After the commencement of the hostilities of the Chanderi State with the Gwalior Durbar in 1829, they were quickly suppressed. A compromise was then made with Raja Mur Pahlad of Chanderi by which it was decided that two-third revenue of the Chanderi State would be given to Gwalior Durbar and one-third would be retained by the Raja but Sindhia continued to excercise control over the state. However, by following the courageous policy of Thakur Mardan Singh, his eldest son, one-third of the Chanderi could be acquired and Banpur was made its capital in 1830.[22] Raja Mur Pahlad died in 1842, and Thakur Mardan Singh ascended to the small throne of Banpur. But his accession was not peaceful as Gwalior Durbar claimed Banpur as forming part of the Chanderi district as conquered by them in 1829-30. However, this claim of Gwalior was not supported by the British and the claim was not admitted.[23]

As referred to earlier, during the Bundela rebellion of 1842, Thakur Mardan Singh had refrained from joining it. It seems that "since English had not supported the claim of Gwalior Durbar over Banpur, Thakur Mardan Singh was sympathetic towards them. In order to suppress the widespread insurrection, the British also developed friendly relations with the Banpur chief who assisted them in apprehending the prominent Bundela rebels."[24] One of its prominent leaders, Madhukar Shah, was captured with his co-operation. In 1844 Sindhia's portion of the Chanderi State was ceded to the British as part security for the payment of the Gwalior contingent and a Deputy Superintendent who administered the new district, was vested with criminal jurisdiction over the Banpur state.[25]

Although Thakur Mardan Singh had faithfully supported the British Government during the trying times of 1842-43, he could not remain aloof from the revolt of 1857. Initially he played a double game negotiating for terms and territories, but eventually became an open rebel and alongwith Raja Bakhat Bali of Shahgarh, made preparations for war even before the actual outbreak of the revolt in this region. By the middle of June he had established his own rule in Chanderi, raised revenue and established a cannon foundry on the European principle, with an excellent boring apparatus at Banpur.[26]

In April 1857 Thakur Jujhar Singh of Nanikpur in the Chanderi State died. His tenure was resumed by the British Government and a settlement was made with his heirs. But one-third of the state was not given to Mardan Singh as had been specified in the original agreement, and he, therefore, induced Jawahir Singh, the heir of Jujhar Singh to revolt in order to compel the Government to restore his tenure. He was also irritated with the British Government because he was denied certain honours to which he considered himself entitled.[27] Thus, the Raja had a number of grievances to be redressed. He also entertained the hope of recovering the entire state of Chanderi, the ancient possession of his ancestors in the event of the overthrow of the British supremacy. During the revolt of 1857 he fulfilled his dream as he established his authority over the Chanderi State and remained in possession of the northern portion of the Sagar district until its capture in March 1858 by Sir Hugh Rose.

Grievances of Raja Bakhat Bali of Shahgarh

During the Bundela rebellion of 1842, Raja Arjun Singh of Shahgarh had supplied 50 matchlockmen for duty at Khimlasa and assured the British Government his full co-operation in the suppression of the disturbances.[28] He died on 2 June 1842 and the heir, Bakhat Bali Shah, nephew of the deceased Raja, succeeded him. As referred to earlier, he captured the prominent rebel leader, Raja Hirde Shah of Heerapur with the whole of his family on 22 December 1842. The latter was coming from Jaitpur and going towards Sagar with his family and other members of the rebel party. The capture of Raja Hirde Shah and his party was a major setback for the insurgents.[29]

The Shahgarh territory was the remnant of the Garhakota state; its remaining parts had fallen either into the hands of the Peshwa's representative at Sagar or those of Sindhia. In 1818 the Sagar territories came under the British by Article XIII of the Treaty of 1817 with the Peshwa Baji Rao II.[30] About this time the Shahgarh chief had received the possession of Garhakota from Sindhia and had been holding it. When the British took possession of Garhakota on behalf of the Peshwa, they expelled the Shahgarh Raja from there who retired to Shahgarh.[31] Raja Bakhat Bali who was the ruler of Shahgarh at the time of revolt still claimed Garhakota as his ancestral property which had been illegally annexed.[32] He entertained hopes of regaining it if the British authority was overthrown. Like Raja Mardan Singh of Banpur, he fulfilled his dream by occupying Garhakota during the revolt of 1857 till its capture by Sir Hugh Rose in February 1858.

We will see later on how both these Rajas had to pay the heaviest price for fulfilling their dreams.

March of Sagar troops for the relief of Chanderi : First sign of mutiny on 13 June 1857

As the Deputy Commissioner of Chanderi had requested the Brigadier commanding at Sagar for succour for the relief of Chanderi, the Raja of Banpur meanwhile had seized the Chanderi district and confined the European officers in early June of 1857. On 13 June Brigadier Sage at Sagar ordered one company of the 31st Bengal Native Infantry, one company of the 42nd Bengal Native Infantry, one troop of the 3rd Irregular Cavalry and two guns (with the two European artillerymen to point them) to go to Lalitpur under the command of Major Gaussen. But Brigadier Sage was doubting whether they would march or not ? In his own words[33] : "They did march; and at the first halt, conspired to murder their officers and return : the 42nd proposed this; the 31st would not agree; so they made a second march. Four men of the 42nd sent a message to the detachment to come back, as a European regiment was coming to punish them. 'It is conscience that makes cowards of us all.' I arrested the messenger and the four sepoys, and tried them by a drum-head court-martial. They were sentenced to imprisonment and hard labour at 6 P.M. and were on their way to Hoshangabad gaol, in irons, at twelve at midnight, where they now are." Thus, the first sign of mutiny was shown by the four sepoys of the 42nd who tried to prevent its march, but were arrested and tried for mutiny and sentenced to six months rigorous imprisonment.

On hearing of the sentence of these sepoys, the excitement was so great amongst the Sagar regiments that the Deputy Commissioner of Sagar very wisely and quietly sent the prisoners off to Hoshangabad under police guard, where they were safely lodged in jail.[34] This step was taken to prevent further repercussions in Sagar.

The detachment intended for Lalitpur reached Malthone on 18 June 1857 and more than once the European officers who accompanied it, were informed that the sepoys were counselling their murder.[35] On the arrival at Malthone, Major Gaussen found the passes north of it were held by large bodies of the Raja of Banpur's rebel troops. It was halted there to protect the northern frontier of the district and keep the Raja of Banpur in check. For this he did not consider his force strong enough; consequently Brigadier Sage ordered it to be strengthened by 250 men of the 31st Bengal Native Infantry, 100 of the 42nd and 50 more *sowars* of the 3rd Irregular Cavalry from Sagar. This detachment joined Major Gaussen on 23 June. The combined forces stormed the fort of Balabehat, on the south border of the Chanderi district which was one of the British police stations but taken possession by the rebels. There were sixteen men in it and the rest had gone to plunder. It was attacked and taken by the British troops on 23 June and all the sixteen men were taken prisoners.[36] In this attack Ensign Spens was killed in blowing up the gateway and Lt. Willoughby had his right leg broken and the detachment lost 6 men, 2 killed and 4 wounded.[37]

Mutiny at Malthone on 25 June 1857

At Malthone Major Gaussen had apprehended a messenger of the Banpur Raja with a letter addressed to the regiment, "telling them that the Boondelas (of which tribe of Rajpoots the Raja is the head) were their friends, that the sepoys had acted well in resisting our interference with their religion, and that as Government had treated the Thakoors very badly, they would assist the sepoys."[38] The Banpur Raja, to whom the sixteen prisoners of Balabehat belonged, also offered "the sepoys twelve rupees a month if they would leave their officers and go over with their arms and ammunition."[39] Major Gaussen then assembled the native officers and consulted them as to what answer should be sent. They at once said that they were faithful to the salt, and if the Raja sent anymore messengers, they would be hanged.[40]

Meanwhile, Captain F. Pinkney, the Deputy Commissioner at Jabalpur volunteered to go to Sagar to proceed with Gaussen's detachment for restoring order in Chanderi and Jhansi. On 20 June he was relieved by Captain Clerk, the Deputy Commissioner of Seoni and Lt. Thomson, Assistant Commissioner of Jabalpur was appointed the Deputy Commissioner at Seoni in his place. He speedily reached Sagar in safety and stayed there as Major Gaussen had already proceeded to Chanderi.[41]

On 25 June some of the men of the 31st and 42nd Native Infantry at Malthone had broken into open mutiny, insisting that the Balabehat prisoners should be brought into their camp from the custody of the police. "On the arrival of the prisoners in camp, the mutineers had surrounded Major Gaussen, and with much gesticulation and vociferation demanded their release from restraint, as they had promised them their lives when they took them prisoners. If they were sent to Saugor, they might be hung. Major Gaussen consulted the other officers and let the prisoners go." He felt that the conduct of the detachment was so bad, that he was obliged to comply.[42]

In consequence of the mutiny at Malthone, the northern part of the Sagar district was infested with dacoits owing to the incursions of the dreaded Bundelas who came from Chanderi and Shahgarh, and who were joined by the Narhat and other Thakurs in the Sagar district.[43] After the mutiny of the Sagar troops at Malthone, there was a general apprehension that "if Saugor rise, Dumoh and Jubbulpore will follow."[44] Thus, there was a great alarm and apprehension amongst the Britishers in these territories.

Meanwhile, the Europeans at Lalitpur confined by the Banpur Raja were sent to Tehri to which place they reached after many trials and narrow escapes, where they were kindly treated through the influence of young Raja of Orchha's tutor, and befriended by Muhammad Ali Khan, Mukhtiar of the Banpur Raja. They were then sent towards Sagar, but seized and imprisoned on the way by the Raja of Shahgarh, who kept them in confinement in an old fort in the jungles for three months in a most wretched condition, allowing them merely one anna a day for food. When threatened by an attack by Captain Millar's Nagpur Movable Column in September 1857, he sent them to Sagar.[45] On 14 September 1857 at 12 P.M. the Lalitpur prisoners, namely, Lt. A.C. Gordon, Deputy Commissioner, Lalitpur, with Captain Sale, 6th Regiment Gwalior Contingent, Captain Irwin, wife and two children, Dr. O'Brien, Mr. Verries Patrol, Quarter Master Sergeant Caroll and wife, reached Sagar. All the party "are pretty well but have been badly treated by the Rajah, *Chupattees* and *Dal* being their only food".[46]

Confinement of the Europeans in the Sagar fort on 29 June 1857

As the mutinous spirit was shown by the Sagar regiments at Malthone, the position in Sagar was causing anxiety. Brigadier Sage suspected the movements of the troops in the Sagar Cantonment. On 27 June he consulted the senior officers as to what should be done. It was resolved to take possession of the old fort in the town of Sagar which was used as arsenal and magazine, and garrisoned by sepoys from the Cantonment. Moreover, it was considered to be the only safe place for the European and the Christian residents, in the event of the mutiny or the rebellion spreading. "Immediate steps were therefore taken to lay in supplies and prepare accommodation for the European families. The bulk of treasure was taken from the Deputy Commissioner Kutcherry and the whole of the powder from the expense magazine and lodged in the fort. The same afternoon the sepoy guard in the fort was, without previous notice, relieved by twelve European artillerymen. Notice was also given at once to the European families, the preparations had been made in the fort for their reception, and nearly all took advantage of it that night."[47]

Orders were then sent for the whole of troops at Sagar to be held in readiness to march to Malthone. This was a ruse. On 29 June, while the weekly guards were being relieved at Sagar, the whole of the rest of the European artillerymen with their guns quietly marched into the fort, where they were at once joined by all the European officers and Christian residents, who had been previously warned to proceed there with a portion of their property.[48] The native army was surprised by this move into the fort, "but attempted no resistance."[49]

The Brigadier then directed the Native Officers of the 31st and 42nd Native Infantry, and of the 3rd Irregular Cavalry, to attend him in the fort. On their doing so, he informed them that notwithstanding their promises of fidelity, there had been a mutiny of a portion of each corps at Malthone, and if they wished to prove themselves true, they must at once give up the bad men, and if they did not do so, he would not trust the European officers to remain longer with the traitors. They expressed great regret for what had happened, and they all volunteered to send good men to Malthone to bring in the bad characters. This was agreed to, and the men selected by their officers marched that evening.[50]

Major W.C. Erskine, the Commissioner, did not agree with Brigadier Sage in his move into the fort of Sagar on 29 June 1857, leaving the native infantry regiments outside without their European officers.[51] In his opinion[52], "this may have a very bad effect not only on the native troops at Saugor, but on those of Nagode, Dumoh and Jubbulpore, and also on the people of this part of country." In his letter of 3 July 1857 to Brigadier Sage, he pointed out fully his fears of the result. At that time all was quiet at Jabalpur and Damoh where there were Bengal troops and all other stations of the Division where there were Madras troops, "but much will depend on the conduct and treatment of the Saugor force for the future."[53] His fears came true on 1 July 1857 when the Sagar regiments mutinied.

The Government of India also did not agree with Brigadier Sage and on 18 July 1857 asked[54] "for an explanation of his conduct in retiring to the fort at Saugor with all the European officers, leaving the native regiments without their officers." Accordingly, Brigadier explained[55] his conduct with regard to this extraordinary and isolated case. He stated that "I had two regiments of infantry (sepoys) and one regiment of native cavalry, and only sixty eight European gunners. I had the fort, magazine and the battering train at one end of the cantonments, and what is called the Artillery-hill at the other; distance between the two is three miles and a quarter. I could not keep both; if I kept the hill, in all probability I should lose the fort, the magazine and the key of the Sagar district. At the hill I had no provisions, and no room to store them, and water had to be brought from below. Things were in this state - the sepoys had the treasury and the fort; in fact we were all at their mercy; and men of the three regiments met at every night and talked openly what they intended to do." In these circumstances he had decided that the Europeans should occupy the fort with magazine and treasure and leave the cantonment. Charles Ball was of the opinion that "the result of this explanation does not appear in any subsequent correspondence, and, therefore, it is reasonable to suppose it was satisfactory."

Mutiny at Sagar on 1 July 1857

Major Erskine had described[56] the mutiny at Sagar in his Narrative of Events as follows : "On the morning of 1 July the position of the 3rd Irregular Cavalry remaining at Saugor, with the exception of some of the native officers and fifty *sowars*, broke out into open mutiny in the Cantonments, went to the *musjid* and sharpened their swords. At the same time Sheikh Ramzan, the senior Subedar present with the 42nd Native Infantry, raised the Mahomedan flag and called for followers by beat of drum. He was joined by the whole of the 42nd, who remained in the station, by a few of the 31st and by all the mutineers of the 3rd Irregular Cavalry and the same day these mutinous troops and the bad characters of the Sudder Bazar and camp followers plundered and injured the property of most of the officers' houses in Cantonments, but did not set fire to them. They also took away about Rs.9,500 worth of copper and silver coins, which could not be removed from the Treasury for want of time and carriage. On the 2 July a portion of the mutineers went towards Dumoh, with a view of inciting the two companies of the 42nd there to join them and carry off the Dumoh treasure amounting to Rs.1,50,000."

On 1 July Sheikh Ramzan, Subedar of the 42nd Native Infantry, had assumed the command in Cantonment and the title of 'General'. The mutineers seized the large saluting gun on the artillery-hill, which had been left there when the rest of the guns were taken into the fort and brought it down to the quarter guard of the 42nd, which the mutineers had made their headquarters. The 31st Native Infantry kept aloof from the mutineers. The native officers of this corps daily went to the fort, and the men protected and conveyed much of their officers' property to them.[57] At this time the Banpur and Shahgarh chiefs intended looting with the mutinous sepoys had proposed an attack on Sagar.[58]

Meanwhile, the men sent out by the 31st to Malthone relieved the Light Company of that regiment which had been the most mutinous, and then they returned to Sagar. Some of the men of this Company expressed extreme contrition for their conduct, but about forty-five at once joined the mutineers of the 3rd Irregular Cavalry and the 42nd Native Infantry. The men, sent out by the 42nd Native Infantry to bring the bad men, were overtaken by the mutineers of that regiment and 3rd Irregulars. They joined them except six who were at once put to death by the mutineers[59] and their heads were sent to Sheikh Ramzan, the rebel Subedar who had assumed the title of General.[60]

As whole of the native troops at Sagar had mutinied, the Commissioner apprehended[61] that "the Regiment at Jubbulpore was almost certain to do so also." However, it came true two months later after the brutal execution of Raja Shankar Shah and his son, Raghunath Shah there on 18 September 1857.

Suppression of the mutiny at Sagar on 7 July 1857

As the Sagar regiments had mutinied, Major Western, the Deputy Commissioner of Sagar, strongly urged[62] the Commissioner on 3 July 1857 the necessity of sending troops for the relief of Sagar. The Commissioner showed his helplessness and stated[63] on 5 July that "Narsinghpore could not possibly furnish about 70 or 80 men for Saugor, and so small a party could be of no avail against your mutineers, and Mr. Plowden, Commissioner of Nagpore, having full occasion for his own troops has refused to send any in this direction, and could not, therefore, send any to Saugor. There is no present hope of aid from without for either you or us."

As the 31st Native Infantry had kept aloof from the mutineers and were loyal to the Britishers, they requested the permission from the Brigadier to attack the mutineers. He permitted them but would not allow their European officers to accompany them. However, Major Western, the Deputy Commissioner, sent out a strong party of the customs peons, who had just been armed with muskets, to make a demonstration in favour of the 31st. They were also accompanied by the officers of the Customs Department, and by Captain Pinkney, who had not been able to proceed beyond in consequence of the mutiny at Malthone, and by Lt. Hamilton, the Assistant Commissioner.[64]

On 6 July the mutineers on seeing that they were about

to be attacked, fired a round shot into the 31st from the saluting gun, and both regiments kept up a desultory fire with their muskets nearly the whole day, but little damage was done on either side. Next morning the mutineers, thinking the 31st would be aided by the artillery of the fort, left the station for the north in great haste, taking with them some conveyances belonging to the officers, but soon abandoned them on the road.[65] After considerable resistance they were driven out of the cantonment with considerable loss and several prisoners were taken.[66]

Major W.C. Western reported[67] to Major W.C. Erskine on 8 July 1857 that the saltuing gun, which was in possession of the mutineers and from which they had fired round shots into the lines of the 31st, was also taken. Six commissariat elephants had also been captured and order had been restored in the Sadar Bazar and Cantonment. The mutineers had fled some towards Damoh and other towards Chhatarpur. He had issued a Proclamation calling upon the chiefs and the police to cut them off whenever they came across them. He further reported[68] that "the arch traitor, Ramzan Subedar of the 42nd Regiment and Dulmeer Khan Moonshee of the same Regiment have escaped, the former had set himself up as Nawab and Governor of the district and the Moonshee as his Naib. They have been the originators and chief movers of the outbreak and I have offered Rs.500 for the former and Rs. 250 for the apprehension of the latter, dead or alive, and I now solicit your sanction to this award."

Meanwhile, on 8 July Nubbee Bux, the Deputy Post Master and a resident of Delhi, was apprehended. He was an active agent in the outbreak and from his knowledge of the dak lines, instructed the mutineers how to cut off the communication. Next day he was hung by the sentence of a court martial on the ramparts of the fort on a charge of the rebellion against the Government.[69]

On 9 July several civil residents of the Sadar Bazar were apprehended on charges of rebellion and robbery and had been made over to the civil powers for trial. A considerable portion of the property carried off by the mutineers and these residents had been recovered in the Sadar Bazar and environs of cantonment and restored to the owners.[70] The Deputy Commissioner of Sagar reported[71] on 20 July that six men, resident of the Sadar Bazar, were hung for rebellion and bearing arms against the government in the recent disturbances. Four troopers and one sepoy had also been hung for the same offence by the sentence of the Court Martial.

After the suppression of the mutiny at Sagar, Major Erskine had resolved to give full *batta* to the well-behaved soldiers of the Bengal Army posted in these territories. On 14 July 1857 he wrote[72] to the Government of India that although it was an unusual measure and the Government might think that he had exceeded his authority in doing so, but the circumstances were peculiar and he had done it after seeking the advice of the senior officers. From the commanding officers of the 50th and 52nd Regiment, he had learnt that "the order has had the best effect on the Native officers and men of those Regiments that it will in every probability keep the men staunch." As he was vested with the extraordinary power of the Chief Commissioner, he had acted promptly and there was no time for reference to higher authority.

Brigadier Sage at Sagar did not agree with Major Erskine in this matter and alleged[73] that he had destroyed the discipline of the Regiments and had given a premium for insubordination. But Erskine was of the opinion[74] that "if by a small addition of pay to our own troops, I manage to keep two Regiments to their duty and several districts undisturbed, I think the Government will not disapprove my conduct." The Government of India, however, approved[75] the measure of giving full *batta* to the well-behaved soldiers of the 50th and 52nd Native Regiments of the Bengal army.

Repercussions in the Sagar district : Further rebellious activities of the Rajas of Banpur and Shahgarh

As almost all the Indian troops had mutinied in Sagar except the 31st Native Infantry, it had its repercussions in the whole district. On 9 July a portion of the 31st Native Infantry and some of the 3rd Irregular Cavalry were sent from Sagar to assist Major Gaussen in his return from Malthone. He arrived at Sagar on 12 July. The greater portion of the Indian officers and men of the 42nd and 3rd Irregular Cavalry with Major Gaussen had deserted.[76] As he retired from Malthone, the Bundelas accompanied by the Raja of Banpur had taken possession of its thanna and the northern portion of the district. They were also joined by the Narhat Thakurs and the plundering became general.[77] Hence, martial law was imposed there.[78]

The Rajas of Banpur and Shahgarh took advantage of this situation and sent emissaries to all the petty chiefs in these territories, telling them to join in the general rebellion. In the Sagar district several chiefs joined the rebels and in the Damoh district nearly all of them joined.[79] They and their followers were in some doubts about the stability of the British rule.[80] Major Erskine was also of the view that "the mass of native chiefs disbelieve in the existence of the British army; and nothing but the existence of troops among them will convince them of their error." Again and again such representations were sent by Erskine to the Governor General and as often as they came, was he compelled to answer that he had no British troops to spare.[81]

On 9 July the Tehsildarees and thannas of Khurai and Benaika in the Sagar district were attacked and taken possession of, the former by the Raja of Banpur's troops and the latter by those of the Raja of Shahgarh.[82] The Qiledar of Balabehat on behalf of the Banpur Raja, with several Bundelas advanced on Khurai and took possession of the fort and Tehsilee on 9 July. The Tehsildar, Ahmad Bux offered no resistance. On the contrary he sided with and invited the rebel chief of Banpur to take possession of the pargana. Peer Ali, the Thanedar of Khurai also joined the rebels with nearly all the police of Khurai. He had received a sword from Lord Ellenborough, the Governor General on account of his bravery in the suppression of the Bundela rebellion of 1842.[83] Major Erskine, later on submitted[84] a detailed report of the Tehsildar and the Thanedar of Khurai who had been implicated in the rebellion there as follows : "No.1 Ahmad Bux Shaikh Tehseeldar and Deputy Magistrate of Khoorye son of Shaikh Mohammad Morad of Jubbulpore. Ahmad Bux from all accounts invited the Raja of Banpoor to Khoorye and made over the Tehsil and Treasure to him without offering the slightest resistance notwithstanding that there was a considerable armed force and a strong fort at his disposal, he has become a servant of the Raja of Banpoor and is at present at Banpoor. No.2 Peer Allee Syed Soomundar son of Meer Amanut Allee of Bhoonkur Pargunnah Kot Kasim Zillah Delhi. Peer Allee was Thanedar of Khooryee on 40 Rs. a month, he was made Soomundar in June last and obtained Rs.10 a month extra, as a head of body of musketeers, jointly invited the Banpoor Rajah to invade Khooryee and took service with him. Peer Allee not only prevented his own men but dissuaded other Government servants from opposing the Raja of Banpoor."

On 18 July a Company of the 31st Bengal Native Infantry, with two European officers was sent from Sagar to Benaika and Lt. Hamilton, Assistant Commissioner accompanied the detachment. On 21 July the rebels near Benaika, having been reinforced from Shahgarh, advanced with one gun to attack the Sagar troops but they were repulsed and their gun, a large brass one, belonging to the Shahgarh Raja, was captured. The Raja then sent a messenger to say that he would give up the Lalitpur European prisoners which were in his custody. Accordingly, the detachment moved out to receive them, but were treachrously fired on. He then sent word that he would exchange them for the gun, but he was evidently false. As the Officer Commanding of the 31st,

Major Lugard, did not think his detachment strong enough to attack the rebels, he withdrew to Sagar, bringing in the captured gun.[85]

At the same time the Raja of Banpur with some 1,400 men, moved down from the north towards Sagar and took up a very strong position at Nariaoli, twelve miles from Sagar. On 25 July a portion of his troops actually advanced to cantonment and fired on an outhouse of the artillery barracks; but on the troops being sent against them from Sagar, they decamped.[86]

On 18 July 1857 Major W.C. Western submitted[87] to the Commissioner the following list of the thannas in the Sagar district which had been taken by the rebels :

"No.	Date on which rebels took possession	Name of rebels
Khorai Tehselee		
1. Narhat	5 July 1857	Bakhat Bali and Pareechut on the part of Shahgarh Raja
2. Malthone	5 July 1857	Raja of Shahgarh
3. Khimlasa	6 July 1857	Raja of Banpoor
4. Khorai	7 July 1857	Raja of Banpoor
5. Erun	8 July 1857	Raja of Banpoor
Benaika Tehselee		
6. Benaika	8 July 1857	Khoman Singh on the part of the Shahgurh Raja
7. Bunda	7 July 1857	Raja of Shahgarh
8. Pancham-nagar	8 July 1857	Raja of Shahgarh
9. Dhamony	7 July 1857	Raja of Shahgarh
Saugor Tehselee		
10. Narioli	14 July 1857	Jawahir of Chundrapoor
11. Rahatgarh	9 July 1857	Nabab Petaree
Rehli Tehselee		
12. Garhakota	14 July 1857	Raja of Shahgarh."

The fort of Rahatgarh on the west border was also taken possession by the Nawab of Ambapani in Bhopal. The police party was driven out there and partly induced to join the rebels.[88] Towards the end of July 1857, most of the Sagar district passed into the hands of the rebels.

The repercussions of the mutiny at Sagar were immediately felt beyond the borders of the Sagar district. In Damoh and Jabalpur where the 42nd and 52nd Bengal Native Infantry were in charge of those districts, its repercussions will be discussed later on.

By the end of August 1857 Sagar district passed into the hands of the rebels except the Sagar fort and town

On 1 August 1857 Major Western reported[89] to the Commissioner the activities of the rebel chiefs of Banpur and Shahgarh who were in almost entire possession of Khurai and Benaika divisions of the district and a great portion of the Sagar Tehsil. They "compel our zamindars and ryots by threat of death or by plundering and burning their villages to join their standards."

On 17 August he again reported[90] that "the rebel chiefs of Shahgurh and Banpoor appear to compel our Malgoozars to join their standards by threatening to burn and plunder their villages and by mutilating them or cutting off their noses." In his opinion[91] "the whole of evil that has fallen on this and the surrounding district has caused by the Rajas of Banpoor and Shahgurh and the disaffection of the 42nd and the 3rd Irregular Cavalry would have no effect on this district, had it not been for the traitor of Banpoor. He took advantage of our difficulties and after deceiving the authorities at Lalitpoor entered the Khorai purganna in the guise of a friend pretending that he came to assist the Government, all the while plundering our villages and inciting our zamindars to rebellion." Since then he had assumed the functions of the Government in the British territory and his agents demanded and received not only for the present, but on account of the balances of the past year and they designated themselves as 'Sircar'. Most of the *ubaridars* and chiefs of the district had joined the rebel Raja.[92]

On 7 August the Tehsildaree and fort at Rehli, to the south of Sagar and west of Damoh, was taken by the rebels of Garhakota, headed by Lachman Singh, a bastard brother of the Raja of Shahgarh and Bodhan Dauaa, his *kamdar*.[93] On 13 August the Banpur rebels advanced from Narioli to Ratona near Sagar but they fled on the approach of the troops sent by Brigadier Sage.[94] Looking to the gravity of the situation, Martial Law was proclaimed in the Sagar district on 13 August 1857.[95]

For the apprehension of the Banpur Raja, the Commissioner offered a reward of Rs. 8,000 which was duly sanctioned by the Lt. Governor of the Central Provinces, Benaras.[96] The Government of India regarded[97] the conduct of the Shahgarh Raja to be deserving of the highest punishment and directed the Commissioner to make every effort for his apprehension. They also authorized him to offer a reward of Rs. 10,000 for his capture "whenever you may think it would conduce to his seizure but for 'live' and not 'dead'".

By the end of August 1857, Major Erskine stated[98] that "the districts of Saugor and Dumoh were, with the exception of the Sudder stations, now entirely in the hands of the rebels, all our police had deserted or driven in, and hundreds of Malgoozars, though well inclined, were forced either to join the rebels, or assist them with men or food, or were plundered and often tortured. No daks were received at Saugor or Dumoh for many weeks; for some time the communication was entirely closed between us, ..."

Thus, by the end of August 1857, the entire district passed into the hands of the rebels except the Sagar fort and town. It was a great landmark in the revolt of 1857 in these territories.

REFERENCES

1. N.E., para 1
2. J.D., B.C., Political File No.18 of 1858, para 4.
3. N.E., para 443.
4. *Ibid*., paras 2-3.
5. *Ibid*., para 20.
6. *Ibid*., para 4.
7. *Ibid*., para 88.
8. J.D., B.C., Political File No.10 of 1857, p. 109.
9. Foreign, Secret, Cons., 18 December 1857, No. 225.
10. *Ibid*., No. 225A.
11. Home Dept., Letters to the Court of Directors, No.75 of 1857, dated 6 August 1857.
12. D.P.Mishra, ed., *History of the Freedom Movement in Madhya Pradesh* (1956), p. 82.
13. M.P.D.G., Sagar (1967), p. 66.
14. *Ibid*., p. 67.
15. N.E., paras 5, 6 and 8.
16. *Ibid*., para 16.
17. Foreign, Secret, Cons., 30 October 1857, No. 560, para 2.
18. N.E., paras 17-18.
19. Charles Ball, *The History of the Indian Mutiny*, Vol. I (1858), p. 436.
20. N.E., para 21.
21. *Ibid*., para 22.
22. *The Imperial Gazetteers of India*, Vol. X (1908), p.164, Vol.XIV (1908), p. 138 and Foreign, Political, Cons., 28 December 1842, Nos. 110-11.
23. C.U.Aitchison, *A Collection of Treaties, Engagements and Sanads*, Vol. V (1933), p. 7.
24. J.P.Mishra, *The Bundela Rebellion* (1982), p. 60.
25. Charles Ball, *op.cit*., p. 17.
26. S.B.Choudhary, *Civil Rebellion in Indian Mutinies* (1957), pp. 206, 215, 218 and 223.
27. *Ibid*.
28. J.D., B.C., Political Case File No. 12 of 1842, p. 97, quoted in J.P. Mishra, *op.cit*., p. 93.
29. J.P. Mishra, *op.cit*., p. 196.
30. C.U. Aitchison, *op.cit*., Vol. III (1909), p. 84.

31. Bundelkhand Agency Records, File No. 3 of 1857, quoted in S.N.Sinha, *The revolt of 1857 in Bundelkhand* (1982), p. 50.
32. Foreign, Secret, Cons., 18 December 1857, No. 235.
33. Charles Ball, *op.cit.*, p. 563.
34. N.E., para 24.
35. *Ibid.*, para 26.
36. *Ibid.*, paras 40-2.
37. Foreign, Secret, Cons., 30 October 1857, No. 560, para 14.
38. N.E., para 43.
39. Charles Ball, *op.cit.*, p. 563.
40. N.E., para 44.
41. *Ibid.*, paras 34 and 45.
42. *Ibid.*, paras 45-6 and Foreign, Secret, Cons., 30 October 1857, No. 560, para 17.
43. N.E., para 48.
44. Foreign, Secret, Cons., 31 July 1857, No. 161.
45. N.E., paras 47 and 179.
46. Foreign, Secret, Cons., 30 October 1857, No. 612, paras 1-2.
47. N.E., paras 49-51.
48. *Ibid.*, paras 52-3.
49. Foreign, Secret, Cons., 31 July 1857, No. 342, para 3.
50. N.E., paras 54-6.
51. Foreign, Secret, Cons., 12 February 1858, No. 109, para 4.
52. *Ibid.*, No.110.
53. *Ibid.*, No.109, para 6.
54. Charles Ball, *op.cit.*, p. 562.
55. *Ibid.*, pp. 562-63.
56. N.E., paras 58-61.
57. *Ibid.*, paras 66-8.
58. Foreign, Secret, Cons., 31 July 1857, No. 357, para 9.
59. N.E., paras 64-5.
60. Foreign, Secret Cons., 30 October 1857, No. 560, para 29.
61. *Ibid.*, 28 August 1857, No. 360, para 4.
62. *Ibid.*, 31 July 1857, No. 357, para 10.
63. *Ibid.*, No. 358, paras 2-3.
64. N.E., para 69.
65. *Ibid.*, paras 70-1.
66. F.P.P. No. C-2277, Enclosure 57 of No.1, para 104.
67. J.D., B.C., Political Case File No. 16 of 1857, p. 118.

68. *Ibid.*, para 5.
69. Foreign, Secret, Cons., 31 July 1857, No. 369, and 30 October 1857, No. 564 and para 4.
70. *Ibid.*, 30 October 1857, No. 564.
71. *Ibid.*, No.573.
72. *Ibid.*, 26 February 1858, No. 126, paras 2-4.
73. *Ibid.*, para 5.
74. *Ibid.*, para 10.
75. *Ibid.*, No.129.
76. N.E., para 12.
77. Foreign, Secret, Cons., 30 October 1857, No. 564.
78. *Ibid.*, 31 July 1857, No. 342, para 15.
79. N.E., para 99.
80. Foreign, Secret, Cons., 30 July 1857, No.342, para 7.
81. Charles Ball, *op.cit.*, Vol. II, p. 150.
82. N.E., paras 100-1.
83. Foreign, Secret, Cons., 30 October 1857, No. 564, also J.D., B.C., Political Case File No. 10 of 1857, p. 1.
84. J.D., B.C., Political Case File No. 10 of 1857, pp. 268-70.
85. N.E., paras 115-16.
86. N.E., para 118.
87. Foreign, Secret, Cons., 30 October 1857, No. 558.
88. N.E., para 117.
89. J.D., B.C., Political Case File No.19 of 1857, p. 19.
90. *Ibid.*, No.23 of 1857, p. 30.
91. *Ibid.*, pp.30-31, para 3.
92. *Ibid.*, paras 4-5.
93. N.E., para 138.
94. *Ibid.*, para 141.
95. J.D., B.C., Political Case File No.23 of 1857, p. 102.
96. *Ibid.*, No.30 of 1857, p. 1.
97. *Ibid.*, No.23 of 1857, p. 82.
98. N.E., para 142.

CHAPTER 5

Spread of the Revolt in the Damoh District

Outbreak of the revolt in Sagar : Panic in Damoh

According to Charles Ball[1] "at the close of September 1857, nearly whole of the territories of Saugor and Nerbudda were in a state of revolt." In the light of this statement, having discussed the outbreak of the revolt in the Sagar district, its spread in the Damoh district, and its further progress in the Jabalpur and other districts upto September 1857 will be discussed in the present and the following chapter to maintain uniformity in dealing with the subject.

The first sign of the mutiny of the Sagar troops on 13 June 1857 when they were sent for the relief of Chanderi; their mutiny at Malthone on 25 June 1857 and consequently, the confinement of the Europeans in the Sagar fort on 29 June 1857, all these proceedings in the Sagar district soon became known at Damoh and Jabalpur. Major Erskine had observed[2] that in these two stations in his division "where there were Bengal troops amongst whom, as well as amongst the majority of the Christian residents, there was much excitement but the sepoy remained quiet doing their duty as usual."

At the time of the outbreak of the revolt in Sagar on 1 July 1857, Damoh was garrisoned by the two companies of the 42nd Bengal Native Infantry. The remainder of this regiment stationed at Sagar had broken out into rebellion alongwith the 3rd Irregulars. The Sagar rebellion created great alarm at Damoh. The bankers hid their wealth on hearing of it and Lt. Nembhard, the Deputy Commissioner of Damoh, resolved to lodge the treasure in the jail-fort.[3] The detachment of the corps at Damoh was greatly excited and the plundering by the Bundelas from Shahgarh had just commenced.[4] Gandharv Singh, a Jagirdar of the Shahgarh Raja, committed a dacoity on 25 June 1857 in the pargana Batiagarh. A day or two after this dacoity, several villages in the north of the district were plundered by the Raja of Shahgarh and his followers.[5]

On 2 July 1857 on receiving an express from Sagar of the departure of the rebels to Damoh with a view of inciting the detachment there to join them and for seizing the treasure, amounting to about Rs.1,50,000, Lt. Nembhard assembled the European officers (only two of them Captain Holt and Ensign Sutherland of the 42nd) and the Indian officers and after consulting them, it was resolved that they and the detachment should enter the jail-fort and defend it against the mutineers.[6]

In the afternoon Bhairon Singh, a Havildar of the detachment who was taking some money to Sagar, returned and stated that he had met some mutineers on the way, and that they would be at Damoh early next morning. The treasure was at once sent to the jail. The detachment were in a very excited and mutinous state and once during the evening rushed to their arms but were quieted by Lt. Holt.[7]

Escape of the Deputy Commissioner to Narsinghpur and its consequences

On the same evening Matadin, Jemadar of the detachment and one or two loyal non-commissioned officers, warned the European officers that their men were not to be depended on, and that certain danger to the European officers would follow, should they enter the jail. These officers were convinced that if they entered the jail, they would not be alive. Moreover, on seeing what had occurred at Sagar in this regiment, all the three European officers alongwith Mrs. Holt left Damoh 'with nothing but clothes on their backs.' They rode direct to Narsinghpur, about seventy miles, where after much suffering from wet and hunger on the road they safely arrived.[8] It may, however, be noted that at the time of revolt only three British officers, one civil and two military, were managing this district.

On 4 July 1857 according to the native officers of the regiment, the jail Daroga and the native Deputy Collector, some thirty five mutineers came from Sagar to Damoh.[9] The infantry portion went to the jail and demanded the treasure which was refused by the Subedar-Major and Ranjit Singh, Havildar. The cavalry portion went in search of the officers, with the intention of murdering them but did not find them due to their escape to Narsinghpur. However, on finding that the Subedar-Major and Ranjit Singh were resolute in not joining them and in not giving up the treasure, the mutineers left Damoh without harming it and plundered some surrounding villages.[10]

The refusal of the Subedar-Major and Havildar in not joining the mutineers was explained[11] by Major Erskine that "the Subedar-Major was a Mahomedan and his family were at Saugor in the hands of the Brigadier, who arrested them; but he was old, and is said not to have had much influence with his men. But Ranjeet Singh was not only a fine gallant soldier, but had great influence, and to his excellent management, pluck in every way and loyalty I ascribe the safety of the treasure." Both of them were promoted by the Government for their good conduct.

Lt. Nembhard later on from Narsinghpur explained[12] to Major Erskine on 9 July 1857 the circumstances why he left Damoh. It is a long explanation. However, it throws light on the circumstances in which he escaped to Narsinghpur. It is worthwhile to quote some excerpts from it. He gave an account of "what happened on the 2nd instant on the night of which we were obliged to fly for our lives from Dumoh. On the morning of the 2nd I received from Major Western an intimation that a portion of the Irregular Cavalry at Saugor had created a disturbance, had demanded their pay and had sharpened their swords and gone off to a musjid. At noon of the day I received an express from Major Western saying that 8 sowars had started for Dumoh with bad intentions. I communicated the fact to Captain Holt commanding the detachment 42nd Native Infantry at Dumoh, got in consultation with him and Ensign Sutherland. It was agreed that for safety sake it would be as well if we transferred the prisoners from the old to the new jail and all the treasure and magazine into the old jail which you are aware is built like a fort. The native officers and Subedar-Major fully approved. I intended to send treasure in, the next day."

At about 7 P.M. a pay Havildar, named Bhairon Singh of the 42nd Native Infantry who had gone to Sagar with some money, returned and stated that as he had met some mutineers on the way, and that they would be at Damoh early next morning, he asked them to send a force of police to stop them from coming to Damoh. But Lt. Nembhard "could not have got together 20 musketeers to oppose the mutineers, besides the idea was preposterous of sending a small body of police to oppose regular troops."[13]

At the same time, the Deputy Collector begged him not to go into the jail, for that there were not twenty men in the whole detachment who were to be trusted, but the treasure was at once sent to the jail. He further stated[14] that "at about 10 P.M. when nearly the whole of the treasure was despatched, the guard came round me in a strange manner, and the two guards in the position of 'charge bayonet' - the bayonets close to me. I saw this and gave myself up for lost, but I turned my side to them, and addressed some joke to the other men of the guard, and by God's will my life was not taken. I stayed among them for a quarter of an hour longer and walked over past the lines (where a most ominous silence was reigning at Captain Holt's quarters). To him I mentioned the evident intention of the men, and we consulted together what we should do and after calm and mature deliberation we agreed that the only course was for us to abandon the station as secretly and speedily as possible for all of us would have been murdered into the jail before morning. We had sent all our property of any value into the jail and therefore we left Dumoh at midnight with nothing but our clothes on our backs. While any hope remained, I was the last man to leave my post and I hope ever will be so, but with a certain knowledge, that if we entered the fort, we should have been massacred before morning, I see not how we otherwise could have acted. But this is no place for me to defend my conduct, I simply and truly report to you matters as they occurred."

Captain Holt, Commander of the Damoh detachment, also explained[15] from Narsinghpur to Brigadier Sage at Sagar, the circumstances why the Deputy Commissioner, Ensign Sutherland and himself had abandoned Damoh. Its copy was also sent to Major Erskine. It is also a long explanation but it gives more details. Some of its excerpts are given here to clarify the whole picture. He also narrated the return of Bhairon Singh with two sepoys while going to Sagar on 2 July 1857 where he was taking some money to the Regimental Head Quarters. He "had been unable to proceed along the road any distance on account of its being crowded with riotous and mutinous persons who he feared would rob him of the money.... He had fallen in with, on the road, six *coss* from Dumoh, a detachment of troops marching on Dumoh the strength of which body, consisted of 25 sepoys of the 42nd Native Infantry and 25 of the Irregular cavalry. He moreover said that he had spoken to some of them, and they stated that they intended to go to Dumoh and take the treasury and that they brought a message from Ramzan-Subedar to Meerhazaree, Subedar-Major, that he should give up the treasure without allowing his men to offer any active opposition as the men of the Regiment (42nd) did not wish to fire on their own comrades. The Havildar added, that upon hearing this, he and the two sepoys with him hurried back to inform me accordingly."

After despatching the treasure to the old jail and prisoners to the new jail, as "I was walking about a short distance from the lines, I heard a confused noise and men calling out loudly to one another and on approaching my bungalow Ensign Sutherland came upon it and I heard him cry out, "Look out Holt, the sepoys are up." And his authority for so saying was, that the orderly who was on duty at his house, rushed to him in a most excited state and called out that "the sepoys were buckling on their belts and coming!" and he saw also, that the sepoy who was at my bungalow cried out to "Everyone to get out of the way as the sepoys were coming!" But however although the men rushed to their arms and buckled on their belts, they were soon persuaded to disperse, some of them expressing a strong desire to retain their arms. Immediately after this I addressed them, and called upon to remain true to their officers and themselves ... but the spirit they manifested was sullen and discontend one."[16]

"When a very short period elapsed, Ranjeet Singh Naik and Matadin Jemadar came up to me and Ranjeet Singh said that if the Deputy Commissioner could not manage to destroy the mutineers marching on Dumoh, with his police, that there would be no hope of saving the treasure and securing the fidelity of the detachment. Matadin Jemadar at the same time said, that there was no doubt that if I took both the companies into the jail, the treachery would take place as No.1 company was in a mutinous spirit and also there was several likewise in the 2nd Company."[17]

There was "no cheerfulness or domestic activity going on in the lines on the night of the 2nd while we were there; but a dead silence reigned, which caused us to imagine that something was being plotted of an insidious and disgraceful nature. At about 11 o'clock on the night of the 2nd, we after a general consultation, determined to leave the station of

Dumoh as we felt perfectly committed that our lives would be taken by the troops in the course of the night, if we did not do so. We, therefore, at about midnight, left the station and made the best of our way to this place, which after many hardships and privations we reached yesterday afternoon, knowing that it was perfectly impracticable to attempt to reach Saugor, leaving everything behind us, with the exception of the clothes on our backs."[18] He also stated[19] that "if I had, had the slightest idea that there was even the most remote chance of the Dumoh detachment remaining "firm", I would have never left my post."

Some excuse for their action may be found in the fact that the 42nd at Sagar had mutinied and there was every reason to suppose that their comrades at Damoh were about to follow their example.[20] Major Erskine was, therefore, satisfied with these explanations of Lt.Nembhard and Captain Holt. He stated[21] that "I think that if they had not left Dumoh on the night of 2nd, some of the bad men of the detachment would then and there murdered them. Their best Jemadar and Havildar told them they could not be answerable for their lives and the change in feeling that took place in the bad men of the detachment owing to their seeing that they could not get away with the treasure."

From the day the Deputy Commissioner had left his district, all was anarchy there.[22] The detachment of the 42nd at Damoh anyhow held the town against the rebels. Meanwhile, the Rajas of Banpur and Shahgarh sent emissaries to all the petty chiefs to join in the general rebellion. In the Damoh district nearly all of them joined it except the Raja of Hatree.[23] Some of the mutineers had taken service with the Shahgarh Raja who had taken some of the thanas in the Sagar and Damoh districts.[24] Major Erskine, therefore, wrote[25] to Major Ellis, Political Assistant for Bundelkhand, Rewa and Nagod on 16 July 1857 that it was reported that "the Shahgurh troops have occupied our Tehseelees of Hatta and Benaika and are about to march on Dumoh, Gurhakota and other places and I request you to warn them that if this is true that the Government will make a severe example of them." Looking to the seriousness of the situation, Major Erskine proclaimed martial law in Damoh.[26]

Recovery of the Damoh district in July 1857

As referred to earlier, Captain Pinkney could not get beyond Sagar, and was of no use in his official capacity there, like the rest in the fort, Major Erskine requested him to try and recover Damoh and its treasure as the two weak companies of the 42nd there were not only holding the place, but had also attacked and driven the rebels out of the town. He requested Brigadier Sage to give him some troops for this purpose. Captain Pinkney anticipated the wishes of Major Erskine. He obtained two companies of the 31st under Captain Finch and two guns, and on arriving at Damoh (45 miles from Sagar) on 16 July 1857, the detachment there at once made over the fort and treasure to him.[27] Captain Pinkney took the charge of the district and Captain Jones of the 42nd Native Infantry took the charge of the two Companies of his regiment at Damoh.[28] Meanwhile, the Subedar-Major of the 42nd aided by the Munsiff, whom Ranjeet Singh, Havildar, took good care to keep in the fort with him, had managed to carry on the duty in the town of Damoh and a few miles around it, keeping the prisoners in jail and the police at their posts.[29]

Captain Pinkney found[30] nearly whole of the Damoh district in insurrection. All the thannas except Damoh and Tejgarh were held by the native chiefs in their own names. He also found[31] that the reports regarding Thakur Kishor Singh of Hindoria were true. On 10 July he (said to be one of the Jagirdars of the Shahgarh State who instigated him to attack Damoh some time before) attacked Damoh and took possession of the Tehsilee office, the thanas, the ruined fort and Deputy Magistrate's office and destroyed all records. Due to the paucity of troops, the Government could not oppose him. He had established a thanna at Damoh and in the name of the Raja of Shahgarh, had called upon the detachment at Damoh to join him "which they refused to do and took up a strong position in the old jail which they armed with three old cannons. Through strategem they induced the rebels to believe that reinforcements had arrived and taking advantage of these twelve sepoys under an officer, made a rally into the town and assisted by some other people, drove off the rebels, killing some ten or twelve of them. The sepoys lost one killed and I fear mortally wounded." He also found[32] that Narsinghgarh, Batiagarh, Hatta, Simariya and Kumharee were in possession of the rebels. The Government officials and police of those places, which had been occupied by the rebels, had mostly joined them.

Rao Krishen Rao, Munsiff and Deputy Magistrate in charge of the Damoh district, also gave his version of the attack on Damoh by Thakur Kishor Singh of Hindoria with more details. He informed[33] on 14 July the Deputy Commissioner, Sagar and the Brigadier Commanding, Sagar, in absence of the Deputy Commissioner of Damoh who had escaped to Narsinghpur, that "on 10 July 1857 Thakur Kishore Singh of Hindoria (said to be one of the Jagirdars of the Shahgurh state) arrived here with some 300 men or musketeers and attacked Dumoh and after a short combat with our 12 sepoys, took possession of the Tehseelee office, the Thanna, the ruined fort and my own office and destroyed all records. I regret to say that owing to the paucity of the troops at the station, the enemies forcibly took possession of the above offices, though a party of 12 men under command of Ranjeet Singh, Havildar of the 42nd Native Infantry was sent to meet them at north entrance of the city Dumoh." He praised "the bravery and smartness of the 12 men and the non-commissioned officer in question, i.e. when the enemies entered the city they killed eleven and wounded 14 by the first shot of their muskets. The loss on our side is one sepoy killed and one wounded,... After a couple of days we have taken possession of all the offices of the city of Dumoh which we had been dispossessed."

On receiving the report of Captain Pinkney, the Government of India considered[34] the conduct of the Raja of Shahgarh to be deserving of the highest punishment and authorized a reward of Rs.10,000 for his capture (and not to be offered for the 'dead' Raja) as he had rebelled and entered the British territory and seized Hatta and Garhakota. On receiving his report, Major Erskine asked[35] him to go to Hindoria to punish Kishor Singh with the instructions : "Go and level Hindoria, or burn every house and if possible catch and hang Kishore Singh - but do not keep the detachment out hunting for him and return to Dumoh." Then aided by the 42nd detachment, on 21 July 1857 Captain Pinkney attacked Hindoria, twelve miles from Damoh. The small British force beat a large body behind the stone walls there and killed many of them.[36] Kishor Singh then, with his 4,000 followers, together with troops of Shahgarh Raja and two heavy guns plundered many villages on the other side of the district and was able to hold Kumharee thanna under his authority for four and a half months.[37]

Meanwhile, on 18 July 1857 three columns of Shahgarh mustering all about 1000 men attacked the town of Damoh but were gallantly resisted by the British troops there, *viz.*, 2 Company of the 42nd, 3 of the 31st, 2 six pounders (worked by 31st) and 80 of the 3rd Irregular Cavalry. They were completely worsted. 31 were killed and 17 were taken prisoners. On the British side, none was killed.[38]

On 19 July 1857 a detachment under Captain Finch, proceeded alongwith Captain Pinkney and attacked a village called Khamkhera, 9 miles from Damoh, held by Pirtee Singh Sodey who had resumed rebellion and plundered several villages. They found the village prepared for resistance and on approaching it, were fired on. The British troops immediately attacked, took and utterly destroyed it. The eldest son of Pirtee Singh and two others were killed and 11 taken prisoners, the rest escaped to the deep ravines. During the attack, a large body of matchlockmen came from Hindoria intending to attack the British troops in the rear, but were kept off by the 3rd Irregular Cavalry.[39]

In the opinion[40] of Captain Pinkney the chief insurgents in the district were the Lodhi Thakurs who were encouraged by the Raja of Shahgarh, whose troops held the thannas of Narsinghgarh, Hatta and Garhakota.

In the meantime, Lt. Nembhard was ordered to go back to Damoh from Narsinghpur and he resumed his charge from Captain Pinkney on 25 July 1857. He was thus absent from the district from 2 to 25 July 1857. Captain Pinkney then returned to Jabalpur to take charge of the Judge's office.[41]

Again in August 1857 the district passed into the hands of the rebels except the Sadar station

The two companies of the 31st and the two guns manned by the 31st and some eighty of the 3rd Irregular Cavalry, as well as the two companies of the 42nd, remained at Damoh and had several engagements with the rebels, in one fight killing some fifty men.[42] On 28 July Rao Swarup Singh, Man Singh and Soney Singh with 200 followers from Balakot joined the Raja of Shahgarh and attacked Damoh but they were driven off with loss. The attack was renewed by them on 5 August but they were again defeated. Consequently, they plundered many villages in the district.[43]

The whole of the Damoh district was then swarming with the rebels, who plundered in every direction and the Shahgarh insurgents were joined by nearly every Lodhi with the exception of a petty Raja of Hatree, who remained faithful throughout.[44] As Damoh was being constantly attacked by large body of rebels with guns, the officers reported that the Bengal sepoys were losing heart from constant fighting and no relief was coming from Sagar as it was also surrounded with the rebels.[45] Most urgent calls were then sent to Major Erskine, the Commissioner of Jabalpur.[46]

By the end of August 1857 according to Major Erskine with the exception of the Sadar stations of Sagar and Damoh, the whole districts were entirely in the hands of the rebels. All the police had deserted or been driven in, and hundreds of Malguzars were forced either to join the rebels or assist them with men or food, or were plundered or tortured until they complied. No daks were received at Sagar and Damoh for several weeks and the communication was entirely closed with the headquarters at Jabalpur. But he further stated[47] that "now and then a tiny note of few lines was received by the hands of a highly paid *hurkara*, and of those poor creatures several mutilated and killed."

Recovery of Damoh on 29 August 1857

In the meantime, on the request of Major Erskine the Nagpur Movable Column under Colonel Millar arrived on 2 August 1857 at Jabalpur from Kamthee, the headquarters of the Madras regular troops. Colonel Millar informed Major Erskine that his column was not to garrison Jabalpur but was placed at his disposal to march on in any place in the Saugor and Nerbudda Territories and it was on no account to be divided.[48] Looking to the serious situation at Damoh which was constantly attacked by large bodies of rebels with guns, and the Bengal sepoys were losing heart from constant fighting, Major Erskine resolved on requesting Colonel Millar to march towards Damoh.[49]

As the most urgent calls for aid were coming from Damoh and the rains were heavy and the guns and carts with the column could not move, the two companies of the 52nd were ordered off on 6 August in advance of the Movable Column to Damoh, with their four officers to Katangi, twenty miles on the Damoh road, to keep boats safe at Hiran river. They were accompanied by Captain Clerk, the Deputy Commissioner of Jabalpur. They marched on 7

August. Shortly after, these two companies reached Katangi. Lt. Oakes, the senior officer in command, received a most urgent call from Damoh and in consequence (in spite of rain, bad roads and swollen rivers) he marched in two days with his detachment to Damoh. Once or twice he was engaged with the rebels near that place.[50]

Due to continuous rains in Jabalpur, the Nagpur Movable Column could not move until 17 August 1857. Major Erskine had also accompanied it as it was his intention to march with the force in the direction of Damoh to settle the district.[51] On 18 August "the force marched to Katangi, crossing the Hiran river. The guns and a portion of the infantry did not arrive until three days later, owing to incessant rains.... On the 26th the Column marched 17 miles to Jabbera, the guns being dragged through mud by the elephants, preceded by the Rifle Company, which was sent ahead to seize the boats on Nohta on the Birma river and on 29th August Damoh was relieved and the rebels all moved off to a distance."[52] Thus, after great hardships on the way to Damoh, the Column reached there on 29 August and relieved it. After the recovery of Damoh, the further plan of action was decided by Major Erskine and Captain Millar. The Madras Column were to clear the country of rebels in the Damoh district and then advance to Sagar for the same purpose.[53]

Recovery of the district

In the meantime, the Simariya pargana of Damoh had been taken by the rebel Rani of Jaitpur, widow of Raja Pareechat. As the Panna Raja had frequently written to Major Erskine offering aid, he told him to attack them and turn them out. Accordingly, the Panna Raja ousted the rebels from Simariya and remained there. His troops with two small guns were under the command of his brother-in-law, Kunwar Shyamlejoo.[54]

On 1 September a detachment from the Nagpur Movable Column was sent to attack the rebels at Balakot, the residence of the rebel Raja Swarup Singh, a Lodhi. The village was taken and a small fort was then set fire to and destroyed. The detachment returned on 2 September.[55] On 4 September a detachment of the Movable Column was then sent to attack Hindoria which destroyed the loopholed house of rebel chief, Thakur Kishor Singh, and returned on 5 September.[56] The fortified building at Hindoria was totally destroyed and rendered forever useless as a residence or place of defence.[57]

Meanwhile, a plot was discovered at Jabalpur that some of the sepoys were conspiring with Raja Shankar Shah to murder the Europeans etc. Consequently, on receiving its news and in consultation with Captain Millar, a detachment was sent to Jabalpur on 7 September consisting of two guns with twenty gunners, an Artillery Officer, 200 of 33rd Madras Native Infantry and a troop of the 4th Madras Cavalry, under the command of Captain Tottenham. They reached Jabalpur on 12 September and encamped in the compound of the Agency-house where all the Christians were assembled.[58]

At Damoh Captain Finch had received peremptory orders from Brigadier Sage to march for Sagar with part of his detachment, including the 42nd Companies stationed at Damoh. Major Erskine asked him to take Rs. 70,000 of the Damoh treasury with him. The Madras Column was to accompany him through the most jungly part of the road. On 8 September they proceeded to Sagar alongwith Major Erskine, and Lt. Dickens was left with a portion of the 31st Native Infantry at Damoh. On 10 September when they were on the way to Sagar, the news came that the Dinapur mutineers had ascended the *ghats* and they were likely to march on Nagod, Rewa and Jabalpur. As the Rewa Raja was not able to oppose them, he had advised Lt. Osborne, the Political Agent there to leave his territory. Major Erskine then decided to return to Damoh, and on the refusal of Captain Finch to take on the treasure with him, kept the treasure. Captain Finch alongwith his detachment of 31st,

42nd and 3rd Irregular Cavalry marched to Sagar and the Madras Column returned to Damoh. They reached Damoh on 13 September just in time to save it as in the meantime, Damoh was again threatened by the rebels and Lt. Dickens had exchanged shots with them.[59]

On 15 September the town and Tehsilee of Hatta in Damoh was taken by the Panna troops from the Shahgarh rebels for the British Government. The Shahgarh rebels were also in possession of the fort, town and thanna of Narsinghgarh. A detachment under Major Jenkins was sent there on 16 September. They took it on 17 September and killed about fifty rebels and thirty three prisoners were taken, of whom thirteen were hung at Narsinghgarh, and the rest taken into Damoh where the detachment returned next day. The fort of Narsinghgarh was also destroyed and levelled.[60]

Mutinies of the 50th Native Infantry at Nagod and the 52nd Native Infantry at Jabalpur : Disarming of the two companies of the 52nd Native Infantry on 20 September 1857

On 18 September Major Erskine had heard of the mutiny of the 50th Native Infantry at Nagod. He immediately called in the detachment from Narsinghgarh, believing that the 52nd would also soon mutiny. The detachment from Narsinghgarh, which included the two companies of the 52nd, returned to Damoh on the evening of 19 September. In the night at twelve Major Erskine received an express from Captain Clerk, the Deputy Commissioner of Jabalpur, telling him about the mutiny of the 52nd Native Infantry at Jabalpur, and stating that the Nagpur rifles with them were not to be trusted. He at once consulted Captain Millar and requested him to disarm the two companies of the 52nd with them, the first thing in the morning, and consulted the senior officers how it was to be done.[61]

At daybreak on 20 September, orders were suddenly

issued for the whole column to march out on the Sagar road, on the pretence of attacking some rebels. The 52nd companies were ordered to form the Advance Guard, and the Madras Rifles the Rear Guard. The 52nd muskets were loaded, having only returned from service at Narsinghgarh the evening before, and the Madras sepoys were ordered to load. The Column then marched the 52nd Companies leading by some 200 paces, the two Companies of the 28th Madras Native Infantry heading the column, then the four guns etc.[62]

On arriving at an open plain about three miles from Damoh, the Column was halted. Major Erskine stated[63] that "the guns deployed to the left, were unlimbered and double shotted with canister. I then told the European gunners of the ruse; the 28th moved to the right, and the Colonel riding upto the 52nd for the first time told the officers what was to be done. The men were ordered to pile the arms; their officers then told them of what had occurred at Jubbulpoor, and that they must quietly give up their arms. They were taken by surprise and hesitated but seeing the guns pointed at them with port fires lighted, they with vehement expressions of loyalty and with much lamentation, piled arms, took off their poaches, and moved to the right. Elephants were at once moved to the front, and on them the arms and accouterments were packed, and the Column marched back to its old ground, where the baggage of the 52nd companies was searched, and all arms found were taken possession of. The Rifle Company (of the 1st Nagpur Infantry) being the Rear Guard, had never left the ground."

Abandonment of the Damoh district on 21 September 1857: Handed over to the Panna ruler

Owing to the mutinies at Nagod and Jabalpur, Major Erskine called[64] a Council of War of the senior military officers on 20 September. At a Council of War, composed of Captain Millar, Major Erskine, Major Jenkins, Captain Ludlow,

Captain Pinkney and Lt. Nembhard assembled at Damoh on 20 September 1857, after disarming the two Companies of the 52nd Bengal Native Infantry, which accompanied the Madras Field Force, the Commissioner laid before the Council two notes marked A and B and the following views of the state of affairs, upon which the subjoined Resolutions were agreed to.

After discussing the authentic intelligence received from Nagod of the mutiny there where the Dinapur mutineers had joined them after arriving there from Banda, and the mutiny of the 52nd at Jabalpur where the mutineers had gone off with their arms and 40 rounds per man, to join some disaffected Thakurs on the Hiran river in the Jabalpur district, they considered that for the protection of Damoh and Jabalpur districts the total reliable force was 500 Infantry and 80 Cavalry, including sick and six guns. After considering the relative position of both the districts, they resolved to give up Damoh and return to Jabalpur. For elaborating the reasons for abandoning Damoh, we will examine the proceedings of the Council of War, in detail.[65]

"The Dumoh district is nearly all lying waste in consequence of the rebellion, and has been plundered from one end to the other by the rebels. Dumoh khas is a large open town forty-five miles from Saugor and sixty-five from Jubbulpore. It cannot be defended by 200 men without guns, and the jail-fort is commanded by a hill within jinjal shot.

The Jubbulpore district has as yet in no way suffered from rebellion, and cultivation is going on as usual. Jubbulpore itself is a large commercial town and cantonment perfectly open, for the defence of which the 165 Infantry and forty Sabres and two guns now there are not sufficient. It is also situated on the north bank of the Nerbudda, and above mid-way on the high road between Nagpoor and Mirzapoor, which is also the main dak road between Calcutta and Bombay. In the event of this district remaining staunch and uninjured, forces operating to the south of Allahabad and Bundelkhand will probably in a great part supplied with grain from this and the districts to the north of Nerbudda. Although insurrection has not actually as yet broken out in the Jubbulpore district, yet disaffection exists to a considerable extent, and only a few days ago a deep-laid conspiracy to murder the Europeans and raise the country was discovered by the Deputy Commissioner, Lt.Clerk, and happily nipped in the bud. It is not improbable but the 50th and 52nd will join the Dinapoor mutineers in an attempt to attack and plunder the town and district.

It thus becomes necessary to decide on the following points :

1st. Shall Dumoh be held or abandoned ? Unanimously determined that it shall be abandoned; that the civil officers and treasure shall accompany the Madras Column, which will return to defend Jubbulpore; that the stamps be destroyed, and that, as it is impossible to remove the records, only the Treasury Accounts be taken away. The 200 of the 31st Bengal Native Infantry, now garrisoning Dumoh will retire to Saugor and join their head-quarters.

2nd. How is the Dumoh District to be temporarily disposed of ?

That koour Shamleyjoo, an officer of the Punnah Raja, now holding Hutta with a considerable force for the British Government, be requested to take the charge of the district; that the police hold the jail and jail-fort until his arrival, which will probably be to-morrow, when they can follow the 31st to Saugor."[66]

It was also resolved[67] that the disarmed men of the 52nd Bengal Native Infantry in camp should accompany the Madras Column to Jabalpur.

As no carriage of any description could be procured except for the treasure and a few records, the stamp papers were burnt. On the morning of 21 September they marched towards Jabalpur alongwith the treasure (about Rs.1,30,000) and the treasury accounts. The same day Kunwar Shyamleju entered Damoh with two guns and a considerable force. Lt. Dickens and party then marched for Sagar and reached there in due time. The Damoh civil officers accompanied the detachment to Jabalpur.

In the *Revolt in Central India from 1857 to 1859*, the following description[68] of the return of the Column to Jabalpur is given :

"The Column left Damoh on the 21st September, 1857 after having been delayed for three days in crossing the river at Nohta, reached Singrampoor on the evening of the 26th September, where intelligence was received that the mutineers, 500 rank and file, with 1,000 matchlockmen, had taken up a position at Kani on the west of the Hiran river, about 12 miles below Katangi. At 2 A.M. on the 27th Colonel Millar sent 12 troopers of the 4th Madras Cavalry, a Company of 33rd Madras Infantry, under Lt. Watson, accompanied by Major Jenkins, Assistant Quarter Master General, to seize the boats on the Hiran at Katangi. The main body marched at 5 A.M. and at the village of Gobra, three miles from Singrampoor, which commands the mouth of the pass, the 52nd mutineers were seen marching along the road in column of sections with colours flying. On being fired at by the guns, the rebels left the road and advanced through jungle on both the sides, but were driven back about half an hour, and were followed up for some miles, a few being killed and some prisoners taken on the hills near Katangi. At the entrance of the town, the body of Lt. Macgregor of the 52nd was found, with the throat cut, a shot in the chest and a bayonet wound in the body." It may, however, be noted that the mutineers had made him a prisoner at Patan on the outbreak of the mutiny of the 52nd Bengal Native Infantry at Jabalpur on 18 September.

"During the first advance, Major Jenkins and Lt. Watson had fallen into an ambuscade, but had succeeded in cutting their way through and concealing themselves in the hills until the arrival of the Column. Lt. Watson was wounded,

F.C. Cartwright, 24th Cavalry, mortally wounded, 2 sepoys wounded, 1 follower killed, and 2 wounded. The two disarmed companies of the 52nd came up shortly after the action and were kept up in the *serai* about a mile from camp that night when ten deserted. The remainder were afterwards sent to Saugor. Next day while the Column was crossing the river in boats and raft, a detachment was sent in search of enemy, but only came on a few stragglers who were cut up and dispersed. The river was not passed by the whole force and its baggage until September 29th and on October 1st, the Nagpur Movable Column marched into Jubbulpore."[69]

Thus, the Damoh district, which had been partially recovered by the march of the Madras Column from Jabalpur, had been again left to anarchy by the return of those troops, which followed as a necessary and immediate consequence of the mutiny of the 52nd at Jabalpur. The southern and western portions of the district were in a state of rebellion. The insurgents had taken possession of the fort of Garhakota on the Sagar and Damoh border. The Mangarh Raja in the east was also in insurrection.[70] As due to the paucity of the British forces, they had abandoned the Damoh district on 21 September 1857 and handed it over to the Panna ruler, it was another landmark in the revolt of 1857 in these territories.

REFERENCES

1. Charles Ball, *The History of the Indian Mutiny*, Vol. II (1858), p. 150.
2. N.E., para 57.
3. *Ibid.*, para 63.
4. *Ibid.*, para 72.
5. F.P. P. No. 2449, Enclosure No. 69 in No. 2, p. 276; and J.D., B.C., Political Case File No. 23 of 1857, p. 166, paras 3-4.
6. N.E., para 72.
7. *Ibid.*, para 73.
8. *Ibid.*, paras 74-5 and Foreign, Secret, Cons., 30 October 1857, No. 563, para 4.

9. Foreign, Secret, Cons., 31 July 1857, No. 356, para 3.
10. N.E., paras 74-5.
11. *Ibid.*, paras 77-8.
12. J.D., B.C., Political Case File No. 16 of 1857, p. 120.
13. *Ibid.*, paras 4 and 6.
14. *Ibid.*, paras 7-9.
15. *Ibid.*, Political Case File No. 13 of 1857, pp. 10-11.
16. *Ibid.*, p. 12.
17. *Ibid.*, p. 13.
18. *Ibid.*, pp. 13-14.
19. *Ibid.*, p. 14.
20. C.P. D.G., Damoh (1906), p. 22.
21. J.D., B.C., Political Case File No. 13 of 1857, p. 14.
22. N.E., para 89.
23. *Ibid.*, para 99.
24. Foreign, Secret, Cons., 31 July 1857, No. 369, para 9.
25. *Ibid.*, No. 377, para 6.
26. *Ibid.*, No. 373.
27. *Ibid.*, 26 February 1858, No. 126, para 11, also F.P. P. , No. 2449, Enclosure No. 69 in No. 2, p. 277, para 8.
28. *Ibid.*, 30 October 1857, No. 573, para 10.
29. N.E., para 119.
30. Foreign, Secret, Cons., 30 October 1857, No. 550, para 4.
31. *Ibid.*, No. 551, para 2.
32. *Ibid.*, para 5.
33. J.D., B.C., Political Case File No. 13 of 1857, pp. 126-27.
34. Foreign, Secret, Cons., 30 October 1857, No. 555.
35. *Ibid.*, No. 552.
36. N.E., para 120.
37. Damoh District, Case File No. GXII, 4 of Rebellion of 1857 quoted in M.P. D.G., Damoh (1971), p. 47.
38. Foreign, Secret, Cons., 26 February 1858, No. 141.
39. *Ibid.*, No. 115, paras 9-10.
40. *Ibid.*, para 14.
41. N.E., paras 121-23.
42. *Ibid.*, para 124.
43. M.P. D.G., Damoh, *op. cit.*, p. 47.
44. N.E., para 125.
45. *Ibid.*, para 133.
46. *Ibid.*, para 136.

47. *Ibid.*, para 142.
48. *Ibid.*, para 131.
49. *Ibid.*, para 133.
50. *Ibid.*, paras 138-40.
51. Foreign, Secret, Cons., 26 February 1858, No. 119.
52. *The Revolt in Central India from 1857 to 1859*, Compiled by the Chief of the Army Staff of the Army Headquarters (1908), p. 39.
53. N.E., para 155.
54. Ibid., para 154, also Foreign, Secret, Cons., 26 February 1858; No. 115, para 15.
55. N.E., paras 159-60.
56. *Ibid.*, para 161.
57. F.P. P. No. 2449, Enclosure No. 69 in No. 2, para 13.
58. N.E., paras 162 and 166.
59. *Ibid.*, paras 169-75.
60. *Ibid.*, paras 176-78.
61. *Ibid.*, paras 190-91.
62. *Ibid.*, paras 192-94.
63. *Ibid.*, paras 195-98.
64. *Ibid.*, Appendix k.
65. *Ibid.*
66. *Ibid.*
67. *Ibid.*
68. *The Revolt in Central India from 1857 to 1859, op. cit.*, pp. 42-3.
69. *Ibid.*, p. 43.
70. F.P. P. No. 2363, Enclosure 2 in No. 10, para 45.

99. F.P. P. , No. C-2363, Inclosure 2 in No. 10, para 48.
100. Foreign, Secret, Cons., 30 October 1857, No. 562.
101. *Ibid.*, No. 566.
102. *Ibid.*, No. 570.
103. F.P. P. , No. C-2363, Inclosure 43 in No. 7, p. 82, para 9.

CHAPTER 6

Further Progress of the Revolt in the Jabalpur and Other Districts

In the Jabalpur District

Situation in Jabalpur one of more anxiety and less action

Jabalpur was the headquarters of the Saugor and Nerbudda Territories and Major W.C. Erskine was its Commissioner. At the time of the revolt of 1857, Jabalpur was garrisoned by the 52nd regiment of the Bengal Native Infantry. While dealing with the outbreak of the revolt in the Sagar district in an earlier chapter, it was referred to that in spite of the inadequate means of communication, the news of the events at Delhi and Meerut reached Sagar and Jabalpur and the next day at Damoh, a week after they had occurred. In the words[1] of Major Erskine, "It did not appear to create any great excitement amongst the natives but a great deal of horror at the cruelties was expressed by the Sepoys and the towns people and much alarm was felt by many of the Europeans at all the stations. Nothing however occurred and the target practice of the 52nd went on as usual."

As the Indian troops stationed at Jabalpur were affected by the news of the Meerut uprising, on 19 May 1857 signs of distrust between the Indian soldiers and their British officers manifested themselves as information was received and transmitted to the Officer Commanding, Colonel Jamieson of "the existence of a bad feeling among the men of the 52nd."[2] The British officers were, thus, put on their guard and preparations were set on foot to meet the mutinous situation.

Very soon excitement prevailed in Jabalpur. At two in the morning of 19 May, Major Erskine was awoke by Major Sleeman, Superintendent of the Thuggee Department, who informed him that the 52nd would rise at daybreak and murder every European. He had heard this from Captain Venrenen, Revenue Surveyor, to whom it was told by Mr. Campbell, one of his uncovenanted Assistants. He hastily dressed and went to Major Sleeman's house where all the European residents were assembled for immediate flight. He disbelieved the story and counselled delay till some sign should be shown by the sepoys who were perfectly quiet in their lines. The officers of the regiment brought their wives and children to Sleeman's house and then went to their lines. Target practice took place as usual and by sunrise most of the Europeans were back in their houses. The sepoys expressed extreme annoyance at this report and the native officers demanded its enquiry. It was conducted at the Commissioner's house on 20 May and it was proved that there was not the slightest foundation in the report. But the men of the 52nd had been getting restive. They were apprehensive because of the open distrust exhibited by the officers towards them.[3]

Again on 22 May there was an excitement in Jabalpur and it was considered advisable that a public building be selected as a shelter in case of danger.[4] There was another panic on 5 June in consequence of Mr. Campbell again spreading a false alarm. Major Erskine ordered him out of the station and recommended more caution to others.[5] Captain Pinkney, the Deputy Commissioner, and the Commissioner then resolved[6] that whatever occurred they would not leave their posts, but all ladies and children were recommended to leave Jabalpur and go to Calcutta or Nagpur.

Although, at times, intelligence from the disturbed districts occasioned much anxiety to the European residents, who had no means of repressing outrage if attempted by the troops, yet nothing to warrant a serious apprehension of immediate danger had occurred. In the language of one who shared the sunshine and shade of the position, was "one day full of hope, and cheered by a feeling of comparative security, and the next by gloomy forebodings, that led them to estimate their lives, as not worth a dav's purchase."[7]

With the news of stirring events in Jhansi on 8 June 1857 in which all the seventy six Europeans were murdered, came the report that Raja Mardan Singh of Banpur had gathered a large body of men at Lalitpur. These news "caused much excitement amongst the Sepoys and the Thakurs near Saugor and at Jubbulpore the sepoys were very uneasy, not apparently inclined to mutiny, but expressed a fear of being disarmed."[8]

On 9 June Major Erskine in a letter to Mr. Plowden, the Commissioner at Nagpur, had expressed[9] his feelings that "I greatly fear, when the Saugor troops hear of the Jhansi affair, that they rise and seize the treasury and magazine at Saugor and if so, I can hardly expect the 52nd to stand quiet here, though we have but very little treasure - some 30,000 rupees. There is a great alarm amongst many of the Europeans here, and I rather think some of them have resolved to send their families towards Seonee, but I hope all the civil officers will stand fast, and I can answer for myself and the Deputy Commissioner."

He also asked Mr. Plowden for a detachment of the Madras force, to strengthen the detachment at Seoni. He further stated[10] : "Here all is quiet, and to all appearance, the 52nd are behaving very well; but there is no saying how long this will last. I feel sure, that if the 52nd heard of a Madras force coming here, it would have the worst effect, but still, I think it would be right to strengthen the detachment at Seonee." He also requested[11] that the object of his letter should be kept 'private'. But on 12 June a rumour prevailed in the Jabalpur Cantonment that "a large force of Europeans or Madrassees was advancing upon the forced marches, for the purpose of disarming the 52nd." The report instantly threw the entire corps into a state of angry excitement, which presently assumed the features of a general mutiny. The officers were treated with disrespect and their orders contemptuously disregarded.

Whilst this disturbance raged in the lines, the Subedar-Major of the regiment, an old and favourite officer, hastened to Major Erskine's quarters and represented the excited state of the regiment, at the same time suggesting, that "a few men of the each company should be allowed to leave to examine the roads and intervening country for a short time, and thereby satisfy the corps that no European troops were approaching in any direction - the assurance of their officers to that effect not being believed! To this extraordinary act of humiliation and confession of weakness the major assented; ..." Some sepoys were sent out on the different roads to see whether the European force was marching up for disarming them. They returned and reported that they had neither heard of nor seen any approaching force and the excitement died down.[12] The situation in Jabalpur was, thus, one of more anxiety and less action.

Attack on the Adjutant on 15 June 1857

The trouble, however, started in an unexpected manner. On 15 June whilst Lt. Miller, Adjutant of the 52nd Regiment was inspecting the guards of his regiment "a man he had passed a pace or two suddenly rushed upon him with the cry of 'Death to the Feringhees!' and accompanied his cry with a downward thrust of his bayonet. The bayonet passed down the sleeve of the Adjutant's jacket, and grazed his arm and side."[13] The Subedar-Major who was standing in the rear, threw his arms round the man and after a severe struggle, in which the Subedar-Major was wounded and risked his own life, the man was secured and confined in the guard-room. The Subedar-Major was rewarded by the Government.[14]

On the attack on the Adjutant, Major Erskine expressed[15] his fear that "had this wretch succeeded in his object of killing the Adjutant, the greater part of the regiment if not all, would have joined the massacre of the Europeans." The Europeans also expressed[16] the feelings of fear : "We are entirely at the mercy of a powerful body of armed men. No place of refuge or rendezevous to fly to in case of revolt; each must seek safety as best he may. The only arrangement we can come to is, that all have agreed to take the same road. Some ladies never take off their clothes at night and all are prepared for immediate flight. Our carriage is drawn up at the door every night, and the horses kept harnessed, ..."

The sepoy was said to be mad, and being pronounced so by the Medical Officer of the regiment. He was sent under a guard of his own corps to the lunatic asylum at Benaras where he was not pronounced mad and was hanged.[17] However, this was not true : "The truth is, the authorities were in too great fright to hang the scoundrel; for the sepoys had swomed they would not eat until they had released their comrade. The men say they will not mutiny unless a European regiment comes here to disarm them. The regiment is not under control. All the ladies have left the station for Seonee and Narsinghpur, and a great many of the male residents have left but to all appearance, all is serene."[18] Thus, ever since this isolated incident, European community had lived in great alarm.

Outbreak of the revolt in Sagar : Reaction in Jabalpur

After the release of the prisoners of Balabehat at Malthone in the Sagar district on 25 June and the confinement of the Europeans in the Sagar fort on 29 June 1857, the British apprehended[19] that "if Saugor rise, Dumoh and Jubbulpore will follow." The Commissioner also apprehended[20] that "if the Saugor force mutinied, the Regiment at Jubbulpore was almost certain to do so also."

The news that the troops at Sagar had rebelled on 1 July 1857, soon became known at Damoh and Jabalpur, the only two other stations where there were Bengal troops. In the opinion[21] of Major Erskine, amongst them as well as amongst the majority of the European residents, there was much excitement, but the sepoys remained quiet, doing their duty as usual. But he was wrong. The men of the 52nd stationed at Jabalpur had assumed an openly hostile attitude towards the Britishers and as such they found the situation deteriorating and a marked change in the conduct and demeanour of the Indian soldiers.

Very soon the spirit of mutiny became manifest as Erskine observed[22] that "on 3rd July three companies took their muskets out of the Bell of arms, with no good intentions, but they were pacified. Some of the neighbouring Thakoors or petty chiefs too were said to be about to join the sepoys against us, and the reports came from Saugor that the mutineers were going to take Jubbulpore after Dumoh."

Shelter of the Europeans in the Agency-house on 4 July 1857

Looking to these serious conditions, it was proposed on 4 July that all females and children at once leave for Narsinghpur and preparations were made accordingly. But seeing that there was every chance of heavy rain shortly falling, this proposal was abandoned. Major Erskine then in consultation with Colonel Jamieson decided[23] that "it would be much better in every way, and cause less alarm to the natives of the town, who were loyal, if all the Christians assemble in the Agency House which I occupied, and which could be blockaded and be made defensible in a short time against musketry, if all worked with a will." It was also thought necessary to place confidence in the sepoys,[24] "for had they seen we distrusted them, they assuredly would not have allowed us to congregate, if they meant mischief. We therefore told the native officers that we were afraid of an attack of the Boondelas and Saugor mutineers, and must barricade ourselves and have a guard from the regiment. They apparently approved of this and seemed pleased."

At 2 P.M. on 4 July notice was sent round to the officers and the Christians in Jabalpur and before 7 P.M. all the ladies, gentlemen and children were assembled in the Agency-house. They sat down for dinner, forty five adults of whom ten were ladies and fifteen children. For the sergeants and uncovenanted members of the service, temporary arrangements were made in the verandahs, tents and out-houses. Pickets of sepoys were posted in the large compound and the officers, sergeants and uncovenanted took it by turns to stand sentry at night all round the house.[25]

According to Major Erskine,[26] "doubtless, that night was of no small danger to the Europeans of Jubbulpoor, for a section of determined men might have shot us all from the large hall door as we sat at dinner, but thanks be to God, all passed off quietly." In the morning of 5 July some thousands of workmen were engaged barricading doors, filling bags and boxes with sand and piling them up in the open verandahs and on the top of the house. Others were bringing in supplies and stores of all kinds. Two small guns (dangerous to the gunners if fired) were dug up and placed in position and the ladies made the powder bags. In the night, "all sat down to dinner with some feeling of security; most of us with good appetites and stout and thankful hearts."[27]

Major Erskine reported[28] to the Government of India on 5 July 1857 that "in Jubbulpore the whole of the Europeans about 40 and their families are now occupying the agency house which is being fortified as fast as possible with the hope of our being able to hold out for sometime against the 52nd Native Infantry should they mutiny (of which at present I am happy to see there appears no sign for the sepoys are perfectly quiet and guarded us last night) or against any mutineers who may arrive from Saugor or from Thakoors or petty chiefs who will rise if the sepoys mutiny."

An officer of the 52nd, writing of the shelter of the Europeans in the Agency-house in his letter, observed[29] that "at this moment I hear the piano and singing. We are a queer lot, we Britons : day after day we hear the atrocities too horrid to write about, and of the murder of friends and relatives and never seem to think of our own fate. Laughing, talking, eating, drinking, music, singing - all seems to go on much as usual."

Disturbances in the Jabalpur district

Meanwhile, the party of the mutineers from Sagar were frustrated in their intentions by the loyalty of the Damoh detachment beyond which station they had not advanced in the direction of Jabalpur.[30] But soon "the plundering parties said to be sent by the Mangarh Rajah have been collecting in the neighbourhood of Jubera and Kuttungee. The Malgoozar of the former village, Deo Kurrun has openly acknowledged himself an enemy of the Government, he took possession of the Thanna and called other Malgoozars to join him telling them that the English rule is at end." Captain Clerk, the Deputy Commissioner of Jabalpur also wrote[31] to Major Erskine on 17 July 1857 that the district around Jabalpur was in a state of turmoil. Dacoities occurred in a large number and the people were loud in their assertion that "the English rule is at end."

As about this time, some villages were plundered and with a view of stopping this, and also to weaken the corps at Jabalpur, the detachments of the 52nd were sent to different Tehsilees and to Katangi on the Hiran river towards Damoh.[32] In doing so, Major Erskine had in mind that "the chances against the Europeans, in case of a mutiny were greatly decreased and the district was restored to order."[33]

On 16 July 1857 Major Erskine reported[34] to the Government of India, that "a portion of the Jubbulpoor district in the direction of Dumoh and also in the Punnah border in the direction of Myhere and Jokai in the Mirzapore road is very much disturbed and I have to-day received reports that from 300 to 500 armed Boondelas have taken possession of a large old fort called Bilehree near the Tehseelee of Sleemanabad on the Mirzapore road." To suppress the rebellion at Bilhari, he sent a party of the 52nd under an officer on the same day. The Bundelas on hearing of it decamped but returned with reinforcements and took possession of the fort. They came on the road at Murwara where they stole the post horses and stopped the up-country and Calcutta daks.[35] Major Erskine then sent Captain Bailey of the 50th Bengal Native Infantry at Nagod with a company to attack the rebels. He also sent Lieutenants Barton and Cockburn at Sleemanabad to move against the rebels. On the arrival of Captain Bailey first, the rebels again fled and the fort of Bilhari was completely destroyed.[36]

By the middle of July, the rebellion had spread to the every part of the district. Major Erskine reported[37] to the Government of India on 18 July 1857 that "all remain quiet at Jubbulpore itself, but the district to the north of the Heerun river particularly on the Dumoh and Pannah frontiers is in a way disturbed state. Dacoitees are hourly reported and some of the petty chiefs in Jubbulpore, Dumoh and Punnah are daily rising and plundering our villages. I have therefore proclaimed martial law in that portion of the Jubbulpore district."

Arrival of Nagpur Movable Column in Jabalpur and its departure to Damoh

As the disturbances at Nagpur had been quelled; and the sepoys of the 52nd seeing themselves trusted, got over their fears of disarmed; and the Europeans having been placed in a place of comparative safety in a case of mutiny, Major Erskine requested the Commissioner and Brigadier of Nagpur, if possible, to send some reliable troops. On 17 July a small body of troops known as Nagpur Movable Column marched from Nagpur to Jabalpur, under the command of Colonel J. Millar, of the 33rd Madras Native Infantry. The troops contained 1 squadron, 4th Madras Cavalry - 92 Sabres; 1 Company 3rd Battalion, Madras Artillery - 65 rank and file, 6 guns; 33rd Madras Infantry - 425 rank and file, Rifle Company, 1st Nagpur Irregular Infantry - 91 rank and file.[38] The cavalry arrived at Jabalpur on 30 July, followed by the remainder of the Column two days later and the 52nd welcome them.[39]

Colonel Millar on reaching Jabalpur informed Major Erskine that his column was not to garrison Jabalpur but was placed at his disposal to march on in any place in the Saugor and Nerbudda Territories and it was on no account to be divided.[40] It was intended to keep the column at Jabalpur to demonstrate military strength and over-awe the dissatisfied elements. However, looking to the serious situation at Damoh which was constantly attacked by large bodies of rebels with guns and the Bengal sepoys were losing heart from constant fighting, Major Erskine had resolved[41] on requesting Colonel Millar to march towards Damoh.

On hearing this, Major Sleeman, Major Gordon, Executive Engineer and Captain Venrenen vehemently protested against the move, declaring that every European left in Jabalpur would be murdered on the column marching. However, Major Erskine had made up his mind for it, thought it better to call a meeting of the senior officers on the subject and the result was that the only actual dissenting voice to the march was of Major Sleeman.[42] The Europeans and the Christian population at Jabalpur on feeling insecured were panicky and loudly protested against the move. They said that it would be suicidal to leave the white men, women and children entirely to the mercies of the disaffected men of the 52nd aided by the local rebel chiefs whose number according to Rice Holmes[43] was no less than one hundred and seventy nine. How this column relieved Damoh on 29 August 1857 is referred to in an earlier chapter.

Martyrdom of Raja Shankar Shah and his son, Raghunath Shah on 18 September 1857

At Jabalpur since the attack on Adjutant on 15 June, the following two months passed away without any attempt at actual mutiny. Meanwhile, trouble was brewing there. Events, however, came crowding soon. The anxious preparations which the Commissioner and the Europeans had made for their defence were not in vain. Throughout August, the Thakurs and Malguzars of the district had been ready for an uprising, and were only waiting for a move from the army. Early in September there were evidences that some of the sepoys and Thakurs had planned to take action. They found a leader in Shankar Shah, the last of the Gond Raja, who, though shorn of territory and power, had still the prestige of belonging to the well-known Gond Royal family of Garha Mandla of Rani Durgavati. Shankar Shah was then a British pensioner having under him three *jagir* villages and was living at Purwa now a suburb of Jabalpur.[44] Several sepoys from the regiment at Jabalpur used to visit him at his house and discuss about the events at Sagar, Damoh and other places. The news of the terrible incidents happening at Cawnpore, Lucknow and Delhi also reached them and deeply agitated them. The rebel sepoys at Shankar Shah's house met Sheonath Singh of Mugirmoha, Devi Singh and Umrao Singh of Bargi and Jagat Singh of Belkheri. They had planned to collect a sufficient force with the aid of some Thakurs, Zamindars and sepoys of the army, and march against the Cantonment on the first day of *Moharrum*.[45]

Early in September "Captain Moxon of the 52nd received information from the Pundits and sepoys of his own regiment, in whom he placed great confidence that mischief was brewing, that some of the sepoys were conspiring with a pensioned Raja named Shankar Shah (a Gond) residing close to Jubbulpoor, to attack and murder the Europeans and though the measures were not completed, they might be ere long." He informed Lt. Baldwin, the Assistant

Commissioner, of this plot. He made an enquiry but thought the information was false.[46]

As the planned uprising did not take place on *Moharrum*, Lt. E. Clerk, the Deputy Commissioner, made further enquiries and reported[47] to Major Erskine at Damoh on 10 September 1857 that "on the last day of *Moharrum* festival a report was spread that there was a plan to attack the Europeans, and station and afterwards plunder the city. The day however passed off peacefully though the report was not altogether without foundation, but how far I am not at present prepared to state."

After a few days, he reported[48] on 19 September 1857 the circumstances which led to the execution of Raja Shankar Shah and his son, Raghunath Shah. He stated that "I succeeded in getting information regarding the alarm on the last day of *Moharrum* and the intentions of the rebels.... Khoosial Chand Seth of Jubbulpore was the first native who came forward and told me that the report was a true one that it had been the intention of Raja Shankar Shah and his son, Raggonath Shah accompanied by several zamindars with their followers and in concert with some of the sepoys of the 52nd to attack the Cantonments on the last day of *Moharrum* - murder all the Europeans, burn the Cantonments and afterwards plunder the treasury and the city, that it had not taken place for two reasons; first they were uncertain how many sepoys would join them, secondly that two of the zamindars of the rebel party had refused to act with them; it was also hinted that an attempt might be made during the *Dussehra*."

On receiving this information he sent a *chaprasee* in the disguise of a *faqir* to find out the more of the alleged conspiracy, and the scheme succeeded admirably, for the Raja and his son were completely deceived by the disguised emissary, and without hesitation disclosed to him their intentions, as well as the means that they had resolved to employ for carrying them into effect. Acting on this information on the morning of 14 September, "I with Lt. Baldwin and a party of 20 sowars and 40 police went to Poorwa without having previously any intimation of my intention to anyone." When they were about a mile from the place the Deputy Commissioner galloped forward with some *sowars* and surrounded the village until the police arrived and arrested the Raja, his son, Raghunath Shah, and some thirteen persons in the house and confined them in a prison. On searching the Raja's house several documents of a rebellious tendency were found, particularly a piece of paper in which the Raja had written a prayer, invoking his diety to aid him to upset the British Government and establish his own. The paper was found in a silken bag in which he kept his fan, near the bed from which he rose as Lt. Clerk and his party entered the house. The poem was written on a scrap of paper torn from a Government Proclamation after the events (massacre) at Meerut and the remainder of the Proclamation was afterwards found in the house. A similar prayer in the handwriting of his son, Raghunath Shah was also discovered.[49]

The poem has been freely translated by Erskine[50] and runs as follows :

> "Shut the mouth of slanderers, bite and eat up backbiters, trample down the sinners, you *Shatrusanharka* (destroyer of enemey, one of the names of *'Devee'* implying here),
> Kill British, terminate them, *Mata Chandee* (another name of the Goddess *'Devee'*),
> Let not the enemy escape, nor the wives and children of such Oh! *Sanharka* (Another name of Goddess *'Devee'*),
> Show favour to Shankar,
> Support your slave,
> Listen to the cry of religion, *Mata Kalika* (another name of Goddess *'Devee'*),
> Eat up the unclean,

Make no delay,
Now devour them,
and that quickly, *Ghormat Kalika* (another name of Goddess *'Devee'*).

After the imprisonment of Raja Shankar Shah and his son, the situation in Jabalpur was alarming. An attempt was made to rescue them but it hastened their end. On the second night of their imprisonment, the Deputy Commissioner heard of a plan on the part of the 52nd to rescue the prisoners. The Madras regiment was turned out and remained under arms all night, and the Raja and his son were removed to the Commissioner's house. During that night a few shots were fired in the 52nd lines, and a bungalow close to the lines was fired and burnt down. Some eight of the 52nd deserted with their arms.[51]

The authorities, however, took precautionary measures to render their rescue impossible. They tried them for plotting against the British *raj*. A Commission, composed of the Deputy Commissioner and two officers, was held on the following day for the trial of Raja and his son. As the proof of their complicity in the plot for the destruction of the Europeans being conclusive, they were sentenced to death by being blown from guns - "this mode of execution being resorted to in preference to hanging, in consequence of the excitement then visible in the lines of the 52nd, which suggested an idea of a possible attempt at rescue; an event that would have been facilitated by the delay afforded while constructing the gallows."[52] Accordingly, at 11 o'clock in the morning of 18 September, they were lashed to guns. "The old man walked upto the guns with a firm stride and haughty demeanour; and but for the defaint tone in which he breathed his last aspirations for revenge, his snow-white hair and venerable appearance might almost have excited a feeling of compassion in the breast of those he had plotted to destroy. The son, Ragonauth Shah, was less determined in his manner, as he placed himself in front of the gun that was to annihilate him."[53] The entire act was made public and people were called to witness the scene. After they were blown away, the half-burnt remains were collected on behalf of the Rani, while European officers looked with a smile of gratified revenge on their lips.[54] Thus, both the father and son died as martyrs.

An officer who was present at the execution of Raja Shankar Shah and his son, in a very graphic description of the incident noted[55] (See Appendix I) that "the old man's (Rajah Shankar Shah's) face was quiet and severe (he never moved a muscle the wholetime before), as was also the young one's (a man of forty)." This particular mode of execution of the rebel leaders by blowing away from guns was chosen to strike terror into the hearts of the people. That it was carried out more as a matter of retaliation and revenge for the atrocities committed elsewhere than as a mode of punishment, is clear from the description[56] (See Appendix II) given by a medical officer of the Bombay Presidency of an execution parade which he considered a "horrible sight" and regarded blowing away from guns as "most appalling."

Mutiny of the 52nd regiment at Jabalpur on 18 September and its march towards Patan, Sleemanabad and Katangi

The brutal execution of Raja Shankar Shah had shocked the people and the troops who followed him. To allay this excitement amongst the rank and file, Colonel Jamieson and others went almost immediately to the lines and explained to the men that the prisoners had merely paid the penalty for treason. They judged from the manner of the men that they had removed all apprehensions from their minds.[57] How wrong the Colonel and his officers were in their estimate of the reaction of the troops of the 52nd soon became manifest.

At 6 P.M. on 18 September "there was reason to believe that the men of the 52nd intended to make some move that night." It was, however, not considered advisable to take any offensive measures against them, as it might have caused the murder of two officers on detached command at Sleemanabad, and one at Patan.[58]

About 10 P.M. that night, whole of the 52nd left Jabalpur, with the exception of one Indian officer and fifteen Rank and File. They rose quickly in a body and left the station, taking with them their arms and ammunition in pouch, and marched by a circuitons route outside the city, went towards Patan, one of the Tehsilees on the Hiran river, where there was a detachment of the corps under Lt. Macgregor, and where they expected some Thakurs with their followers to join them. When it became known, the lines magazine and the property of the 52nd which they had evidently in a panic left behind them, were secured by the Madras troops.[59] Expresses were at once sent off to the officers at Sleemanabad and Patan, warning them what had occurred, and ordering them into Jabalpur at once.[60]

The mutineers on reaching Patan confined Lt. Macgregor, took his horse from him and would hardly give him enough to eat. They were joined by the men of the Patan detachment who had a considerable quantity of ammunition. They plundered Patan and crossed the river. There a rebel Thakur of Narsinghpur named Mirbhan Singh, and his followers joined them and marched towards Katangi. Lt. Macgregor was also compelled to accompany them. They were joined by the detachment of the corps there.[61]

In a letter[62] (See Appendix III) to Colonel Jamieson the mutineers had explained their reasons for the desertion and mutiny and announced their intentions respecting Lt. Macgregor. They stated that they had been told that the officers had given orders to the Madras sepoys to "seize all the arms of the regiment and kill all men; then you will receive thirty rupees per man as reward and be promoted to Subahdar Bahadoors." They added that they had sought an assurance from the Colonel on the subject of the alleged order, and were informed that the Madras sepoys were not under his (Colonel's) authority. "Then having become helpless we came away here." The sepoys offered to release Lt. Macgregor and send him to the Colonel if the men of the regiment who were left behind at Jabalpur were sent to them. Otherwise the sepoys "having bound him, we will take him to Delhi." Colonel Jamieson replying[63] (See Appendix IV) to the men of the 52nd, told them that he would not send the men demanded by the insurgents. He also advised them to return bringing Macgregor with them. He threatened the sepoys that "if Lt. Macgregor in anyway hurt, or any robbing takes place, you will not escape."

From Katangi a portion of the mutineers proceeded to Sleemanabad where Lieutenants Barton and Cockburn were on duty with a detachment of regiment. Upon their arrival, the two officers were ordered by the rebels to depart for Jabalpur. Their men "expressed their regret at parting with these officers and did not molest them, but said they must make the best of their way towards Delhi. Some of them shook their officers by the hand, robbed the Tehseelee of the little money then was there, the Pay Havildar handing one of the officers of the balance of his pay, and marched off quickly towards Nagode. The two officers safely reached Jubbulpoor, and the men procuring carriage sent in the officer's baggage to Jubbulpoor."[64] This singular treatment of the British officers provides a sharp contrast to the fate that befell the captured insurgents at the hands of the British.

It was believed in Jabalpur and the sepoys said to themselves, that on being joined by the Thakurs, they would return to Jabalpur, plunder the treasury and city, burn the cantonment, and murder the Europeans. But their hopes were disappointed as they evidently feared two guns at Jabalpur.[65]

Immediately after the uprising of the 52nd Infantry at Jabalpur on the night of 18 September, orders were given to the Madras Column at Damoh to return to Jabalpur. The mutineers and rebels then advanced against the Movable Column and the action with them is, however, referred to in detail in an earlier chapter regarding Damoh.

Repercussions in the Jabalpur district till Sept. 1857

During this time, the Jabalpur district continued to be in ferment. The remnant of the 52nd, numbering some five hundred and thirty men, even after its defeat at Katangi by the Madras Column, continued to ravage the country. In Sihora and Sleemanabad, the Thakurs plundered in all directions and Debi Singh, Jagat Singh and Bahadur Singh assembled their forces in Bargi pargana to the south of the Narmada. These three, according to the official reports, were in league with Raja Shankar Shah in his meditated attack on the Europeans.[66] Reports from Patan spoke of a strong party of 1000 rebels who later attacked the town and burnt public buildings.[67]

Lt. Clerk had reported[68] in detail to Major Erskine that during this time throughout the district except the immediate neighbourhood of Jabalpur, villages were daily plundered. He corroborated the situation of Sihora, Sleemanabad and Bargi referred to earlier. He offered a reward of Rs. 200 a head for the apprehension of three rebel zamindars of Bargi. The Thanna of Kundam was attacked on 1 October 1857 and burnt by Moorat Singh, Thakur of Narainpur and the police were driven out, but after destroying the Government property and *Bania's* shops the rebels appeared to have been satisfied and spared the village. Thus, at the close of September 1857 the situation in the Jabalpur district was very much disturbed.

In the Narsinghpur district

In July 1857 a certain amount of panic had seized the people in the Narsinghpur district as Captain Ternan, the Deputy Commissioner, reported[69] to Major Erskine on 28 July 1857 that "the copper currency is being exchanged to silver in the Bazars at 19 annas for the Company's rupee," but the peace of the district remained undisturbed.

In August 1857 inroads by the Bundelas and the Bhopal rebels were made into the Chawarpatha pargana, north of the Narmada, and the town and thanna of Tendukhera was plundered. In fact, all to the north of the Narmada, except the districts of Jabalpur and Mandla, were in a state of anarchy and all the forts were held by the rebels while all to the south of Narmada was in perfect peace.[70] Thus, the situation in this district to the north of the Narmada river was disturbed.

In the Hoshangabad district

In July 1857 in the Hoshangabad district, a plot was discovered to rob the Tehsilee treasury of Harda and the Najeebs in charge of it were most mutinous. But as Mazhar Zameel, the Deputy Magistrate, maintained a bold front, they were unable to do much harm there and about Rs. 30,000 were sent to Hoshangabad under a strong guard of police.[71]

The Nemawar pargana, which is on the right bank of the Narmada and had been ceded to the British by the Sindhia in 1844, was also disturbed. On 3 July much alarm was created by the *sowars* from Indore, bringing exaggerated accounts of the rising at Indore to the effect that the Holkar had rebelled and blown away the Resident and all the British officers with guns. As the rebels from Indore were fast advancing, the commanding officer at Hoshangabad informed[72] Major Erskine that he could not resist them with a weak wing of the Madras Native Infantry and two guns. In panic he, therefore, proposed that the other wing of the regiment should join him from Narsinghpur. He also suggested that the Narsinghpur station and district should be abandoned and the whole troops in Hoshangabad, Narsinghpur, Betul, Seoni and Jabalpur should retire to Kamthee, the headquarters of the Madras troops.

The Commissioner was doubtful of this news and required its confirmation. He was of the opinion[73] that "such a retreat on our part would be disgraceful and would not only deliver up the fine valley of Nerbudda to anarchy, but probably endanger the Southern-Central India and at any rate lose us all my districts and the northern part of Nagpoor." As he was also invested with the powers of the Chief Commissioner, he ordered the troops at Narsinghpur, Betul, Seoni and Hoshangabad to stand fast unless actually driven in. To instil loyalty in them he put them on full *batta*.

The news from Indore was false though some of the Holkar's troops had murdered some of the Europeans. As these false reports reached Nagpur, the Commissioner Plowden and Brigadier Prior at Kamthee ordered[74] all the Madras troops at Narsinghpur, Hoshangabad, Betul and Seoni to fall back on Kamthee in the event of Holkar's troops advancing against them.

Major Erskine resisted such interference of the Nagpur authorities and reported[75] the same to the Government of India that "Mr. Plowden, Commissioner of Nagpore Province, should not issue direct orders to troops serving in my division.... Moreover, to retire before a rebellious army without first firing a shot would I respectfully submit destroy forever the confidence of the natives of Central India in the British Government and give the whole of the rich valley of Nerbudda upto plunder. A general order to retire on information of the approach of an enemy must as Brigadier Prior did, became known, and not only does it dishearten our own soldiers but gives confidence to the enemy." The Government of India concurred[76] in his views respecting the interference of the Commissioner of Nagpur with his troops serving within the Saugor Division. Its result was that the five districts alluded to were not lost and remained intact. Major Erskine then recommended that both at Hoshangabad and Narsinghpur some building be fortified and intrenchments be made. He also ordered extra *batta* to be given to all Bengal troops in the division who might remain loyal.[77]

Meanwhile, the police at Harda broke out into open mutiny and raised the Mahomedan standard, but Mazhar Zameel, the Deputy Magistrate, again kept a bold front. The rebels on seeing that they could not succeed, nine of them deserted, leaving their muskets. Six men were afterwards captured and the rest have since been brought to trial. Some were hanged and other imprisoned for life.[78]

In another large commercial town of Seoni Malwa there was considerable alarm when the falseness of the Holkar's rebellion arrived. Ali Husain, the Munsiff, also an Assistant Magistrate, saved the situation there as he not only allayed the fears of the people but kept the police to their allegiance.[79]

In another large town with a fort, Sohagpur, dacoities had commenced. J.C. Wood, the Deputy Commissioner, sent J.L. Thornton, one of the Deputy Magistrates who had a great influence over the *ubaridars* or petty Rajas who held their jagirs there, and over the police. Very soon he put down the dacoities.[80]

On 8 July Colonel Durand and his party arrived at Hoshangabad from Indore. Major Ludlow, its Chief Engineer, was also with them. He laid down the necessary intrenchments at the *Kutcherry* for the protection of the residents, in case of attack from Bhopal, Indore or elsewhere. From 13 to 15 July, other fugitives from Sehor, Augur, Seepree arrived at Hoshangabad.

Towards the end of July 1857, several dacoities had occurred in the Nemawar pargana but the robberies were for the most part in Holkar's villages which were strongly mixed up with the ceded pargana of Nemawar. The police at Harda and round about it had greatly been increased owing to the proximity of the Holkar's and Sindhia's territories near the Nemawar pargana. The *ghats* on the Narmada were strongly guarded by the police and no person was allowed to cross over to Bhopal and further down to the Nemawar pargana without special permission and *vice versa* and no one came over to Hoshangabad side without special sanction previously obtained.[81]

In September 1857 in the Nemawar pargana, the Mewatees of Satwas had risen in rebellion. Ramkishan, a Maratha Pandit of the Sindhia's territories had also appeared there with the other rebels. He called himself the Agent of Sindhia. He took possession of Nemawar and hoisted the Maratha flag there. He also commenced collecting revenue and at the same time the mutinous police joined him.[82] Thus, in this district also the situation was very much disturbed.

In the Mandla district

It may sound strange but it is true that during the revolt of 1857 Lt. H.F. Waddington, the Deputy Commissioner of Mandla administered the Mandla district from Jabalpur. As there had been no house in Mandla, the Lt. Governor of the North-Western Provinces permitted him to reside at Jabalpur during the hot weather and rains. He was called at Jabalpur in June 1857.[83]

Early in July signs of rebellion were visible in the Mandla district as two Malguzars had refused to pay revenue and the others said the British Government must go. Later in the month four of the chief landlords talked treason.[84]

Major Erskine reported[85] to the Government of India on 1 August 1857 that a day before he had received information that in Sohagpur and Mhow, some of the Taluqdars were collecting matchlockmen and powder and that the British Government had not a single solider in the district. He was, therefore, obliged to send some of the 52nd Native Infantry there.

The Deputy Commissioner of Mandla reported to Major Erskine on 3 August 1857 that on 29 July the Tehsildar of Sohagpur had informed him that Guroor Singh, *Surburahkar*, and next of kin of Rani Sulochna Kunwar of Sohagpur *Khas*, Balbhadra Singh, Taluqdar of Kothee Nigwanee, Jag Mohan Singh, Taluqdar of Jaitpur, Lachman Singh, brother of Balbhadra Singh, had been showing symptoms of bad feeling towards the Government and the inhabitants of Sohagpur were in a state of excitement in consequence. They all were the relatives of the Raja of Rewa.[86] Guroor Singh had refused to pay his revenue. He in conjunction of Balbhadra Singh had beaten a Government *chaprasee* in the streets of Sohagpur as they thought that the British power was to end in India.[87]

On 10 August 1857 he again reported[88] that *Surburahkar* of Ramgarh had informed him that the Raja's immediate attendants had shown the signs of excitement. He was of the opinion that as its Raja Bikramjit Singh, was insane, he was automation in the hands of the Rani and Sookai Dewan who were at the head of affairs and the real managers of the family.

He again reported[89] on 5 September 1857 that as on 1 September Guroor Singh and Balbhadra Singh had created a disturbance in Sohagpur, the whole of the establishment Revenue and Judiciary had been obliged to abandon Sohagpur and were returning towards Shahpura. He again reported[90] on 9 September that the Tehsildar of Sohagpur arrived at Jabalpur at 9 P.M. on the last evening. He found it quite impossible to oppose the numerical odds against him there. Shamjee Lal, Tehsildar of Shahpura was also in a state of great alarm. He made for Mandla not even making arrangements for the conveyance of the treasure to a place of safety or yet of his own family. The Deputy Commissioner was afraid that Ramgarh would be the next to go for the Raja's people had been showing the disaffection lately. As he had no troops he was helpless to do anything.

On 28 September he again reported[91] that on 25 September Tehsilee and thanna of Shahpura were attacked by a number of armed men, supposed to be the men of the district. The whole of the Government servants were put to flight and the Government *Kutcherry* and thanna buildings were burnt. Bijai Singh, Thakur of Shahpura was mixed with, if not the originator of this attack. He stated[92] that "two-thirds of my district have thus risen in rebellion against the Government and as I hear that Garoor Singh and the Ramgarh Raja and probably Bijai Singh have an idea of paying Mandla a visit." He was in panic as he ordered all the Sohagpur, Shahpura and Ramgarh fugitives to go at once to Mandla and the treasure of Rs. 5,000 from Shahpura to Mandla.

On 26 September a few government officials who had held out at Ramgarh were obliged to quit and the treasure amounting Nagpur Rs. 650 was taken possession of by the Raja's people, headed by Seetaram, brother of the Rani, Sookai Deewan of the Raja and his son, Hiralal. He was convinced that Bijai Singh of Shahpura and the Ramgarh Raja had formed a resolve to attack Mandla. He again reported[93] on 5 October 1857 that the whole of Sohagpur, Shahpura and Ramgarh had risen in rebellion but no symptoms of disaffection were apparent in the Mandla pargana.

In his opinion although it would be inexpedient to attempt to put down the rebellion in Sohagpur, Shahpura, Ramgarh and Mandla, he requested[94] Major Erskine that a small guard could be spared to accompany him to Mandla. It would have excellent results as "in the first place, it would be exceedingly inconvenient if the rebels took possession of the Mandla fort and secondly, the flame would not reach Seoni." His request was not granted and he remained at Jabalpur as a dumb spectator.

In the Seoni district

Lt. W.B. Thomson, the officiating Deputy Commissioner of Seoni, reported[95] on 27 July 1857 to Major Erskine that "the effects of the present outbreak in North-West have been scarcely felt in this district owing partly to its isolated position and partly to the presence of the Madras troops. Various reports had been circulated by ill-disposed persons which had frightened the more ignorant classes of the population and led the Mahajans and Sarafs to curtail their money dealings but beyond this the district had not been affected upto that time."

He again reported[96] on 1 August 1857 that "in consequence however of the reports of the mutiny of Saugor and Dumoh troops which reached us on the 4th and 5th and as it was thought that the 52nd Native Infantry at Jubbulpoor might follow their example, considerable alarm was created here." As he had no official intelligence of any disturbance, at first he gave these reports no credit. On 9 July when he learnt the true state of affairs through the letters of Major Erskine and "since it has been made known that Saugor, Dumoh and Jubbulpore are safe, the alarm which had been created by the reports of the 4th and 5th instant has been dissipated."[97]

By the end of September the thannas of Kundam and Bargi in the Jabalpur district were attacked and driven in. As Bargi is on the south side of the Narmada, it was the first appearance of the rebellion near the Seoni district, and there was much alarm in Seoni lest the rebellion should spread south. The Deputy Commissioner addressed the Thakurs and sent a messenger to them, advising them to be firm to the Government. According to the advice of Major Erskine, a company of the Madras Native Infantry was sent from Seoni to Dhuma near Bargi.[98] The district remained quiet and continued to be so the Deputy Commissioner hoped if nothing serious took place at Narsinghpur or Jabalpur on which it bordered[99].

In the Betul district

Captain I.N.H. Maclean, the Deputy Commissioner of Betul, reported[100] to Major Erskine on 6 July 1857 that the district under his charge was perfectly quiet and the feeling of the inhabitants was very much in favour of the government. He again reported[101] on 13 July 1857 that the news of Maharaja Holkar's attack on Indore had caused a slight panic and he found it to enlist parties of matchlockmen to guard the passes and roads leading into the district from the direction of Indore and Elichpur i.e. Berar. He had also information "about Shrodeen Patel of Betul, a powerful landholder and a dissatisfied man, who had taken an opportunity of leaving the boundary of the district where he was sent to settle a dispute and had proceeded to Holkar's camp. He had a large number of followers and relations and was not to be trusted. It was the general opinion in Betul that he was only waiting for an opportunity to show his disloyalty." Having his suspicions confirmed about him, he at once disarmed him and his relatives.

He again reported[102] on 20 July 1857 that since Shivdeen had returned to Betul, he did not think that he had held any communication with the Holkar's people, but he had him still closely watched. Meanwhile, Captain Rich, commanding the regiment at Betul, informed him that he had received order to fall back on Kamthee in the event of authentic information being obtained of the approach of the Holkar's army. He told that officer that "I protested against anything of the sort and that whatever he did, I would not leave the district until forced to do so. I think any order of this kind under present circumstances is most injudicious and if known in the district, would cause want of confidence in Government, the reverse of which it has been my endeavour to instil among the people." However, nothing happened in this district till September 1857.

In the end, it may be worthwhile to quote a private letter[103] written on 16 October 1857 by Major Erskine to the Secretary to the Government, Central Provinces at Benaras under whom he was working, in which he had described the condition then prevailing in the Saugor and Nerbudda Territories. It was forwarded to the Government of India with a note that in the following extract of his letter "the condition in these territories is better described than in any official document in his possession." It runs as follows :

"The people here, even the chiefs appear to take little notice of our successes in Delhi and Lucknow, indeed it is questionable if they believe the reports; and from all I can learn, they only look to local matters. ... In all around the Jubbulpore district, numerous thakoors have risen with their followers and are plundering every village not close to Jubbulpore. At Jubbulpore we have 400 Madras Infantry in the station and they have to guard the city, station, magazine, treasure, artillery park. ... The Narsingpore and Hoshangabad are the troubled districts. ... Dumoh is not in our possession. Saugor and Mandlah are in a state of anarchy and without troops I am helpless. ... We want more infantry. Madrassees might do, with a few hundred Europeans, but Mr. Plowden (Commissioner of Nagpur territory) at present has none to send us. I earnestly hope you will soon be able to send us some assistance to enable me to restore peace here and in the rest of the Saugor and Nerbudda districts."

REFERENCES

1. N.E., para 10.
2. J.D., B.C., Political Case File No. 4 of 1858.
3. N.E., paras 11-12.
4. *Ibid.*, para 13.
5. *Ibid.*, para 14.
6. *Ibid.*, para 15.
7. Charles Ball, *The History of the Indian Mutiny*, Vol. I (1858), p. 435.
8. N.E., paras 17-18.
9. Charles Ball, *op. cit.*, p. 436, also F.P. P. No. C-2277, Inclosure 57 of No. 1, p. 27.
10. Charles Ball, *op. cit.*, p. 436.
11. *Ibid.*
12. *Ibid.*
13. *Ibid.*, p. 437.
14. N.E., para 27.
15. *Ibid.*, para 29.
16. Charles Ball, *op. cit.*, p. 437.
17. N.E., para 28.
18. Charles Ball, *op. cit.*, p. 437.
19. Foreign, Secret, Cons., 31 July 1857, No. 161.
20. *Ibid.*, 28 August 1857, No. 360, para 4.

21. N.E., para 57.
22. *Ibid.*, para 79.
23. *Ibid.*
24. *Ibid.*, para 80.
25. *Ibid.*, paras 81-2.
26. *Ibid.*, para 83.
27. *Ibid.*, paras 84-5.
28. Foreign, Secret, Cons., 31 July 1857, No. 356, para 2.
29. Charles Ball, *op. cit.*, Vol.II, p. 143.
30. Foreign, Secret, Cons., 30 October 1857, No. 568, para 7.
31. *Ibid.*, para 8, also J.D., B.C., Political Case File No. 16 of 1857.
32. N.E., para 97.
33. *Ibid.*, para 113.
34. Foreign, Secret, Cons., 31 July 1857, No. 373, para 1.
35. N.E., paras 109-11.
36. *Ibid.*, para 112.
37. Foreign, Secret, Cons., 30 October 1857, No. 547, paras 1-2.
38. N.E., para 114.
39. *Ibid.*, paras 127 and 129.
40. *Ibid.*, para 131.
41. *Ibid.*, para 133.
42. *Ibid.*, paras 134-35.
43. T. Rice Holmes, *History of the Indian Mutiny* (1885), p. 49.
44. M.P. D.G., Jabalpur (1968), p. 103.
45. *Ibid.*
46. N.E., para 146.
47. J.D., B.C., Political Case File No. 20 of 1857, p. 217, para 8.
48. *Ibid.*, No. 19 of 1857, pp. 246-7, paras 2-3.
49. *Ibid.*, paras 4-7.
50. N.E., Appendix I.
51. *Ibid.*, para 180.
52. Charles Ball, *op. cit.*, p. 145.
53. *Ibid.*
54. R.M. Martin, *The Indian Empire*, Vol. II (1860), p. 491.
55. Charles Ball, *op. cit.*, pp. 145-46.
56. *Ibid.*, p. 145.
57. M.P. D.G., Jabalpur, *op. cit.*, pp. 105-6.
58. N.E., paras 182-83.
59. *Ibid.*, paras 184-85.
60. *Ibid.*, para 186.

61. *Ibid.*, para 188.
62. Charles Ball, *op. cit.*, pp. 146-47.
63. *Ibid.*, p. 147.
64. N.E., para 187.
65. *Ibid.*, para 189.
66. M.P. D.G., Jabalpur, *op. cit.*, p. 107.
67. *Ibid.*
68. F.P. P. , No. C-2449, Inclosure No. 67 in No. 2, p. 272, also J.D., B.C., Political Case File No. 19 of 1857, p. 349.
69. Foreign, Secret, Cons., 30 October 1857, No. 589.
70. N.E., para 143.
71. *Ibid.*, para 62.
72. *Ibid.*, paras 90-1.
73. *Ibid.*, para 92.
74. *Ibid.*, para 93.
75. Foreign, Secret, Cons., 26 February 1858, No. 115, paras 1-2.
76. *Ibid.*, No. 120, para 1.
77. N.E., paras 94-6.
78. *Ibid.*, para 103.
79. *Ibid.*, para 104.
80. *Ibid.*, para 105.
81. Foreign, Secret, Cons., 30 October 1857, No. 582.
82. N.E., para 167.
83. *Ibid.*, para 32.
84. *Ibid.*, para 98.
85. Foreign, Secret, Cons., 26 February 1858, No. 153.
86. J.D., B.C., Political Case File No. 12 of 1857, p. 42, para 1.
87. *Ibid.*, para 7.
88. *Ibid.*, p. 47.
89. *Ibid.*, p. 137.
90. *Ibid.*, p. 133.
91. *Ibid.*, p. 70.
92. *Ibid.*, para 4.
93. *Ibid.*, p. 73.
94. *Ibid.*, para 5.
95. Foreign, Secret, Cons., 30 October 1857, No. 584, paras 2-3.
96. *Ibid.*, No. 592, para 2.
97. *Ibid.*, paras 3-5.
98. N.E., paras 218-19.

CHAPTER 7

Suppression of the Revolt in the Sagar and Damoh Districts

As Charles Ball had observed[1] that "at the close of 1857 nearly whole of the territories of Saugar and Nerbudda were in a state of revolt," the events in all the districts except Sagar upto September 1857 in the preceding two chapters were described. It may, however, be noted that the revolt came to a climax more slowly in this region than other parts of the North India. Now, while dealing with the suppression of the revolt in these territories in this and next chapter, it will be seen that in the long run, it proved far more troublesome to suppress.

Events in the Sagar district upto the end of 1857

While dealing with the outbreak of the revolt in the Sagar district, we had narrated the events there till August 1857 when the entire district passed into the hands of the rebels except the Sagar fort and town. It was a great landmark in the revolt of 1857 in these territories.

On 17 September the Banpur rebels from Nariaoli (12 miles to the west of Sagar) advanced to the Rahatgarh Gate of the city of Sagar and fired a few shots at the guards, but finding them on the alert, they retired. Next day Brigadier Sage, Commandant Sagar, sent out a detachment under Colonel Dalyell of the 42nd to attack the Nariaoli rebels and the Deputy Commissioner also sent 200 customs *chaprasees* under their European officers. But they found the place too strong and the attack failed. Colonel Dalyell was killed and Lt. Prior, the Executive Engineer, badly wounded. Next day the detachment returned to Sagar.[2] The sepoys were much dispirited by this incident and Major Erskine anticipated very bad effect from this reverse.[3]

On 6 September a large body of rebels headed by Bodhan Dauaa, *Kamdar* of Raja Lachman Singh of Shahgarh, advanced on Rehli from Garhakota. They were at first beaten back by the police under Girdhari Naik, but as the ammunition of the British was falling, they had to retire towards Sagar. On 11 September Rehli was retaken without opposition and Chhatar Dauaa and others were arrested.[4] On 14 September, Mr. Bell, Collector of Customs, with his Assistants and 200 *chaprasees* brought in Chhatar Dauaa and 31 rebels from Rehli to Sagar. W.C. Western, the Deputy Commissioner reported[5] to Major Erskine on 21 September 1857 that "Chhutter Dowa was tried and convicted of rebellion. This man has taken an active part in the present disturbances and has committed numerous outrages in the Rehlee division. Beharee Lall, the late Qanungo of Rehlee and Nand Kishore, his relative, were also tried and convicted on the same charge with Chhutter Dowa. Bihari Lall had assisted the rebels with his counsel and many documents are in my possession proving that he had endeavoured to incite the Thana and other landholders to rebel against the state. These three culprits were hung in the Kuttra to the north of the fort at Saugor, after having been paraded through the streets of the city, whilst their offence was proclaimed to the public by the common crier. The populace evinced the greatest pleasure at the execution of these rebels and upward of 4000 people of Saugar attended to witness it."

In early October the Deputy Commissioner of Sagar having resolved to secure Rehli, requested Brigadier Sage to aid him with troops. This he did and Lt. Dickens of the 31st, Ensign Grant of the 42nd and 100 sepoys of the 31st were sent to Rehli. But before their arrival, the fort had been recovered by a resident of Rehli named Girdhari Naik and his brothers. He was at once made Qilledar till relieved by

Lt. Dickens.[6] On 13 October the Shahgarh rebels from Garhakota joined by the mutineers of the 52nd, again attacked Rehli but were speedily repulsed with loss by Lt.Dickens and his sepoys.[7] On 26 December Rehli was again attacked by the 52nd and rebels from Garhakota, but were driven off by Lt. Dickens.[8]

On 2 October the rebels had assembled at Mynpanee on the road from Sagar to Narsinghpur. Brigadier Sage, therefore, sent a detachment against them, they fled. The detachment was then ordered to patrol the road. This had a very good effect and the dak was re-established to Narsinghpur and Jabalpur.[9] On 19 January 1858 Brigadier Sage placed the detachment on the Narsinghpur road at the disposal of the Deputy Commissioner of Sagar for the purpose of attacking the rebels who had assembled near the road. Whenever the troops showed themselves, the rebels fled.[10]

On 17 October a considerable body of Pathans and Rohillas from Rahatgarh came near to a hill four miles west of Sagar but were driven away by the police.[11] On 15 December, Brigadier Sage sent a party to attack the rebels at Bhapel, on the Rahatgarh road, but failed.[12]

The names of rebels connected with the Sagar rising were Jungah Singh, Bulbhuder Singh, Taluqdar of Sohagpur, Lachman Singh, the brother of the Raja of Shahgarh and Nawab Kandar Khan Pindari[13]. The most famous of the Sagar rebels was Daulat Singh for whose apprehension a reward of Rs. One Thousand was offered[14] by a Government proclamation on 15 October. He was a resident of Bamoree and was a follower and acting under the orders of the rebel chief of Shahgarh. He "has plundered numerous villages in close proximity of Saugar, murdered many of the inhabitants and is daily committing acts of atrocity and torture. Several of our cultivators and other Ryots have come into Saugor with their noses cut off and otherwise mutilated, the work of Daulat Singh. He has moreover threatened to hang every Lambardar that aids the Government in any way and carried out his threat in the person of Har Govind, the Lambardar of Jhagree who was hung by him at Kurrapoor a few days ago." The Lt. Governor at Benaras, duly sanctioned[15] the offer of a reward of Rs.1,000 for his apprehension.

Thus, the situation in the Sagar district till the end of 1857 was very much disturbed. Now and then there were attempts of the revolt made by the rebels and mutineers in its different parts before the arrival of Sir Hugh Rose in the district in January 1858.

Capture of Rahatgarh by Sir Hugh Rose on 29 January 1858

The tension in the territories to the north of the Narmada continued for a long time due to the non-availability of the British forces. In fact, as the year drew to a close the daring of the rebels increased, whilst the handful of British, shut up in the stations at long distances from each other, and powerless to interfere effectually, could do little more than hold their own. After the suppression of the revolt of 1857 in the major centres of India, the counter offensive was launched by the British to quell the uprisings in the Bundelkhand and the Saugor and Nerbudda Territories. With the arrival of Major General Sir Hugh Rose, the commandant of the Central India Force, in early 1858 in the Sagar district, the turn in tide began in favour of the British.

In December 1857 there were some changes at Indore, the British headquarters of the Central India. On 16 December 1857 Sir Robert Hamilton assumed office at Indore as Agent to the Governor General in Central India. Next day Sir Hugh Rose, a distinguished soldier and statesman, took over the command of the forces of the Central India. As the intelligence received at Indore made it desirable that the relief of Sagar should be undertaken as soon as possible, the general plan of the coming campaign was decided. The advance of one column under Sir Hugh Rose operating from Mhow, would sweep the country from that place to Kalpi on the Yamuna, relieving Sagar and recapturing Jhansi. At the same time a Madras force under General Whitlock was to cross Bundelkhand from Jabalpur to Banda. The Central India Field Force, consisted of two Brigades, which were assembled, the first at Mhow under Brigadier Stuart and the second at Sehor. A portion of the Hyderabad Contingent Field Force, under Major W.A. Orr, formed an advance guard to this Brigade. Sir Robert Hamilton and Sir Hugh Rose joined the second Brigade at Sehore on 8 January 1858.[16]

Before his departure to the Sagar district, the importance of Rahatgarh in it was realised by Sir Hugh Rose. He observed[17] that "a hundred miles from Sehore and twenty five miles south-west of Saugar, the fortress of Rahatgurh, 'a place of traditional strength' formed the key of Western Frontier of Saugor and Bundelkhand, the former of which was partially and the latter completely in the hands of the rebels. It is situated in the midst of hills, nullas and dense jungle on a high rock on the left bank of the winding river, Bina, which is very difficult to cross. The fort, as strong as Maratha art could make it, commanded all the country and the road from Bhopal and Central India to Sagar." At that time the fort was garrisoned by *Walayties* and Pathans under command of Nawab Muhammad Fazil Khan, a relative of the Regent of Bhopal, a man of energy and courage who having failed in an attempt to usurp the power of the latter, had became a chief leader of the rebels. The Shahzada of Mandsor and other rebels of note had also assembled at Rahatgarh.

He further observed[18] that the rebels of Sagar and Bundelkhand had selected Rahatgarh "as a place of importance where they were determined to make a stand. The garrison in the same sense, declared that they would die or held it. Their selection was a good one." If the rebels at Rahatgarh could have made a successful resistance to his force, "the moral effect would have been most unfavourable. Rebellion would have been extended in every direction, and

I could not have relieved Saugor, which would have been in a worse state than ever." Meanwhile, the Raja of Banpur had already sent troops from Khurai across the river Bina to cut off the supplies of his force from Udaipur and other parts of the Sindhia's territory. He "would have cut off my communication with the West my only base; and I should have been left destitute of supplies, with the fort of Ruthghur in my front, and swarms of rebels on every other side, perfectly acquainted with their dangerous country and attacking my rear from their two fortified camps, Nariaoli and Kooreye."

In the opinion[19] of Sir Hugh Rose, as there was no British force available in Sagar and Bundelkhand to control the rebellion, the Raja of Banpur, Fazil Muhammad Khaṇ and others by their acts of most barbarous cruelty, intimidated and crushed the well-disposed chiefs and rendered their sway paramount. All persons, on the mere suspicion of being friendly to the British Government, were mutilated and their noses and hands cut off. Moreover, the rebels made war cheaply, paying their followers with the plunder of the thriving villages. Under these circumstances, and knowing that one of the chief objects of the defence of Rahatgarh was to prevent the relief of Sagar, he was determined to reduce Rahatgarh by an immediate attack. He arrived at Rahatgarh on 24 January 1858.

He besieged the Rahatgarh fort from 25 to 28 January 1858. A practical breach was effected on 28 January and preparations were made for stroming it in the following morning, but the rebels fled during night towards Khurai.[20] On the same day the Raja of Banpur advaned to Rahatgarh with his force from Narioli and Khurai but failed in his attempt to relieve it.[21] The garrison despite their determination that they would hold Rahatgarh or die, had not been able to stand the shelling or meet the approaching assault. At sunset of 29 January Muhammad Fazil Khan, the Nawab of Ambapani, the Nawab Kamdar Khan, a pensioner of the British Government and a son of the great Pindari chief taken by Sir John Malcolm in 1818, were hanged over the gate of the fort and next day, seventeen more, most of them rebels of note were executed.[22] Major Boilean destroyed the defences of the fort of Rahatgarh as much as the allowance of the powder would permit. He blew in completely the main gateway.[23]

After the capture of Rahatgarh, the rebels under the Raja of Banpur had concentrated at Barodia, on the left bank of the Bina river, with a small fort and dense jungle on each side. It was about twelve miles from Rahatgarh on the road to Khurai and twenty nine miles to the north of Sagar. The object of the rebels in concentrating this place was to prevent or endanger the British advance to Sagar, by retaking Rahatgarh, or by placing themselves in their rear, on the road from Bhopal to Sagar, to cut off as they had already attempted to do, the supplies coming from the states of Sindhia and Bhopal. It was, therefore, necessary to drive them out of Barodia.[24] Consequently, Sir Hugh Rose immediately moved out and attacked them. They were quickly defeated and about 100 killed and many wounded. On the British side one was killed and six or seven were wounded.[25]

Sir Hugh Rose then not being sure that his camp with the seize artillery and numerous stores, left under a small guard at Rahatgarh, would not be attacked, he marched back to Rahatgarh on the same night. At Rahatgarh in the encounter with the rebels four or five hundred of them were killed, a nephew of Muhammad Fazil Khan was also killed and the Raja of Banpur wounded. The *Walayties* and Pathans fought with their usual courage even when dying springing from the ground and inflicting mortal wounds with their broad swords. On the British side two were killed and twenty one wounded. The result of this victory exceeded expectations. The communications with the west and Sagar were completely opened.[26] The rebels were driven with much loss from their strong position and they evacuated Khurai as well as Narioli from where they had threatened and molested Sagar, stopping all direct communication by the direct road *via* Bhopal and Sehore to Indore and Mhow. There was now nothing to prevent his march to Sagar.[27]

Relief of Sagar on 3 February 1858

Sir Hugh Rose then marched from Barodia to Sagar on 1 February 1858 and entered the town on 3 February 1858. Sir Robert Hamilton reported[28] to the Government of India on the same day that "as we approached the town I may say the whole native population in addition to the Europeans (ladies and all) came out to welcome the column whose arrival spread the greatest joy and confidence amongst all classes." The number of Europeans 173 men, 67 women and 130 children had been confined in the fort since 29 June 1857, without much more than bare necessities and deprived of all ordinary convenience and comforts[29]. The officers and men with their families who had been confined in the fort for more than seven months were then emancipated. They returned to their barracks and residences in the cantonment. The mortality during this period had amounted to twenty two, of these some were from cholera and small pox when terrible diseases broke out in the fort. Sir Robert Hamilton praised the Europeans during this trying period, cut off from all communication, and with the knowledge that succour could not be sent them for many weeks, performed their duty well and nobly maintained the character of their country.[30]

Before the arrival of Sir Hugh Rose's force, the rebels of the Bundelkhand, Shahgarh, Sagar and other districts, had not only invested Sagar but also occupied the forts of Sanodha and Garhakota to the east, and Narioli and Khurai to the north-west. The fort of Rehli to the south-east was held by Lt. Dickens. The relief of Sagar had opened the roads to the west and north permitting of communication on Mhow and the Agra Grand Trunk Road. It remained to open communications from Sagar towards the east and cut the rebel line from Jhansi to the Narmada. As the best means of doing this, Sir Hugh Rose was determined to capture the fort of Garhakota, which was garrisoned by the sepoys of the 52nd and other regiments that had mutinied.[31]

Capture of Garhakota on 11 February 1858

On 8 February Sir Hugh Rose sent Captain Hare with his detachment of all arms of the Hyderabad contingent to Sanodha, ten miles on the way to Garhakota, which he captured. After despatching some parties to destroy small forts and to clear the district of the rebels, General Rose marched on 9 February to Garhakota[32] and reached there on 11 February.

The rebels fired on them from the fort. General Rose not only returned the fire sharply, but commenced arrangements for a siege, but in the night the rebels evacuated the fort and fled in the Shahgarh direction. They left all their cattle and stores and their 13 guns loaded. No doubt they were intimidated by the energy of the investment, the lesson of Rahatgarh and fear for their line of retreat. In any case, with the numbers at his disposal, it would have been impossible for the General to have made a complete investment. His troops were strictly speaking, only sufficient to guard the camp and artillery. His force was unusually weak as he had left a large number of it at Sagar. The rebels were, however, overtakn by a column under the command of Captain Hare of the Hyderabad Contingent, and about 100 were killed. On the British side, the casualities during the operations amounted to only four wounded. The defences of the fort were demolished by a party of sappers left for the purpose.[33]

In his report to the Government of India, Sir Robert Hamilton wrote[34] : "I cannot but consider it most fortunate that the fort at Garhakota has been so easily obtained, for it is beyond exception the strongest and most difficult I have seen in Bundelkhand, indeed as formidable as any I have met within India. We have not only saved a great deal of time, but we have not lost a life; whilst the impression which the fall of this celebrated fort will make throughout this country will be far greater than can be conceived, it being deemed impregnable."

After the fall of Garhakota, the Raja of Shahgarh abandoned Shahgarh and met the Raja of Banpur at Serai to plan their future operations. The rebels from Garhakota and Shahgarh assembled at the fort of Maraura. The road towards this fort led through dense jungles and dangerous ground full of passes, rocky hills and winding streams, well-suited to the rebels who were adept in guerilla warfare.[35]

When Sir Hugh Rose arrived at Sagar from Barodia, the Banpur rebels at once fled from Nariaoli and Khurai and the police re-occupied those posts. The taking of Garhakota made nearly all large bodies of rebels leave the Sagar district, consequently, the police returned to their outposts, except at Malthone in the north, which was still held by the Banpur Raja, and Patan, Dhamoni and Panchamnagar all in the north, which were held by the Shahgarh rebels.[36]

The Central India Field Force then returned to Sagar from Garhakota to prepare for a further advance. They had to halt there till the supplies could be collected. It was no easy matter as the most parts of the district had been for sometime in the hands of the rebels and greatly plundered. The consumption of the grain alone in the camp was 1,735 *maunds* daily and thirty days supply was needed and to provide for carriages for it. With the utmost exertions of the Deputy Commissioner, and his establishment, the supplies were collected.[37]

On 23 February the Deputy Commissioner reported that the supplies were ready for Sir Hugh Rose's force and on 27 February he marched towards Malthone, leaving a small detachment at Sagar to bring on the bulk of his supplies. On learning General Rose's intention of leaving no troops at Sagar, Major Erskine requested him to remember that without leaving troops in Sagar, the place could not be considered relieved or safe, but Rose informed him that he could not leave a man at Sagar.[38] Certain civil officers, Major Western, the Deputy Commissioner of Sagar, and recently appointed Captain Pinkney, Superintendent of Jhansi, Captains Ternan and Maclean, officiating Deputy Commissioners of Jaloun and Jhansi, joined General's force.[39]

In the meantime, due to the delay in the movements of General Rose's force from Sagar, the rebels had regained courage and again occupied the strong positions in the Shahgarh and adjoining districts such as forts of Surahi and Maraura and the difficult passes in the mountain ridges which separate the Shahgarh and Sagar districts.[40]

Before General Rose left Sagar on his way to Jhansi, most of the posts had been recaptured in the Sagar district, except Malthone which was held by the Raja of Banpur. J.L. Thornton, the Assistant Commissioner of Hoshangabad, was, therefore, sent on 3 March to Malthone with the detachment under Major Scudamore. On reaching Malthone, the fort was evacuated by the rebels. The police was put in possession of the fort and the thanna was re-established.[41] Thornton[42] stated that "a salt peon who had gone over to the Boondelas and who the villagers said one of their leading men, was taken up and brought into camp by me. He was tried by a Drum-Head Court Martial and executed the same evening. Confidence has been restored in Malthone and the inhabitants are returning to their houses."

Victory of the British forces in the battle of Madanpur pass on 3 March 1858

Sir Hugh Rose then decided to take Jhansi and to get into communication with the first Brigade under Brigadier Stuart which was to arrive at Guna on about 28 February. He would make a combined attack on Jhansi with both Brigades.

He anticipated resistance at the three passes, the pass of Narhat and fort of Karnalgarh near Malthone and the passes of Madanpur and Dhamoni, leading to Jhansi. Resistance was also anticipated at the forts of Surahi, Maraura and Talbehat. At Talbehat it was said the Raja of Banpur intended to make his last stand. General Rose was determined to force these obstacles, accordingly, he gave orders to Brigadier Stuart, commanding the 1st Brigade to move from Guna westwards and take Chanderi while he forced his way northwards and crossing the Betwa, he would then march with both Brigades against Jhansi.[43]

In the meantime, General Rose had directed Major Orr to reconnoitre the passes while he was detained for supplies at Sagar. As supplies having come into Sagar, he marched on 27 February from Sagar and reached Rajwas on 1 March. Here he was joined by the force under Major Orr, who had collected information which decided the General to select the pass of Madanpur for his point of attack. In order to deceive the rebels as to his intention, and prevent the Raja of Banpur from coming from the pass of Narhat to the assistance of the Raja of Shahgarh who defended Madanpur, a feint was made against Narhat by the force under Major Scudamore, who was sent to the town of Malthone, while the real attack was carried out against Madanpur.[44]

In the battle of Madanpur pass on 3 March 1858, which had been occupied by the sepoys of the 52nd and other regiments and by 7,000 picked Bundelas, the British force defeated the rebels and they retired from Madanpur, through the jungle, towards the fort of Surahi. Major Orr and Captain Abbott pursuing along the road through the jungle came up with a rear of the insurgents, consisting principally of the 52nd Bengal Native Infantry, and killed a number of them, including Lal Tribedi, the Havildar Major, who was the instigator of the mutiny in the regiment, and whom they had made their commanding officer. Three hundred rebels were killed. The cause of the defeat of the rebels was that the sepoys and the Bundelas quarrelled, the former declaring that the latter had run away and left them to fight at the pass, and general mistrust and panic ensued in the rebel camp. After this battle, General Rose got into the rear of the other two parsses of Narhat and Dhamoni and the insurgent's line of defence, upon which the rebels abandoned them. On 4 March, the fort of Surahi, a fortified palace of the Raja of Shahgarh, fell into the hands of the British troops and Sir Hugh Rose took possession of Maraura, an ancient fort with a double line of defences in an important position on the road from Sagar to Jhansi and from Shahgarh to Malthone. This enabled General Rose to advance towards Jhansi without any opposition.[45]

After the capture of Madanpur pass, in a telegraphic message[46] sent to the chief of the staff on 4 March 1858, Sir Hugh Rose stated that "yesterday the troops under my orders forced the pass of Muddunpore after a short but very rigourous resistance. The troops British and native behaved very gallantly. The pass is extremely strong. The enemy suffered severely. They numbered four or five thousand Pathans and Boondelas and 600 or 700 sepoys of the 52nd and other regiments. I sent Major Orr in pursuit. He cut up 50 or 60 rebels of whom a large share were sepoys. The enemy scattered in every direction abandoning the perfect little fort of Serai a sort of arsenal which is the property of Raja of Shahgarh in which I shall leave a small force to keep up my communication with Saugor. This success enables me to communicate with my 1st Brigade at Esanghur or Chundeyree and gives me the command of whole country upto Jhansi with the exception of two or three forts which I can take."

The success in the battle of Madanpur pass had some important results. With this victory ended the last vestiges of popular revolt in the Sagar district. By the beginning of March, a regular administration was restored in it and police and revenue-offices re-established.[47] Moreover, the whole country betwen Jhansi and Sagar, to the east of the river Betwa, which since the outbreak of the rebellion, had been in the hands of the insurgents, was now with the exception of Talbehat, restored to the British Government.[48]

Surrender of the Rajas of Shahgarh and Banpur

After his defeat at Maraura on 4 March 1858, the Raja of Shahgarh with the Bundelas left it towards Narhat leaving the fort gates locked. On opening the gates the fort was found empty with everything in confusion indicative of the most hasty retreat. The British flag was then hoisted on the fort of Maraura and a proclamation[49] was issued on 7 March 1858 notifying that "the Shahgarh state had been attached consequent to the rebellious conduct of the Rajah whose power has ceased." It was duly approved by the Government of India.[50] Mr.Thornton, Assistant Collector of Hoshangabad who had been attached to the force in charge of the districts, was established at Maraura.[51] It was also approved by the Government of India.[52]

The British force under General Rose then advanced towards Banpur. They reached there on 10 March 1858 and occupied it easily as the Raja was said to be at Chanderi and other members of his family had retired to Talbehat enroute to Jhansi. The town was quite deserted and the palace empty. Sir Robert Hamilton then issued a Proclamation[53] notifying on the same day that "the landed possessions of the Banpur Rajah are confiscated on account of the Raja Murdun Singh having rebelled against the British Government and they therefore are incorporated in the Lullutpore district from this date." Captain Maclean, the Deputy Commissioner of Chanderi was also appointed in charge of Banpur. It was duly sanctioned[54] by the Government of India.

After occupying Shahgarh and Banpur, whose Rajas had created disturbances in the Sagar district during the revolt of 1857, peace was restored in those states. But Chanderi continued to be a stronghold of the rebels. It was absolutely necessary for the British to capture it, to enable the 1st Brigade on the west and the 2nd Brigade on the east of the river Betwa to join each other for an attack on Jhansi. After many encounters with the rebels, the 1st Brigade captured Chanderi on 17 March 1858. The fort was dismantled as much as it was possible. The 1st Brigade then marched towards its important goal to effect a junction with the 2nd Brigade. Sir Hugh Rose heard of the storming of Chanderi on 18 March 1858. He commenced his advance towards Jhansi on the next day.[55]

On 3 April the town of Jhansi was stormed and taken by the British force under Sir Hugh Rose. He laid down the siege of its fort, and after many encounters with Rani Laxmi Bai of Jhansi, she left it desperation on the night of 4 April 1858 to Kalpi. The British then occupied the Jhansi fort.

At Jhansi, General Rose received a communication by the Rajas of Banpur and Shahgarh that "if their lives are spared and they are not imprisoned, they will do a service to the British Government." On receiving this message, Sir Hugh Rose sent a telegram to the Governor General on 20 April 1858 that in his opinion,[56] "it would produce excellent results and break up the rebel confederacy as the two Rajas resign all pretensions to Raj and would consent to be confined anywhere in India." The Governor General had no objection in promising[57] that the lives of the Rajas would be spared but "any further favour shown must however depend on the nature of service which may be rendered by them." He was further informed[58] that the detaching of such persons as the Rajas of Shahgarh and Banpur from the rebels in Bundelkhand was of the utmost importance. The bare promise of life was not sufficient in the case of Shahgarh Raja. He should be assured that no indignity would be put upon him and that he would receive a liberal assistance. The same terms might be extended to others who were not implicated in the murder of Europeans.

After some time, Raja Mardan Singh opened negotiations

with Captain Maclean, the Deputy Commissioner of Chanderi. As he had not imbued his hands with the blood of any European, Captain Maclean proposed to Sir Robert Hamilton that lenient terms be offered to Raja, let his life be spared, but let him be informed that he would not be tried but would be banished from the country.[59] Hamilton forwarded the same proposals to the Government of India in reply to which he was authorised to offer the Raja 'life, honour and a liberal subsistence' of eight hundred rupees per month on the condition that he would be required to reside under surveillance at Lahore.[60] The Raja surrendered to J. Thornton, Assistant Superintendent, Shahgarh on 5 July 1858 at Maraura.[61]

Like Raja of Banpur, Raja of Shahgarh sent a petition to Sir Robert Hamilton in which he prayed for life subsistence allowance.[62] He also surrendered to J. Thornton on 6 July 1858 at Maraura.[63] He was sanctioned a monthly stipend of Rs.1,400 and was sent to Lahore where he had to survive under surveillance.[64]

Regarding the Shahgarh territory, Hamilton had suggested that it should be attached as a separate district to the Jhansi division, but the Lt. Governor of North-Western Provinces proposed that it should be divided between the districts of Chanderi, Sagar and Damoh. The proposal of the Lt. Governor was approved by the Government of India.[65] Thus, both the Rajas of Shahgarh and Banpur had to pay the heaviest price of participating in the revolt of 1857. Their states had been confiscated and they were banished from their states.

It may, however, be noted that after the capture of Garhakota, Sir Robert Hamilton was of the opinion[66] that "there may be a rebellion in the district but there are no organised bodies, at least Major Western has never so stated, nor has he mentioned the name of a single petty leader". But in the opinion[67] of Major Western, the Deputy Commissioner, the principle leaders of the rebellion in his district "were the ex-Rajas of Shahgurh and Banpoor and their agents. I am decided of the opinion that had these petty Rajah had not invaded this district, notwithstanding of the mutiny of the troops, that the inhabitants would not have joined the rebellion."

Supression in the Damoh district

Capture of Damoh by the rebels and mutineers on 24 October 1857 and its re-capture by the Panna ruler

As referred to earlier, on recieving the information of the mutinies of the 50th Bengal Native Infantry at Nagod and the 52nd Bengal Native Infantry at Jabalpur, the two companies of the 52nd Native Infantry were disarmed on 20 September 1857 on their return from Narsinghgarh. On the same day it was also unanimously resolved in the Council of War at Damoh to give up Damoh and return to Jabalpur. Accordingly, the town and fort of Damoh and the district was abandoned and handed over to Kunwar Shyamleju, brother-in-law and the Agent of Panna Raja. While returning from Damoh, the Nagpur Movable Column had fought successfully on 26 September with the mutineers of the 52nd Native Infantry at Koni, about 12 miles from Katangi and then it returned to Jabalpur on 1 October 1857.

After the 52nd mutineers were beaten off by the Nagpur Movable Column, they, about 300 of them accompanied by their rebel friends, and led by Devi Singh, a rebel Malguzar of the Jabalpur district marched to Damoh on 24 October 1857 where they attacked the Panna troops whom they soon beat.[68] They then went to the jail which was most gallantly defended by the jail-guards but the latter falling short of ammunition and food were obliged to give in. At the same time they were attacked by the prisoners. They surrendered on condition of their lives being spared. On the 52nd getting into the jail, the guards nearly to a man were murdered. The mutineers and rebels then plundered the town of Damoh, burned the records and public buildings, blew up the *kutcherry* and gutted the Deputy Commissioner's house, but did not burn it down, owing probably to its belonging to an Indian. After some days at Damoh, they joined the Shahgarh rebels at Garhakota and they daily plundered all around,[69] until they were driven out by Sir Hugh Rose when he captured Garhakota on 11 February 1858.

After a few days, the Panna troops having been reinforced, returned to Damoh and held it unopposed. Kunwar Shyamleju then ruled the Damoh district till 4 March 1858 when he made over its charge to Major Erskine on his arrival at Damoh with General Whitlock and his force from Jabalpur[70].

Re-occupation of Damoh by Major General Whitlock on 4 March 1858

As Sir Hugh Rose had advanced from Sehor to Rahatgarh in January 1858 to begin his campaign in the Central India, General Whitlock with a Madras Column was marching from Nagpur, to undertake operations in the Saugor and Nerbudda Territories. The plan of campaign in Central India provided for the advance of a Madras Column from Jabalpur to co-operate with Sir Hugh Rose in the relief of Jhansi, and to move through the eastern part of Bundelkhand and suppress the revolt in that area. In November 1857, Major General Whitlock was appointed to the command of the column which was to be concentrated at Jabalpur for the advance on Banda, in the south-east of the North-Western Provinces. The Madras Column under General Whitlock reached Jabalpur on 3 February 1858.[71]

It was reported[72] to the Government of India in the weekly report upto 6 February 1858 that "the entrance of the force under Sir Hugh Rose, which had just reached the Sagar district ... and of General Whitlock's Column which was daily expected, will doubtless change the whole face of affairs in the division." We will see later on how the hopes of the British were fulfilled by the arrival of these forces in the division.

As Whitlock's force was sent for service in the Saugar and Nerbudda Territories, Major Erskine laid his plan before him "which was to march in two columns by different routes to Dumoh, clearing the rebels out as he went, leaving garrisons at Jubbulpore and Dumoh and then marching on Saugor." General Whitlock informed him that he quite approved the plan and would carry it out,[73] but this he never did as the events would prove afterwards.

On 11 February the 4th and 6th Madras Light Cavalry, which had been ordered to Allahabad, marched from Jabalpur, but had not gone far when the news was received that Nana Sahib had crossed into Bundelkhand with a large force. Consequently, General Whitlock ordered them to halt until his force could overtake them.

On 17 February General Whitlock's force marched from Jabalpur, accompanied by Major Erskine, the Commissioner, as he had resolved sometime before to accompany him. On 24 February they reached Jukehi which had been completely destroyed by the Rewa troops. Here he met the loyal Raja of Nagod, and information having been received that the report of the Nana's entry into Bundelkhand was erroneous. The 4th and 6th Madras Cavalry then resumed their march to Allahabad. During their march to Jukehi, the Commissioner had asked General Whitlock "to send a small body of troops out to Ramnugger, twelve miles off, to destroy the small fort there and on the 20th I asked him to destroy the little fort of Bhutgaon, both of which have given us much trouble." But the General replied that he could not spare time or troops.[74]

While continuing their march, on 28 February Erskine again asked Whitlock to destroy a small fort called Murdangarh, occupied by some 200 rebels. Another place, Mangarh on the route, the seat of a Gond rebel Raja who had about 500 armed followers, was to be destroyed. He was of the opinion that "these rebels should be attacked as they advanced, for independent of their power of doing mischief in Jubbulpoor when we had gone, they would, unless attacked, think we could not, or dared not touch them." However, nothing was done. Neither were the strong places destroyed nor the rebels once attacked between Jabalpur and Damoh.[75]

The Madras Column then left the Deccan road on 26 February, marched by seven stages to Damoh. On the way Erskine again asked Whitlock to attack the noted rebel, Thakur Kishor Singh of Hindoria, 12 miles from Damoh. He was most anxious about it. But nothing was done and he was allowed to continue his plundering unmolested.[76]

On 2 March General Whitlock's force entered the Damoh district and on 4 March marched into the station at Damoh and Kunwar Shyamleju made over the district to Major Erskine.[77] Thus, Damoh was re-occupied by the British forces under General Whitlock on 4 March 1858. The public buildings and records had been utterly destroyed there. Several bodies of rebels still held various posts in the district but the thannas and tehsils had been re-established.[78]

Major Erskine was not happy with the attitude of General Whitlock in not attacking the rebels on the way from Jabalpur to Damoh. In his opinion[79] "I cannot doubt had the rebels been attacked as I wished, my division would have much sooner be restored to peace that it has been, particularly as the very rebels, I wished him to attack are those who have plundered ever since, and some of whom will not submit to our authority and retain places they seized."

On 4 March Erskine wrote a memorandum to Whitlock that in his opinion, "the rebels should have been attacked as your force advanced and after leaving a garrison at Dumoh, it should proceed to Saugor." As they advanced from Jabalpur, he had informed him several times "where the rebels were, and that I wished them to be attacked and their strongholds to be destroyed; but for reason unknown to me, but which I do not presume to question for a moment, we have passed all these places and left the rebels intact."

Whitlock acknowledged the receipt of this letter and in person assured Erskine that he could not divide his force or undertake the expeditions as he wished.[80]

On 5 March General Whitlock went to Sagar and divided his force contrary to his assurances. Some went to Sagar and some to proceed to Jabalpur to escort treasure. The rest of his force remained at Damoh under the command of Brigadier Carpenter. On 8 March Major Erskine asked Carpenter to attack the rebels at Hindoria but he informed that General Whitlock had forbidden him from doing so. On 12 March Whitlock returned to Damoh from Sagar. Erskine had a long conversation with him but it ended in his not consenting to do anything against the rebels, who were plundering close to Damoh. Erskine on seeing that it was no use to remain with him, resolved to go to Sagar.

On the same day the General received orders from the Government to proceed to Nagod and Panna *via* Hatta. As Hatta was close to a village, called Jatashankar, where there were 500 rebels with two guns, Erskine asked him to attack them, but he did not do so. General went out of the Damoh district and Erskine went to Sagar.[81] He reached Narsinghpur on 30 March and returned to Jabalpur on 3 April 1858.[82]

It is not necessary to describe in detail how the rebels in the Damoh district were captured and the rebellion suppressed after the re-occupation of Damoh by General Whitlock on 4 March 1858. The most prominent and turbulent of them, Thakur Kishor Singh of Hindoria was so strong that even General Whitlock avoided a clash with him. He alongwith other rebels, however, surrendered[83] before Major Erskine in December 1858 on condition that no further action would be taken against them. The revolt was thus finally suppressed in the Damoh district in December 1858 and peace was restored.

Thus, the victories of Sir Hugh Rose in the Sagar district and General Whitlock in the Damoh district broke the spell of popular resistance in these districts.

REFERENCES

1. Charles Ball, *The History of the Indian Mutiny*, Vol. II (1858), p. 150.
2. N.E., paras 216-17.
3. F.P. P. , No. C-2363, Inclosure 2 in No. 10, para 43.
4. J.D., B.C., Political Case File No. 19 of 1857, pp. 277-78.
5. F.P. P. No. C-2449, Inclosure No. 70 in No. 2, p. 278.
6. N.E., para 231.
7. *Ibid.*, para 242.
8. *Ibid.*, para 307.
9. *Ibid.*, para 230.
10. *Ibid.*, para 340.
11. *Ibid.*, para 274.
12. *Ibid.*, para 306.
13. F.P. P. , No. 2363, p. 193 and No. C-2449, pp. 614 and 850.
14. J.D., B.C., Political Case File No. 30 of 1857, p. 15.
15. *Ibid.*, No. 35 of 1857.
16. *The Revolt in Central India, 1857-59* (1908), pp. 85-6.
17. Foreign, Secret, Cons., 26 March 1858, No. 249.
18. *Ibid*.
19. *Ibid*.
20. N.E., para 344, also F.P. P. No. C-2449, Inclosure No. 1 in No. 34, p. 845, para 20.
21. *The Revolt in Central India, 1857-59, op. cit.*, pp. 89-90.
22. *Ibid.*, p. 91.
23. Foreign, Secret, Cons., 28 May 1858, No. 704.
24. *The Revolt in Central India, 1857-59, op. cit.*, pp. 91-2.
25. N.E., para 345.
26. *The Revolt in Central India, 1857-59, op. cit.*, p. 94.
27. Foreign, Secret, Cons., 28 May 185, No. 101, para 5.
28. *Ibid.*, para 4.
29. *Ibid.*, No. 704.
30. *Ibid.*, No. 101, paras 1-3 and 6.
31. *The Revolt in Central India, 1857-59, op. cit.*, p. 95.
32. F.P. P. C-2449, Inclosure No. 1 in No. 35, p. 845.
33. *The Revolt in Central India, 1857-59, op. cit.*, pp. 95-7.
34. *Ibid.*, p. 97.
35. Foreign, Secret, Cons., 26 March 1858, No. 284.
36. N.E., para 372.
37. *Ibid.*, paras 351 and 373.

38. *Ibid.*, paras 385-86.
39. *Ibid.*, para 390.
40. *The Revolt in Central India, 1857-59, op. cit.*, p. 98.
41. Foreign, Secret, Cons., 28 May 1858, No. 112.
42. *Ibid.*, paras 4-5.
43. *The Revolt in Central India, 1857-59, op. cit.*, p. 98.
44. *Ibid.*, p. 99.
45. *Ibid.*, pp. 100-2.
46. Foreign, Secret, Cons., 26 March 1858, No. 303.
47. M.P. D.G., Sagar (1967), pp. 71-2.
48. *The Revolt in Central India, 1857-59, op. cit.*, p. 102.
49. Foreign, Secret, Cons., 26 March 1858, No. 55.
50. *Ibid.*, No. 57.
51. *Ibid.*, 13 August 1858, No. 134.
52. *Ibid.*, No. 136.
53. *Ibid.*, 20 May 1858, No. 211.
54. *Ibid.*, No. 212.
55. S.N. Sinha, *The Revolt of 1857 in Bundelkhand* (1982), pp. 110-11.
56. Foreign, Secret, Cons., 28 May 1858, No. 190.
57. *Ibid.*, 191.
58. *Ibid.*, 13 August 1858, No. 138.
59. Foreign, Political, Cons., 3 September 1858, No. 115.
60. *Ibid.*, No. 117. The income of Banpur was estimated to be Rs. 60,000 per annum.
61. *Ibid.*, Nos.120-21.
62. F.P. P. , No. C-2449, Inclosure 13 in No. 16, p. 160.
63. Foreign, Political, Cons., 3 September 1858, Nos.123-24.
64. *Ibid.*, No. 118. The income of the Shahgarh territory was estimated to be Rs. 1,75,000 per annum.
65. *Ibid.*, 29 July 1859, No. 65.
66. J.D., B.C., Political Case File No. 1 of 1858, p. 233.
67. *Ibid.*, No. 42 of 1858, (no paging) para 2.
68. F.P. P. C-2449, Inclosure No. 2 in No. 21, p. 569.
69. N.E., paras 232-34.
70. *Ibid.*, para 235.
71. *The Revolt in Central India, 1857-59, op. cit.*, p. 171.
72. F.P. P. , C-2449, Inclosure No. 1 in No. 34, p. 845, para 20.
73. N.E., para 375.

74. *Ibid.*, paras 374, 376-77.
75. *Ibid.*, paras 378-80.
76. *Ibid.*, para 383.
77. *Ibid.*, paras 391-92.
78. F.P. P. C-2449, Inclosure in No. 36, p. 860.
79. N.E., para 402.
80. *Ibid.*, paras 393-94.
81. *Ibid.*, paras 395-401.
82. *Ibid.*, para 409.
83. Damoh District Records, File No. 128, 31 December 1858, p. 136.

CHAPTER 8

Suppression of the Revolt in the Jabalpur and Other Districts

In the Jabalpur district : Events upto the end of 1857

During October 1857 plundering had become very common in the Jabalpur district in every direction. Sehora, Sleemanabad, Patan and Katangi all the tehsils were affected. The British had very few troops to send out. On 6 and 7 October a detachment was sent to Sehora and a second detachment to Bargi, where much plundering was going on. The rebels fell back in the jungle.[1] On 20 October the thanna of Majholi, which had been driven in, was re-established.[2]

On 21 October a large body of the rebels crossed the Hiran river and attacked the town and tehsilee of Patan. The Deputy Collector, Tehsildar and police went to meet them, but after exchanging a few shot, the Tehsildar and some of the police being wounded, they gave way and fled away before the superior numbers. The rebels then entered Patan. They destroyed the government buildings and burned and plundered many houses in the town. A small force was sent to Patan from Jabalpur but the insurgents fled into the jungle. To protect Patan, 100 infantry under an officer and a troop of cavalry were left at the place.[3]

On 25 October the thanna of Burtulla, on the road leading from Damoh to Mirzapur, was attacked by the rebels and mutineers who plundered the town and burned the dak bungalow and thanna. During the next few days other posts were driven in and the rebels were very formidable in the villages near Mirzapur road. These rebels plundered and took away many dak horses.[4]

On 7 November the town and the dak of Gosalpur were plundered by the rebels from Neemkheda. A troop of the 4th Cavalry under Captain Tottenham was sent out. They caught up the rebels, killed several and took seventeen prisoners. Captain Tottenham continued the pursuit to the village of Ramkheria where the rebels were hiding in the houses. He was dismounted whilst attempting to get into a house, was mortally wounded by a gun shot and died on the next day. On the same day his party was reinforced by Captain Clerk's detachment and also by more of the 4th Cavalry sent out from Jabalpur under Colonel Cumberledge. They proceeded to Ramkheria on 9 November and destroyed the house from which Captain Tottenham was killed but all the rebels had fled.[5]

On 14 November on receiving an intelligence from Rao Anirudh Singh of Kaimooree, a faithful Thakur to the British, that a party of rebels from Mangarh in Damoh district intended attacking him, a detachment was sent out under Major Jenkins, Assistant Quarter Master General of the Nagpur force. He drove the rebels with a loss of twelve. Several prisoners were taken but he was shot through the heart by a rebel from behind a bush, but Lt. Oaks of the 52nd immediately shot the rebel.[6]

The rebels in the hills near Katangi were still causing great trouble and were plundering all the villages near Koni, on the right bank of the Hiran river. On 21 December a detachment was sent to Koni which drove the rebels out but they took their position on the top of a nearly perpendicular hill covered with bush jungle. As the British force was insufficient, on 26 December Colonel Millar marched from Patan to attack the rebels at Koni pass. They successfully drove them out.[7]

Suppression of the Bargi rebels

On 30 November the rebel leader of Bargi, Devi Singh Gontia, attacked and burned the thanna of Shahpur on the road to Narsinghpur. A part of cavalry was sent after them, but they escaped to Bargi and the police were re-established there.[8]

As the Bargi rebels were becoming very bold, it was necessary to undertake measures for their destruction. Major Erskine, therefore, proposed a plan to Colonel Munsey, the Commandant at Jabalpur, to attack them at their headquarters at Nawal Pahar but he did not think it safe. Erskine then proposed another plan in which Munsey would give some slight assistance. On the day of the attack on Nawal Pahar, he would allow the Company of the 26th stationed at Bargi thanna to join and the cavalry to patrol the north bank of the Narmada.

His plan[9] was as follows : Two Companies of the 28th Madras Native Infantry were on their way up from Hoshangabad with two six-pounders; Captain Woolley's detachment alongwith Captain Ternan, the Deputy Commissioner of Narsinghpur, was near Sankul and had two six-pounders, with some Hyderabad Cavalry; and Lt. Thomson, the Deputy Commissioner of Seoni and Captain Waddington, the Deputy Commissioner of Mandla, were at Dhuma, with a Company of the 1st Nagpur Irregular Infantry. He called on all these three officers and troops to move simultaneously on Nawal Pahar and Colonel Munsey permitted the Company at Bargi to co-operate.

On 7 December the detachment under Captain Wooley in Narsinghpur, joined by the two companies of the 28th from Hoshangabad, forced the passage of Sunere river which was held by the rebels amounting to 1,500 under Devi Singh Gontia and other leaders. The other detachments also advanced. Captain Woolley arrived at Cherapur on 10 December where the rebels had been in force. The rebels fled but Captain Ternan with a detachment came upon the insurgents and captured their guns and tent. Four days later they caught the leading rebel, Devi Singh and hanged him. Some rebels under Bahadur Singh fled towards Mandla.[10] This victory completely settled the Bargi pargana. It was a turning point in the rebellion in the Jabalpur district. From that day a rebel had not been seen to the south of the Narmada river.[11]

Martyrdom of Thakur Sarju Prasad Singh of Bijairaghogarh

One of the heroic figures of this movement in the Jabalpur district was the young Thakur Sarju Prasad Singh of Bijairaghogarh, which once formed a part of the Maihar State. On the death of Thakur Durjan Singh of Maihar in 1826, his property was divided between his two sons, Bishnu Singh taking Maihar and Pragdas Singh the estate of Bijairaghogarh. By a *sanad* dated 29 February 1828, the British Government recognised Thakur Pragdas Singh as chief of Bijairaghogarh. For about nineteen years he conducted the affairs of the estate with great success and introduced many useful reforms. He died in 1845 and was succeeded by his son, Sarju Prasad Singh, who was then only a boy of five years. The Government, therefore, took over charge of the minor chief and brought the estate under the Court of Wards. Thus, during the revolt of 1857 Thakur Sarju Prasad was a youth of seventeen years and his estate was managed by the Superintendent of Nagod. Towards the end of October 1857, when the events, that had recently happened in Jabalpur following the execution of Raja Shankar Shah, had been agitating the public mind, young Thakur Sarju Prasad rose in revolt. The Tehsildar, Sabir Ali, was killed and the dak horses were captured and large bodies of armed men covered the important Jabalpur-Mirzapur road so that neither the dak nor could travellers pass along the road.[12]

On 4 November Major R.S. Sullivan marched from Jabalpur with a wing of the 4th Cavalry to support the infantry and artillery on the Mirzapur road, which had moved towards Chaka to check the Bijairaghogarh rebels. On 6 November the rebels surprised this detachment when they were advancing from Gosalpur to Khailwara, and opened fire from two guns. Some thousand matchlockmen at Murwara on the Mirzapur road opposed them. Captain Clerk repulsed them and took their guns. The rebels, who numbered some 1,500 to 2,000, left 60 dead on the field. On the British side, five men were wounded and one killed.[13]

As the Bijairaghogarh rebels remained a great force on the Deccan or Mirzapur road, they completely cut off the direct communication between the north-west and Calcutta and Bombay. Not a soul could pass and all who attempted it were searched and plundered, some killed and others mutilated. Major Erskine was, therefore, very anxious to open this road. He applied to Colonel Munsey, the Commandant at Jabalpur, to send troops to attack the rebels. But a detachment under Colonel Byng did not consider himself strong enough to attack and the British troops did nothing upto 29 November and called for reinforcements.[14] As Colonel Byng failed to open the Deccan road, Colonel Whistler was sent out. On 23 January he attacked the rebels at Ramnagar, killing several of them and taking a few prisoners. One sepoy was killed. On 27 January the force advanced and re-established thanna at Sleemanabad.[15]

As the Jabalpur troops failed to capture Bijairaghogarh and suppress the rebels, the main attack on them came from the Rewa troops, which succeeded in it. Captain Osborne Willoughby, the Political Agent at Rewa also reported[16] to the Government of India about the rebellion of Thakur Sarju Prasad. He also apprehended about the rising at Maihar. He was, therefore, determined[17] to march on Bijairaghogarh with a view of capturing it and clearing the road.

On 21 January 1858 he captured Khailwara fort on the road to Bijairaghogarh. He then reported[18] to the Government of India from Khailwara that "my force will immediately march to Bijairaghogarh and I have no doubt of speedily taking it as I have received information that Sarjoo Pursad has taken to the jungle leaving only a small force to defend it."

After the capture of Bijairaghogarh he again reported[19] on 9 February 1858 that the forts of Khailwara and Bijairaghogarh had been wrested from the rebels and three guns captured at the former and thirteen guns and one mortar at the latter place. He had dismantled the fort at Bijairaghogarh as much as the small means at his disposal. Some of the rebels captured in the Bijairaghogarh fort were sentenced to death but Sarju Prasad and others had escaped in the hills and jungles.

The rebels connected with the rebellion at Bijairaghogarh[20] were Lala Chhatar Singh, Deewan Sarda Prasad, Deewan Mukund Singh, Deewan Dal Ganjan Singh, Buddha Singh, Ganeshju, Beeju Bhisti Jamadar, Shivlal Baree Qiledar and Ram Prasad Thanedar of Khailwara.

As Thakur Sarju Prasad had managed to escape, he wandered about disguised as a *faqir*. The British succeeded in capturing him in 1864. He was taken to Jabalpur where he was confined for a long time. He was then tried for a rebellion and was sentenced to transportation for life and forfeiture of all his property. Rather than face this sentence, Sarju Prasad committed suicide at Benaras and may, thus, be considered as one of the early martyrs in the struggle for freedom. The territories of Bijairaghogarh were confiscated and formed a part of the Murwara tehsil of the Jabalupur district[21].

Rebellious activities in 1858 till their suppression

In 1858 the activities of the rebels continued unabated till their suppression. On 2 January Colonel Byng attacked and dispersed some rebels from Neemkhera.[22] The rebels at Narainpur in the east of the district were giving much trouble. Major Erskine asked Brigadier Lawrence to send a detachment for its suppression. Accordingly, under Colonel Cumberlege a detachment was sent and the troops on the Mirzapur road were directed to make a combined attack on the rebels. On 5 January the troops of Colonel Cumberlege on their way to Narainpur were attacked and they lost an elephant. The rebels were then driven off. Next day twenty men with arms in their hands were seized by Colonel Cumburlege and being recognised as some of the rebels were tried by court martial and executed. His detachment returned to Jabalpur without effecting anything. The other part from Sehora under Colonel Whistler alone drove them out but did not recover the elephant.[23]

On 25 February the rebels under Devi Singh attacked Jabera on the Damoh road, and closed the direct road between Jabalpur and Damoh. They took up positions at Singrampur and Jabera and also at Konda, a place near Majholi. On 28 February in consequence of General Whitlock's forces being near, the Burtulla thanna was re-established on the road between Jukehi and Damoh. On 1 March Lt. Walters, who was at Sihora, attacked the rebels near Majholi and killed several, taking their ammunition and several prisoners, but he was severely wounded.[24]

On 26 March the Deputy Commissioner of Jabalpur taking advantage of the troops passing between Damoh and Jabalpur, re-established the thannas at Jabera and Singrampur. But they were soon driven in again by strong bodies of rebels under Devi Singh and Mirbhan Singh. Several attempts to take over these places failed[25].

On 2 April a large body of rebels attacked the police post at Piprod on the Mirzapur and Jabalpur road, but the rebels were driven by the daffadar of police. On 5 April the rebel leaders, Bhao Singh and Himmat Singh of Neemkhera, attacked the Burtulla thanna but the rebels were driven out. On 14 April the Tehsildar of Patan attacked some rebels and killed three. On 16 April the rebels attacked the village Hurdua, and carried off the Malguzar and his daughter as they had assisted the police with information. On 26 April 500 rebels under Randhir Singh, Pratap Singh, Devi Singh and Himmat Singh attacked and destroyed the thanna of Majholi. On 29 April the thanna of Katangi was again attacked but the rebels were driven off.[26]

As plundering was still going on in Jabalpur, on 9 May the Nagpur rifles under Lt. Pereira and some of the Sleeman's *Najeebs* under Captain Cib went out into the Katangi hills. Each party met with rebels, some 26 rebels were killed including their leader, Jagat Singh, a sepoy of the 52nd. Major Erskine stated[27] that since that time nothing worthy of note had occurred.

In a statement[28] of the *Koorseenashins* who had joined in the revolt in this district, were Raja Mehpal Singh Gond of Bhutgaon Kunoja, Rao Chandra Hans Gond of Murdongarh, Thakur Ram Bux of Murwara, Thakur Issoredas of Khireni, Laxman Singh Gond of Narainpur and Gajraj Singh and Jawahar Singh of Garhaghat. Their estates were confiscated after the supression of revolt.

Since the proclamation of Amnesty ordered by the Governor General in May 1858 was issued in these territories, Major Erskine observed[29] that "peace has greatly been restored and many rebels have given in. Still, however, some remain bitterly opposed to us."

In the Narsinghpur district : Events upto the end of 1857

In October 1857 the Narsinghpur district was in a great danger. The district north of the Narmada river was again invaded by Nawab Ali Khan of Bhopal with 150 Pathans from Rahatgarh. He was also accompanied by some local rebel leaders, 500 matchlockmen, and some customs *chaprasees* who had joined the rebels some time before. They entered the Chawarpatha pargana and plundered and burned Tendukhera and Belkhedi and committed other depredations. At the same time, Mirbhan Singh, a local rebel leader, moved down to Heerapur on the right bank of the Narmada river about fifteen miles from Narsinghpur, and threatened it. The rebels of the Bargi pargana in the Jabalpur district threatened the south-east of Narsinghpur, so that the district was threatened from three directions at the same time.[30]

Captain Ternan, the Deputy Commissioner of

Narsinghpur, gave more details of these events in his weekly reports to Major Erskine, the Commissioner. He reported[31] on 19 October 1857 regarding the Chawarpatha pargana where the plundering was going on that "it is a notorious fact, however, that the main body of the plunderers consists of the villagers of the Chawarpatha pergunnah. It is also equally notorious that nearly every Talookdar and Malguzar of the pergannah of any substance, is aiding and abetting such plundering."

He again reported[32] on 27 October 1857 that Captain Woolley marched from Chhindwara to village Soonwarah in Bargi pargana. It belonged to Shiv Bux Lodhi, a head rebel on that border who had been plundering several villages. The rebels ran off and the example made had good effect. Since then the Bargi rebels had not entered this district. Captain Woolley then crossed the Narmada and entered Heerapur which he found completely deserted. The village of Heerapur, the headquarters of the rebels, had been burnt to the ground. The small *ghuree* (fortress) which commanded the village was also destroyed. Some matchlockmen of the Delheree and Patera Rajas and Rao Soorut Singh of Narsinghpur had also accompanied Captain Woolley across the river.

Captain Ternan was anxious to save the British position in his district. Hence, he, accompanied by the two companies of the Madras Native Infantry under the command of Captain Woolley, marched to Sankul opposite Heerapur to oppose Mirbhan Singh, a noted rebel leader who occupied a small fort commanding the village. The guns opened fire on him and he quietely fled. This had an excellent effect in other direction. The rebels at Tendukhera evacuated that place.[33] On 17 November Mirbhan Singh burnt the village and thanna of Sankul and went back the same evening. A detachment under Lt. Walton was sent against them. The rebels did not take to their heels and faced the British force. When a few volleys were fired, they fled with considerable loss and confidence was restored in that part of the district.[34]

Captain Ternan alongwith the Captain Woolley's detachment then went to the north of the Narmada river on the Sagar road. With the co-operation of a detachment under Captain Roberts of the 31st and Captain Mayne of the 3rd Irregularsfrom Sagar, they cleared north of the Narmada of the rebels. In his weekly narrative ending 29 November 1857, Captain Ternan reported[35] that he marched on 23 November 1857 against Singhpur, held by the rebel leader, Dal Ganjan Singh, who "was attacked as he was leaving the village surrounded by 150 or 200 matchlockmen. He and his whole party being charged by the cavalry were driven into a sugarcane field where their total discomfiture was effected by the arrival of infantry and guns. Of the whole number, only 43 came out of the field alive among whom Ganjan Singh himself who was hanged on the same evening in Deori before an immense crowd. Next day 22 more were hanged under martial law."

Chawarpatha pargana cleared off the rebels in January 1858

In Jaunary 1858 the Rahatgarh and Bhopal rebels again invaded the Narsinghpur district. On 9 January 1858 about 4,000 rebels from Rahatgarh and Bhopal including 250 Pathan horses under Abdul Muhammad Khan of Bhopal, Balbhadra Singh of Sahajpur in Sagar and other leaders aided by Delun Shah of Madanpur, Narwar Singh of Dhilwar and others of Narsinghpur district, attacked Tendukhera on the north of the Narmada. The police and some matchlockmen under Rao Soorat Singh of Imjhira and Nizam Shah defended the place. Many rebels were killed and they retreated. In retaliation the rebels destroyed the fine *pakka* house of Rao Soorat Singh and all his valuable property was plundered. Tendukhera and some villages were burnt. The troops with Captain Ternan advanced against the rebels and the troops from Sagar patrolling the road co-operated, the rebels then fled upto the *ghats* towards Rahatgarh.[36]

After clearing off the Chawarpatha pargana, Captain Ternan then alongwith the troops made a long march and dashed on 17 January 1858 into the village of Madanpur of the rebel leader Delun Shah. Before anyone there was well awake, he surprised all and captured some rebels amongst whom were a son and grandson of Delun Shah and killed others. Delun Shah managed to escape. Captain Ternan shot three rebels and Doctor Bradby dragged two from the earthen jar.[37] The son of Delun Shah and 15 rebels were hanged at Dhilwar on 17 January 1858. Most of them were concerned in the rebellion of these parts of 1842-43.[38] This cleared the Chawarpatha pargana of all rebels of any consequence.

Capture and execution of Delun Shah on 16 May 1858

In March 1858 Captain Gordon, the new Deputy Commissioner, alongwith Lt. Walton of the 28th Madras Native Infantry took Mirbhan Singh and Delun Shah by surprise in the jungles at a day-break and killed many rebels and would have seized Delun Shah had the ground been good. In reteliation Mirbhan Singh had once or twice come down to Heerapur but never dared to cross the Narmada river. He had also attacked Bumhoree but was repulsed.[39]

On 16 May Delun Shah, who had long been hiding in the jungle, attacked Madanpur, his former residence which was, in the meantime, given to Nizam Shah for his help to the British government. He compelled Nizam Shah to take to flight. He gallantly met the police who beat him off, followed and seized him. He was tried by the Deputy Commissioner (as Special Commissioner) and hanged.[40] This settled the Narsinghpur district.

In this revolt most of the chief malguzars of the district were either passive or actively helped the British officers with their horsemen and retainers. For their active help they were recommended for rewards. These rewards consisted mostly of a grant of landed property, with *khilat* of shawls, sword, shield and remission of *jumma* for life or a privilege of obtaining a chair.[41]

Rao Soorat Singh and Nizam Shah were rewarded[42] for their loyalty to the British. The title of Raja and Bahadur was conferred on Rao Soorat Singh. The settlement with the Raja of his state of Jhingree at half *jumma* for two generations was sanctioned and a *khilat* of Rs. 5,000 and a sword not costing more than Rs.200. Nizam Shah was bestowed the forfeited states of Dhilwar and Madanpur at half-*jumma* for two generations and a *khilat* of Rs. 2,000 and a sword not costing more than Rs.200.

In the Hoshangabad district : Events upto the end of 1857

As referred to earlier, there was trouble going on in the Nemawar pargana. Lt. Wood, the Deputy Commissioner of Hoshangabad had reported from time to time that the Mewatees had been assembling in the Nemawar pargana for the purpose of plunder. They had taken possessin of the fort of Satwas. They were aided by Thakur Daulat Singh of Raghogarh who had taken possession of the Nemawar Tehsilee and thanna. They were joined by a man named Ramkishan who styled himself as a *Kamdar* (*agent*) of Sindhia. Their hands had been further strengthened by the treachrous conduct of Kalyan Singh, a Jamadar of police.[43] They were too strong for the police who were obliged on 3 October to retire to Harda. The rebels plundered the town of Nemawar and confiscated and tortured several of the most respectable inhabitants who refused to rebel. As the Mewaties violated many local women there, this enraged the people and they rose against them. But they did not muster enough armed men to dislodge the rebels from Satwas.[44]

It was the intention of the rebels to cross over the Narmada from Nemawar and to pillage Harda. The Deputy Magistrate of Harda fearing that Harda would fall into the hands of the rebels, asked for help. The Deputy Commissioner was then determined to proceed to Harda,

56 miles from Hoshangabad. On 8 October he proceeded with a small detachment of the 28th Madras Native Infantry and two guns, marched twenty three miles towards Nemawar and next day moved on twenty one miles. On arriving at the old city of Handia on the south bank of the Narmada on 12 October, they found the rebels in great force on the opposite bank. The rebels at once commenced firing from behind the walls of the temples at the water's edge, but were dispersed by the fire of the guns. Next day Lt. Wood crossed over and the police succeeded in capturing Ramkishan, the pretender who was tried and hanged.[45]

Intelligence was then received that Satwas was still held by the rebels under Lal Khan, a Mewatee Malguzar and Kalyan Singh, a Jamadar of police, who had been deputed to oppose these rebels, had publicly joined them. As the Harda police volunteered to go to Satwas, they were permitted and in the morning of 16 October they arrived and captured Kalyan Singh and Lal Khan, with a few rebels. But Thakur Daulat Singh and his band had fled on hearing of the approach of the guns. It was satisfactorily proved that Kalyan Singh and Lal Khan were the chic leaders of the rebellion. At first Kalyan Singh reported that he had taken possession of the place for the Government; but in the trial he admitted that he had exchanged *pugrees* with the rebel Thakur Daulat Singh as a pledge to act with him against the Government. Both Lal Khan and Kalyan Singh were hanged under the provisions of the Act XIV of 1857. Ram Singh, son of Kalyan Singh, not being equally guilty was sentenced to transportation for life. The fort of Satwas was destroyed and the detachment marched back to Hoshangabad.[46]

Suppression of the disturbances again in the Nemawar pargana in January 1858

At the close of December 1857, the Mewatees were again plundering in the Nemawar pargana. Lt. Wood resolved again on attacking them and the troops left Hoshangabad for Nemawar on 11 January 1858. On 12 January he received two expresses from Narsinghpur informing him that 4,000 rebels from Rahatgarh had taken possession of Tendukhera in Narsinghpur and they intended moving down to Hoshangabad. This information made Lt. Wood to retrace his steps, but his object had been effected as the rebels had fled and since then Nemawar had been tranquil.[47]

On 19 June 1858 Sir R.Hamilton, Agent to the Governor General for Central India, informed Lt. Wood that Thakur Daulat Singh of Raghogarh had taken poison as his body was brought into his camp and recognised.[48] Thus, the last important rebel leader of the Hoshangabad district had committed suicide and peace was restored.

In the Mandla district : Events upto the end of 1857

As referred to earlier, two-thirds of the Mandla district was in rebellion at the close of September 1857. As the whole of Sohagpur, Shahpura and Ramgarh had risen in rebellion, on 12 October 1857 Captain Waddington, the Deputy Commissioner of Mandla who was residing at Jabalpur, wished to go out into his district. As Major Erskine had no troops to send with him, he refused.[49] At last the Deputy Commissioner having collected a few police and ten men of the 52nd Native Infantry, who had remained loyal, was allowed to proceed to Mandla. He marched on 22 and reached Mandla on 25 October.[50]

On reaching Mandla, he sent out a party of police who attacked a small party of rebels at Ramnagar and killed a few. On hearing that a large body of rebels was coming down on them, they retired to Mandla. The rebels then took the thanna of Naraianganj on the road from Mandla to Jabalpur and thus cut off the communications between the two districts.[51]

On 11 October the village of Ghugri was looted by men who came from the direction of Ramgarh. As a small party of rebels were located between Ramnagar and Ghugri, who were robbing the travellers, a small force was sent to Ghugri and another to Ramnagar on 28 October, the rebels fled and the police occupied Ghugri.[52] At this time Captain Waddington reported[53] to Major Erskine that only one third of the district was under the Government control. As the oppression carried on by the Ramgarh Raja, the Taluqdars of Sohagpur, Kothi Nigwani and Shahpura, the people were generally most anxious for the re-establishment of the British Government.

In the meantime, combination of Khuman Singh of Mokas, Bijai Singh of Shahpura with the Ramgarh rebels attacked Ghugri and on 6 November the Tehsildar and others were driven out of it.[54] The rebels also assembled close to Mandla in large bodies with the design of attacking it. The police were called in and all the Government property (records etc.) were taken into the town. The rebels did not attack Mandla but contented themselves with plundering the villages all round.[55] On 20 November the thanna of Naraianganj, which had been re-established, was again driven in.[56]

Escape of the Deputy Commissioner to Seoni on 26 November 1857

On 23 November the rebels appeared again in large bodies and surrounded the Mandla town. Next day all the available police were sent against them. The rebels at first fled, but being reinforced turned and drove in the police, but a ball from the Deputy Commissioner's rifle turned the rebels once more.[57]

As the rebels had resolved to attack Mandla again, they gathered around it in large numbers. The Deputy Commissioner's ammunition too began to fall short, his retreat to Jabalpur was cut off and worse than all, some of the town's people began to show treachery and reports were heard that some rebels were about to go round to the south of Narmada to cut off the retreat to Seoni. Under these circumstances, Captain Waddington's position was becoming every day more embarassing, he considered it advisable to retreat on Seoni. Major Erskine also advised him to do so as he could do little or no good without troops and was needlessly endangering his life. He, therefore, escaped to Seoni on 26 November 1857 but the rebels did not enter the town of Mandla.[58]

On reaching Seoni he was ordered by Major Erskine to assist the Deputy Commissioner of Seoni in the Dhuma direction in the suppression of the Bargi rebels.[59] As referred to earlier, it was carried out on 7 December which completely settled the Bargi pargana. On their way they occupied Kedarpur from the rebels. In accordance with the orders of Major Erskine, Captain Waddington moved to Mandla with the Nagpur Column under Lt. Barton to clear the banks of the Narmada river of the rebels. In the Mandla district except Mandla and Mhow, it was entirely in the hands of the rebels. His little army consisted of a few police, one company of the Irregular Infantry and fifteen men of the 52nd. He started on 31 December to Mandla through the hills and dense jungle.[60]

On 4 January 1858 Captain Waddington re-established the Jabalpur police at Narainganj and captured a noted rebel, Asajeet, who was tried and hanged. To open the road between Jabalpur and Mandla, it was necessary to move on Mokas, the headquarters of the rebel, Khuman Singh. On 7 January Captain Waddington and Lt. Barton drove the rebels and took possession of Mokas. So precipitate was the flight of the rebels that they left behind them a loaded jinjal and never fired on the British troops and the road to Jabalpur was cleared.[61]

Return of the Deputy Commissioner to Mandla on 15 January 1858

Captain Waddington had returned to Mandla after an absence of one and a half months and after re-establishing the Seoni thanna of Kedarpur and the Jabalpur thanna of Narainganj. After dispersing all the rebels near Narmada, he reached Mandla on 15 January 1858 and found everything as usual. His force was very small, being only eighty five soldiers of the 1st Nagpur Irregular Infantry, about thirty police and his district being very large about 8,900 miles of hills and jungles. He could do little beyond settling the immediate neighbourhood of Mandla.[62]

Capture of Ramgarh on 2 April 1858

After some time, troops were reinforced to Mandla as a 2nd company of the Nagpur Infantry under Lt. Cockburn reached there on 23 March 1858. On 29 March a little force consisting of 130 of Irregular Infantry, 15 of 52nd Native Infantry, 80 police and 100 matchlocks totalling 325, under Lieutenants Barton and Cockburn was sent to Ramgarh as it was very much disturbed. On 31 March the Deputy Commissioner took possession of the rebel village of Ghugri without opposition and planned to attack Ramgarh as the rebels had resolved to make their stand there.[63]

On 1 April three signal shots were fired by the rebels from a hill near Ramgarh as the *ghat* was occupied by them. On 2 April the Mandla force advanced and attacked the *ghat* and the rebels fled, leaving three of their party dead on the field. The troops then pushed on for Ramgarh. Lt. Barton, who commanded the party, made a dash at the place from two sides, when the rebels evacuated Ramgarh. The Deputy Commissioner at once took possession of the Raja's house and established his headquarters there. The rebels were then reinforced from several places. The Thakur of Shahpura put himself at their head. On 9 April they mustered strongly on the side of the hill to the north of the town, intending to attack Lt. Barton's force from three sides. They were completely routed leaving twenty five dead. On the British side only one man was wounded.[64] Thus, Ramgarh was captured and the Raja Bikramjeet Singh was deposed and his estate was confiscated.

Re-occupation of Shahpura and Sohagpur

On 24 April Shahpura, another Tehsilee of Mandla was re-occupied without opposition by Lt. Barton's detachment. On 27 April the *Gurhee* of Singhpur was occupied as the rebels fled.[65] The Ramgarh Raja, Raja Bijai Singh of Shahpura, Bahadur Singh of Lodhee Pipariya, the Narainpur Thakurs, Mahipal Singh of Bhutgaon were all in the Rewa territories where they were living with the knowledge of the Rewa Thakurs who had taken blackmail from them.[66]

Sohagpur was the only place now remained to be occupied. This was a small but strong fort and could not be attacked without guns and the British troops were not having any guns. They marched towards Sohagpur on 25 May. General report was that about 300 rebels were at Sohagpur and their spirits were buoyed up by a belief that a force was coming from the Rewa territories to their relief.[67]

Major Erskine then asked the Commissioner of Nagpur for a large force to proceed from Raipur to assist Lt. Barton. Accordingly, he sent Captain Baron Von Mayern with 250 of the 3rd Irregular Infantry and eight Irregular Cavalry to surround Sohagpur. Guns in time came from Rewa and both these detachments surrounded the fort. The Rewa garrison were about 300 matchlockmen with some half dozen small guns. The Sohagpur rebels were expecting assistance from them instead they opposed them. The first shot was fired on the fort on 15 June and continued at the rate of about 20 rounds per diem until 18 June. On the same night the Sohagpur rebels evacuated the fort and had gone to the Rewa territories. Since then the Raipur and Rewa detachments returned to their posts. The Mandla district was settled and quiet.[68]

In this context, the report[69] of Captain Waddington from Sohagpur on 12 July 1858 is very signficant. He stated that "the Ramgarh Ranee and Bijai Singh have been sending petitions and messages - the last accompanied with a rupee as *nuzzur* being to the effect that they were coming to throw themselves at his feet - I do not believe that they will." It means that the Rani of Ramgarh was very much alive in July 1858 after the capture of Ramgarh on 2 April 1858 as it is commonly believed that like Rani Durgavati she ended her life by piercing the dagger in her heart on the battlefield to avoid capture.

As some of the rebels of the Mandla district had sued for pardon including Raja Bikramjeet and Aman Singh, son and heir of the Ramgarh family, Captain Waddington submitted on 30 July 1858 an outline of the known facts of the Ramgarh family. He stated[70] that Raja Bikramjeet was a helpless and confirmed idiot so much so that his estate was placed under the Court of Wards management and it was therefore certain that he had nothing to do with the rebellion. His son, Aman Singh, although about 20 years of age was wanting in intelligence but sufficiently wise to understand the nature of acts he performed. He was generally engaged at the rebel thanna of Muhidwanee where Bijai Singh of Shahpura and others were occasionally summoned by orders issued in the Raja's name with the view of demonstrating the Raja's power and of holding up Aman Singh to the people as his representative. He also went on one or two occasions with the rebel forces towards Mandla and was present during the attack on the British at Ramgarh on 9 April 1858. The only point for decision "is whether in the present circumstances his guilt may be overlooked and the deprivation of his estates considered a sufficient punishment." The second son, Sher Singh was about 8 years old and therefore too young for any guilt and one still younger died in the jungles subsequent to the flight of the rebels from Ramgarh.

He further stated[71] about the Rani of Ramgarh that "I turn to the Ranee and cannot help feeling disposed to treat leniently a woman, who with a mad husband and uneducated and ignorant son must have naturally been constrained to live on the advice of and be guided about the people about her.... I consider her in every respect guilty of instigating the rebellion and the only point for consideration was whether she should be considered as the victim of circumstances, and that she could not have acted otherwise even if inclined to do so and whether the subsequent inconvenience she has suffered and the confiscation of her husband's estate is sufficient punishment for the crime." Although "it must appear that the Raja and his second son are innocent and that Aman Singh, the eldest son is a fit subject for merciful consideration, I have suggested that the deeds of Ranee have wrought their own punishment."

Settlement of the Mandla district

During September 1858 the rebels had mustered very strong to attack Sohagpur and Shahpura simultaneously. As a third of Nagpur Irregulars were prostrate with fever, and Shahpura being inadequately defended, Captain Waddington was determined on evacuating Sohagpur and concentrating the troops at his disposal at Shahpura.[72] The rebels were said to muster about 2,000 fighting men under Ran Mast Singh, a rebel Thakur of the Rewa state. There was, however, a great hindrance to a speedy restoration of peace as the Rewa authorities were giving shelter to all the rebels of the Mandla district.[73]

As Thakur of Shahpura was tired of the rebellious activities, on 12 February 1859 he gave in his submission to the authorities at Shahpura and its Thanedar reported that the Thakurs of Sohagpur wished to follow his example. They also surrendered and a thanna was established at Sohagpur and the revenue was collected through a small force. Captain Waddington hoped that "before a fortnight elapses I will be able to report that there is not a rebel in arms throughout the length and breadth of the district."[74]

After the suppression of the revolt in the Mandla district, Sohagpur Taluq was handed over to the Maharaja of Rewa for his help in suppressing the Sohagpur rebellion. The *ubari* tenures of Ramgarh and Shahpura were confiscated, the family of the rebel Raja of Ramgarh being granted a small pension at the expense of the cultivators, who had joined in the revolt.[75]

In the Seoni district

As referred to earlier, the districts of Seoni and Betul, south to the Narmada river, were least affected by the revolt. However, to complete our narrative, the main events in these districts are as follows. In October 1857 Lt.Thomson, the Deputy Commissioner had reported[76] that the district was generally quiet except the Dhuma thanedaree. Some villages bordering on the Jabalpur district were burnt by the rebels under a Jabalpur Thakur. Dhuma itself was reported to be threatened by the rebels.

In November 1857 he moved out to Dhuma towards Jabalpur to re-assure the Thakurs. Some of them joined him with small contingent and afforded him good information. Had they rebelled, the whole of their followers would have risen, and the rebellion would have rapidly spread south. But as it happened there was little or no rebellion in Seoni, though some villages towards Mandla, Jabalpur and Narsinghpur were plundered by rebels from those districts. The customs line was also once attacked.[77]

As referred to earlier, while suppressing the Bargi rebels in the Jabalpur district in December 1857, Major Erskine had asked the Deputy Commissioners of Seoni and Mandla who were at Dhuma with a company of the 1st Nagpur Irregular Infantry to move on Nawal Pahar, the headquarters of the Bargi rebels.[78] On 7 December the detachment under Captain Woolley in Narsinghpur joined by the two companies of the 28th from Hoshangabad also advanced and captured Cherapur on 10 December where the Bargi rebels were in force. The rebels fled but Devi Singh, the leading rebel, was caught and hanged. Some rebels under Bahadur Singh fled towards Mandla.[79]

This victory completely settled the Bargi pargana. It was a turning point in the revolt of 1857. From that day a rebel had not been seen to the south of the Narmada river.[80] The Deputy Commissioners of Seoni and Mandla then established police posts between the two districts to check the Mandla rebels. On 20 December on receiving the information that Bahadur Singh, the rebel of Bargi, was hiding in the jungle to the east of Dhuma, Captain Waddington started on 21 December to catch him and on the way re-occupied Kedarpur. As attempt to catch Bahadur Singh failed, he was driven further eastward and most of his followers had deserted him. On 25 December the Kedarpur police were re-established.[81] In accordance with the orders of Major Erskine, the Deputy Commissioner of Seoni then made over the whole of the Grenadier Company of the Nagpur Irregular Infantry (commanded by Lt.Barton of the 52nd Native Infantry) to the Deputy Commissioner of Mandla to clear the banks of the Narmada of the rebels in the Seoni, Jabalpur and Mandla districts and to return to Mandla.[82] It was discussed earlier with reference to the Mandla district.

In the Betul district

During the revolt the tranquility of this district was scarcely disturbed. As referred to earlier, there had been some signs of disaffection on the part of Shivdeen Patel, one of the chief men, but it had been detected early enough to prevent anything serious occurring. The Deputy Commissioner of Betul reported[83] to Major Erskine on 21 October 1857 that Shivdeen and Ramdeen Malguzars, having been found guilty of rebellion, were sentenced under provisions of Act XIV of 1857, to seven years imprisonment and their property was confiscated. Thereafter, nothing of consequence happened in the district.

After suppressing the revolt in the Saugar and Nerbudda Territories, Major Erskine reported[84] to the Government of North-Western Provinces on 10 August 1858 that "I can now with confidence and pleasure state that peace is restored to my division of eight districts, for although we have some leaders still at large, their followers are but few."

Causes of the failure of revolt in the Saugor and Nerbudda Territories

The causes of the failure of the revolt of 1857 have been analysed at length by the historians. In this context, the observation[85] of Dr. K.M. Panikkar aptly summarizes its causes, "If during that period (i.e. May to August 1857) a reasonable central government could have been established and the activities of the rebels co-ordinated, the British would have found it difficult to maintain their position in the interior, and they would have been compelled to withdraw to their coastal fortification."

This observation of Dr. Panikkar is also true to this region. The major weakness of this movement was the absence of the proper co-ordinated organisation. As one district after another came to the possession of the popular leaders, it would have settled down to an orderly life but in its absence all law and order for a time disappeared from it. The villagers had to flee in terror and when they came back they found their homes destroyed and properly looted. This "happened time and again in many places, and after some months of experience, the people began to long for a respite from this uncertainty, even at the cost of their liberty. Any power that held out a promise of orderly, secure administration was welcome."[86]

There were leaders in this region but there was no such leader who could unify and organise the activities of all in one direction i.e. the liberation of the whole region. The insurgents had no unified command although there were leaders of great stature in the different districts as follows: in Sagar the Rajas of Shahgarh and Banpur; in Damoh Thakur Kishor Singh of Hindoria; in Jabalpur Raja Shankar Shah and his son, Raghunath Shah and Thakur Sarju Prasad Singh of

Bijairaghogarh; in Narsinghpur, Raja Delun Shah of Madanpur, Raja Narwar Singh of Dhilwar and Mirbhan Singh; in Hoshangabad Thakur Daulat Singh and in Mandla, the Rani of Ramgarh and the Thakurs of Sohagpur and Shahpura. No doubt, the revolt threw up leaders of genius and daring in different parts of the region, but there was no co-ordinating centre to direct the command of the regional commanders.

The main cause of the failure of this revolt in this region, like other parts of India, was that these rebels were acting without concert, each for his own individual interest and without sympathy with the mutinous sepoys.

The British forces, on the other hand, had the advantage of a strong and watchful central authority which directed the military operations in the different theatres of war. Moreover, the British had superior military equipment in this trial of strength. Although the armies of the popular leaders during 1857 had larger numbers and the general support of the people, they were unable to withstand the better equipped British army. The breech-loading guns of the English troops and their heavier field guns outranged and silenced the muzzle-loading and hand-made guns used by the insurgents. The cavalry units of the British army led by persons who had seen many wars in India and abroad, were better skilled in the latest methods of warfare than our own leaders. The British with their control over widespread telegraph system and postal communications were in a position to know every thing more quickly and act upon it according to the needs of the situation.

Thus, the British suppressed the revolt in these territories by their superior strategy and savagery and termed them as suppression. The policy of ruthless suppression thus secured the position of the British and they felt themselves strong enough to embark upon a policy of reprisals and repression. Hence, a reign of terror was let loose in these territories.

REFERENCES

1. N.E., paras 228-29.
2. *Ibid.*, para 246.
3. *Ibid.*, paras 253-54.
4. *Ibid.*, paras 258-59.
5. *Ibid.*, paras 268-71.
6. *Ibid.*, para 272.
7. *Ibid.*, paras 309-17.
8. *Ibid.*, para 291.
9. *Ibid.*, paras 292-94.
10. *Ibid.*, paras 295-98.
11. *Ibid.*, para 299.
12. D.P. Mishra, ed., *History of the Freedom Movement in Madhya Pradesh* (1956), p. 79.
13. N.E., paras 264 and 266.
14. *Ibid.*, paras 289-90.
15. *Ibid.*, paras 346-48.
16. Foreign, Secret, Progs., 27 November 1857, Nos. 157-59.
17. *Ibid.*, No. 160.
18. J.D., B.C., Political Case File No. 1 of 1858, p. 73, para 5.
19. Foreign, Secret, Cons., 26 March 1858, No. 187.
20. *Ibid.*, 26 February 1858, No. 74.
21. D.P. Mishra, *op. cit.*, p. 80.
22. N.E., para 320.
23. *Ibid.*, paras 321-25.
24. *Ibid.*, paras 387-88.
25. *Ibid.*, para 404.
26. *Ibid.*, paras 422-24 and 426-27.
27. *Ibid.*, para 430.
28. J.D., B.C., Revenue Case File No. 20 of 1858, p. 48.
29. N.E., para 431.
30. *Ibid.*, paras 247-48.
31. J.D., B.C., Political Case File No. 19 of 1857, p. 330, paras 4-5.
32. *Ibid.*, pp. 370 and 378.
33. N.E., paras 249-50.
34. *Ibid.*, para 276-77.
35. J.D., B.C., Political Case File No. 10 of 1857, p. 925, paras 2-4, also F.P. P. No. C-2449, Inclosure No. 4 in No. 22, para 36.

36. N.E., paras 332-36, also J.D., B.C., Political Case File No. 1 of 1858, p. 199.
37. *Ibid.*, para 337.
38. J.D., B.C., Political Case File No. 1 of 1858, p. 220, para 7.
39. N.E., para 403.
40. *Ibid.*, para 432, also J.D., B.C., Political Case File No. 36 of 1858.
41. Record on the Mutiny of 1857 (Collectorate Narsinghpur), quoted in M.P. D.G. Narsimhapur (1971), p. 66.
42. J.D., B.C., Political Case File No. 10 of 1858, p. 203.
43. *Ibid.*, No. 23 of 1857, p. 326.
44. N.E., paras 221-22.
45. *Ibid.*, paras 323-26, also F.P. P. , C-2449, Inclosure No. 2 in No. 21, paras 30-1.
46. N.E., paras 238-40, also F.P. P. , C-2449, Inclosure No. 8 in No. 21, p. 575.
47. N.E., paras 329-31.
48. J.D., B.C., Political Case File No. 36 of 1858.
49. N.E., para 241.
50. *Ibid.*, para 255.
51. *Ibid.*, paras 256-57.
52. J.D., B.C., Political Case File No. 12 of 1857, p. 83, paras 2-3.
53. *Ibid.*, paras 4 and 8.
54. *Ibid.*, p. 87, para 3.
55. N.E., para 275.
56. *Ibid.*, para 283.
57. *Ibid.*, paras 284-85.
58. *Ibid.*, paras 286-87, also J.D., B.C., Political Case File No. 12 of 1857, p. 98.
59. N.E., para 288.
60. *Ibid.*, paras 301-3.
61. *Ibid.*, paras 326-28.
62. *Ibid.*, para 339.
63. N.E., paras 406-7.
64. *Ibid.*, paras 411-15.
65. N.E., para 416.
66. J.D., B.C., Political Case File No. 12 of 1857, p. 209, para 5.
67. *Ibid.*, p. 220, paras 2-3.
68. N.E., paras 416-20, also J.D., B.C., Political Case File No. 12 of 1857, p. 238, paras 2-3.

69. J.D., B.C., Political Case File No. 12 of 1857, p. 265, para 4.
70. *Ibid.*, p. 278, paras 2-4.
71. *Ibid.*, paras 5 and 7.
72. *Ibid.*, p. 351, para 2.
73. *Ibid.*, paras 3 and 5.
74. *Ibid.*, pp. 24-5, para 2.
75. C.P. D.G. Mandla (1912), p. 40.
76. F.P. P. , C-2449, Inclosure No. 67 in No. 2, para 12.
77. N.E., para 282.
78. *Ibid.*, paras 292-94.
79. *Ibid.*, paras 295-98.
80. *Ibid.*, para 299.
81. *Ibid.*, paras 300-1.
82. *Ibid.*, para 302.
83. F.P. P. , C-2449, Inclosure No. 8 in No. 21, p. 575.
84. N.E., para 434.
85. K.M. Panikkar, *A Survey of Indian History* (1954), p. 201.
86. D.P. Mishra, *op. cit.*, p. 90.

CHAPTER 9

Aftermath of the Revolt

Tatya Tope in the Saugor and Nerbudda Territories

Sometime after the suppression of the revolt in the Saugor and Nerbudda Territories, alarm was again spread with the arrival of Tatya Tope. He remained here nearly for a month from his entry in the Sagar district in the middle of October 1858 to his exit to Khargone on 19 November 1858. His arrival was too late. It was a delayed excercise. It created some ripples in these territories and beyond this it did nothing as we will examine it in detail.

Tatya Tope, the general of Nana Sahib's army, was one of the foremost leaders of the revolt of 1857 who harassed the British Generals more than any other revolutionary leader. As he was a great guerilla fighter, he lived to be a terror to the British armies. He was a capable general and could raise and organize an army even after severe reverses.

After the martyr's death of Rani Laxmi Bai on 20 July 1858 at Gwalior, Tatya Tope and Rao Sahib (brother of Nana Sahib) left Gwalior being accompanied by some rebels. In the words[1] of Dr. Anil Baran Ganguli: "At that stage Tatya Tope was absolutely helpless. He had no arms and ammunitions. He had not enough of food stuffs for maintaining the rebel army. Practically he had no large group of army at that time under his command. But neither Tatya Tope nor Rao Sahib became disheartened because of the dark picture in front of them. They became determined to take recourse to guerilla warfare in the lines of Shivaji, the great Maratha leader who had evolved it courageously at one time."

According to Dr. Dharam Pal[2] the most remarkable career of Tatya Tope began after he was driven from Gwalior after his defeat there by Sir Hugh Rose. "For almost one year he defied all the attempts of the British columns to capture him. Tatya Tope always outwitted and outmanoeuvred them. Even when the net seemed to be fast closing round him, he would effect a miraculous escape and by his daring initiative carry out some counter-stroke which would baffle the enemy. In the marathon race he was never really beaten" until betrayed by one of his trusted friends.

The great deeds performed by him at Jhansi, Kalpi, Gwalior and Central India, although constituted a bright and unforgettable chapter in the struggle for freedom, are outside the scope of this research-project. Here we are concerned with the events that occurred in many parts of the northern districts and south of the Narmada of these territories as a result of his presence.

During September 1858 after capturing Isagarh in Malwa, the Maratha force was split up. Tatya Tope marched on Chanderi while Rao Sahib advanced towards Lalitpur. Tatya Tope was hopeful that Sindhia's troops garrisoning Chanderi would join him. But they did nothing of the kind. After trying in vain to persuade them to come over to his side, Tatya Tope moved twenty miles south to Mungaoli on the left bank of river Betwa. Here he was overtaken by Major General Michel, who was commanding the British forces in Malwa, and defeated him on 10 October 1858. Tatya Tope fled across the Betwa to Lalitpur where he found Rao Sahib. The latter marched south-east about fifteen miles to Sindhwa. Michel, however, had anticipated this move, so he hurried after Rao Sahib and defeated him on 19 October 1858. Rao Sahib rejoined Tatya Tope at Lalitpur.[3] Both of them then united their forces and marched to Khajuria, with the intention of crossing the Betwa there and then moving southwards. But they were turned by Colonel Liddell at the Sairas Ghat. They then retraced their steps to Jakhlone and thence to Itawah and Khurai in the Sagar district. General Michel arrived at Lalitpur on 22 October and heard of the movements of Tatya Tope. The rebels proceeded in the Sagar district *via* Pali, Narhat Balabehat to Kanjia while General Michel proceeded *via* Malthone.[4]

Battle of Khurai on 25 October 1858

The intelligence of Tatya Tope with a large body of rebels having crossed the Betwa near Chanderi caused considerable alarm throughout the northern portion of the Sagar district. Major Western, its Deputy Commissioner reported[5] to Major Erskine on 18 October that the disaffected took advantage of it to spread false and alarming reports of the extent and resources of the rebels. He feared that some of the Narhat Thakurs with some designing Mukhtiars had been mainly instrumental in spreading these alarms. He further regretfully reported[6] that officer commanding at Maraura had left that place on account of this intelligence and the retirement of the 42nd from Malthone had the very worst effect. He had received information on 17 October that General Michel was in close pursuit of Tatya Tope. He had divided his force into columns, one was at Balabehat, the other at Malthone and the other near Jakhlone so that these parts might remain secure.

Major Western again reported[7] on 1 November that on 23 October General Michel overtook the Peshwa's army under Tatya Tope, Rao Sahib and Nawab of Banda. He at once commenced the attack and nearly 250 were killed. The rebels then fled *via* Barodia leaving Rahatgarh 4 miles to the east towards Bagrodh and their cavalry in search of forage plundered the villages of Chudamow, Jhilla and Moondra. On 24 October these rebels had plundered Khimlasa.

On the night of 24 October Michel heard that the rebels were at Khimlasa and knowing that they would move during the night, he marched on Khurai at 2 a.m. on the 25th and at dawn discovered the rebels crossing his front just beyond that place. Tatya Tope with his troops passed two or three hours afterwards to the south, losing on the way 40 men who were cut up by Colonel Bechar with a body of newly raised cavalry of the Central India Horse.[8]

Tatya Tope crossed the Narmada on 30 October 1858

After the battle of Khurai on 25 October 1858, where Tatya Tope had lost one wing of his army, he found himself at bay in the Central India and Bundelkhand. He, therefore, accompanied by Rao Sahib, crossed the Narmada about 40 miles above Hoshangabad to proceed towards the recently annexed Nagpur territory with the intention of inciting the Marathas there to revolt.

In the opinion of G.B. Malleson if it had happened twelve months earlier, the mutiny might have extended over to the whole of Western India. He stated[9] that the significant movement of Tatya Tope towards the Nagpur territory "if carried out twelve month earlier, would have produced an effect fatal for the time to British supremacy; a movement which would have roused the whole of the Western Presidency, have kindled revolt in the dominion of the Nizam, and have in its working, penetrated to southern India."

However, it was now too late to stir up in these territories the leaders and the people "who had been terrorised and subdued by an exhibition of force and merciless suppression, whose spirits had been shocked by mass hangings and executions, in which the innocent and offender shared the same fate. Villages that had been burnt down, families rendered destitute by the execution of their bread-winners, fields and farm-yards destroyed, could not now rise again in support of Tatya Tope and his men[10]." Tatya Tope's rushes and forays were, therefore, not accompanied with disturbances in the civil population.

Meanwhile, on 22 October 1858 George Plowden, Commissioner of Nagpur, reported[11] to the Government of India that on 18 October 1858, the Kotwar of the village of

Etawah, in the district of the Chhindwara, brought to the Thanna of Assair (ten miles from Chhindwara in a direct route from Bhopal and Hoshangabad) a flag of the colour of red ochre, a coconut, a betel nut and a green betel leaf and reported that those things had come, village to village from Chhindwara and had been given to him by a Kotwar of a neighbouring village. He had no doubt that the red ochre flag and its accompaniments had been put into circulation through the emissaries of Nana and Tatya Tope to signify their arrival in this way to arouse the people and expected that the subjects of the Bhonsla would flock to his standard. The Commissioner then took immediate measures by alerting the officers of the neighbouring districts to be ready to meet the situation.

Following in the wake of red-ochre flag, Tatya Tope crossed the Narmada with a great force reported to be 2,500 strong at Sandia Ghat near Fatehpur towards the end of October 1858. So sudden and unexpected was this eruption of the rebels across the Narmada that when the first information of it was received by the Deputy Commissioner of Narsinghpur from Nagpur on 3 November 1858, the rebels were already in his district and in his close proximity.[12]

Captain Baldwin, the Deputy Commissioner of Hoshangabad reported[13] on 6 November 1858 that on 30 and 31 October, Tatya Tope with the Banda Nawab and some of the petty chiefs and a force variously stated from 2,500 to 5,000 crossed the Narmada at Sandiya Ghat and went off to Fatehpur.

When Tatya Tope crossed Narmada, the Fatehpur Raja met him and presented him *nazar* and conducted him to Fatehpur by a short cut so as to evade the British troops lying in wait for him. Tatya Tope halted with him for a night and after receiving necessary supplies and guides from him, he continued his march. The Fatehpur Raja was accused of giving him supplies and guides and fell into a sad disgrace for a long time. An investigation was made but nothing proved against him.[14]

On 2 November on hearing of Lt. Kerr's advance from Sohagpur to Fatehpur, he deserted the latter place and entered the Pachmarhi hills in the Chhindwara district. He went to the Mahadev hills in Pachmarhi where Bhabut Singh, zamindar of Harrakot, joined him. In a semi-official note[15] of 19 November 1858, the Deputy Commissioner of Betul spoke of reports that a large body of rebels with guns was at Pachmarhi intending to move towards Betul. This was supposed to be the portion of force which crossed the Narmada with Tatya Tope and to have been left by him at Pachmarhi.

Tatya Tope in the Betul district

It is, however, to be noted that the peace of the Betul district was scarcely disturbed except when Tatya Tope passed through this district. From Pachmarhi Tatya Tope marched into the Betul district and reached Multai on 5 November. He halted for a day at Multai with his troops. He took bath in the river Tapti. It is said that he called all the Brahmans at that place and gave them a golden *asharfi* each which was afterwards confiscated by the Government. His troopers were directed to pay for their provisions and they did so, afterwards another trooper (probably from the Banda Nawab territories) came along and took away the money.[16] Though heads of Deshmukh and Deshpande families of Multai with a number of villagers joined his army, yet he did not get the anticipated support which he expected from the people in general at Multai, and elsewhere. He was convinced that once he reached the Maratha region, the people would offer him support. With almost super-human courage and tenacity he eluded his pursuers and did cross the Narmada. When he reached the other bank, he could not find a single village which would give him shelter. Everybody turned against him so that he had to fly again and take resort in the forests.[17] Thus, the people were showing no inclination whatsoever to join him or even to afford him the assistance in nature of supplies which was readily given in Rajputana.[18]

At Multai Tatya found that the roads to the plains were in the possession of the British forces. He was in a way shut out in the Betul district by the Britishers from further progress towards west or south. Multai was completely plundered and all the government buildings were burnt down. He made a turn north-westwards through Atner and Bhainsdehi into Nimar and reached Khargone on 19 November 1858.[19]

Tatya Tope's martyrdom : Betrayal and hanging at Shivpuri on 18 April 1859

At Khargone he found his progress impeded in all directions. Sir Hugh Rose preventing his advance into Khandesh, and General Roberts cutting him off from Gujarat, a small force was also moving towards him from Achalpur, in order to see that he did not enter into Berar.[20]

Meanwhile, General Michel following the track of the rebels after defeating them at Khurai, reached Hoshangabad on 7 November where he was joined by Brigadier Parke. Michel crossed into Betul while Parke crossed the Narmada at Hoshangabad and marched to Charwa, eighty miles south-east to Indore. Michel also moved in the same direction on learning the Tatya Tope's movements, while the troops at Asirgarh barred the way to the south across the Tapti river.[21] It is not necessary to trace in detail the course of Tatya Tope from Khargone onwards.

Finding himself surrounded on all sides, he crossed the Tapti and proceeded towards Baroda and then to Rajasthan. His last days were embittered by the desertion of companions and the final betrayal by his trusted colleague, Raja Mansingh who having rebelled against Sindhia, had joined Tatya Tope. Major Meade of Meade's Horse entered into negotiations with Mansingh for the betrayal of the fugitive. He led a party of the 9th Bombay Infantry on 7 April 1859 to the secret hiding place where Tatya Tope slept. They seized him while asleep, rudely awakened him and took his captive to Meade's camp and then to Sipri (Shivpuri), where he was court-martialled. He was charged with rebellion and waging war against the British Government between June 1857 and December 1858. He was sentenced to be hanged. The sentence was carried out at Sipri(Shivpuri) on 18 April 1859.[22]

As we have seen, for sometime he roamed about in the Narmada territory and held out 'fighting as he fled and flying as he fought'.[23] An officer who took part in the pursuit of Tatya Tope paid glowing tributes to him as he wrote[24] : "Each fresh Commandant who took the field fancied he could catch Tantia; prodigious marches were made, officers and men threw aside all luggage, even their tents, and accomplished forty miles daily - the rebels did fifty. The end was, all our horses were sore-backed and the halt of a week or ten days rendered absolute necessary." Moreover, "they had the very best of information and never trusted themselves to the open country when any force was near. We had the very worst of information, even in the territories of professed friendly Rajas. The sympathy of the people was on their side."

According to Dr. Radhakrishnan,[25] the ex-President of India : "One of the outstanding leaders on the Indian side was the Maratha soldier Tatya Tope. His constant harassment of an enemy far superior in equipment and his skill in utilising difficult terrain evading encirclement have gained him a recognised place in the history of Guerilla warfare."

Aftermath of the Revolt

Consequences of the stringent measures taken by the Government of India

The revolt of 1857 was put down with a relentless repression which led to a reign of terror in the country. It appeared that the authorities in England were not satisfied[26] with the repressive measures taken by the Government of India for the punishment of those who had been guilty of mutiny, desertion and rebellion during the recent disturbances in India. In the first place it had been a matter of complaint against the Government in India that the country was not put under martial law after the occurrence of mutinies.

In reply[27] to it, the Government of India recapitulated on 11 December 1857 the repressive measures taken them in order to clear the misunderstanding. They reported that the country was put under martial law wherever it was necessary and as soon it could answer any good purpose to do so but the power of trial by court martial did not extend to persons guilty of rebellion unless taken in the Commission of an overt act. Under these circumstances,[28] "the Government of India might have been much embarassed had Indian martial law had alone been relied upon and seeing that the number of officers at the disposal of Government was in many parts of the country wholly insufficient for the trial of mutineers and rebels, the Government of India took a course much more effectual than the establishment of martial law." Having first, by Act No.VIII of 1857, strengthened the hands of the officers by giving them greater powers for the assembling of Court Martial, and by making the proceedings of those courts more summary, the Government adopted measures which should give them the services not of their military and civil officers but of independent English gentlemen.

On 30 May when it was known that the mutiny of the sepoys had been followed in many places by rebellion of the populace, Act No.XI of 1857 was passed.[29] By this law persons guilty of rebellion or of waging war against the Government or of aiding or abetting therein, were liable to the punishment of death, and to the forfeiture of all their property, and the crime of harbouring rebels etc. was made heavily punishable. The supreme and local executive governments were empowered to issue a commission in any district in a state of rebellion for the trial of rebels or persons charged with any other crime against the state or with any heinous crime against person or property. The Commissioners were empowered to act singly, and were vested with absolute and final powers of judgement and execution without the presence of law officers and assessors. Finally, the possession of arms in any district in which it might be prohibited by the executive government was made penal.

By Act No. XIV of 1857,[30] passed on 6 June, provision was made for the punishment of persons convicted of exciting mutiny or sedition in the army, the offender was rendered liable to the punishments of death and forfeiture of all his property, and persons guilty of harbouring such offenders were made liable to heavy punishment. Power was also given to general courts martial to try all persons, whether amenable to the Articles of War or not, charged with any offence punishable by this or preceding Act. The supreme and local executive governments were authorised to issue commissions in any district for the trial by the single Commissioner, without the assistance of law officers or assessors, and with absolute and final power of judgement and execution, of any crime against the state or any heinous offence whatever the term 'heinous offence' being declared to include every crime attended with great personal violence, committed with the intention of forwarding the designs of those who were waging war against the state.

By Act No. XVI of 1857,[31] all heinous offences committed in any district under martial law or in any district to which this Act might be extended, were made punishable by death, transportation or imprisonment and by forfeiture of all property and effects.

These enormous powers had been largely excercised. They had been entrusted not to military officers only but to civil officers and trustworthy persons not connected with the Government, who, under martial law properly so called, would have had no authority and the law had thereby been put in force in parts of the country where there were few troops and no officers to spare for such purpose. In all the three Acts Nos. XI, XIV and XVI, European British subjects were expressly exempted from their operation.[32]

By Act No. XVIII of 1857,[33] power was given to Sessions Judges and to any person or persons, civil or military, to whom the Executive Government might issue a commission for the purpose, to try for mutiny or desertion, any person subject to the Articles of War for the native army, with final powers of judgement and execution. Police officers were empowered to arrest without warrant persons, suspected of being mutineers or deserters. Zamindars and others were made penally responsible for not giving early intelligence of persons suspected of mutiny or desertion resorting to their estates.

Lastly, by Act No. XXV of 1857,[34] the property and effects of all persons amenable to the Articles of War for Indian army, guilty of mutiny, were declared forfeit, and stringent means were provided for the seizure of such property and effects and for the adjudication of forfeiture in all cases, whether the guilty person be convicted, or whether he died or escaped before trial.

In conclusion,[35] the Government of India argued that "not only therefore is it not the case that the martial law was not proclaimed in districts in which there was a necessity for it, but the measures taken for the arrest, summary trial and punishment of heinous offenders of every class, civil as well as military, were far more widely spread and certainly not less stringent than that could have resulted from martial law."

Thus, the British officers were armed with summary powers to stamp out all signs of disaffection and break the determination of those who showed any independence of spirit. By an exhibition of unashamed and ruthless power they kept down the people of India, and curbed their spirit to rise against them for a while. Against this background we will examine the aftermath of the revolt in the Saugor and Nerbudda Territories.

Cruel reprisals in the Saugor and Nerbudda Territories

Court martial and immediate hanging of the rebels

Like other parts of India, all the above-mentioned Acts passed by the Government of India for the suppression of revolt in the country were also enforced in these territories. Particularly Act XVIII of 1857[36] was enforced with great severity in the districts to the north of the Narmada. This legislation gave summary powers to the Deputy Commissioners. Section II of this Act empowered them to try cases of desertion and mutiny. Section III conferred upon the police officers to apprehend any person without warrant. On the mere suspicion of his being a mutineer or deserter, the Deputy Commissioner was empowered to sentence the offender to death or transportation of life and the sentence passed by him was final. The sentence of death was to be carried out without any delay, or at such time as he might direct.

The innumerable instances of the imposition of the court martial and immediate hanging of the rebels were enumerated while discussing the suppression of the revolt in these territories in the preceding two chapters. Where the officers were not available for the court martial, the drum-head court martial was held and the British never missed any opportunity of cruelly repressing the revolt.

Wholesale destruction of the villages

As the number of lives lost by hanging, execution, indiscriminate shooting and wholesale burning of villages must have been enormous, the people were terrified. The British were so blinded with rage and hatred that they resorted to wholesale destruction of villages. Villages everywhere were burnt down and destroyed. It would appear that a common method to strike a terror into the hearts of the people, was to set fire the whole villages in a most indiscriminate way which was carried on with such thoroughgoing ruthlessness that Major Erskine was alarmed at the wholesale burning of villages and depopulation of wide stretches of territory.[37] In a circular,[38] dated 30 October 1857, he wrote to the District officers as follows :

"The Commissioner has observed that in some instances there still exists an inclination to destroy entire villages which have been inhabitated by persons who have rebelled against the state.... although the measure was not entirely prohibited by the Government, yet a wholesale destruction of property by the officers of Government without due regard to the guilt or innocence of those who were affected by it was reprehensible.... The wholesale destruction of villages or property is hereby prohibited without the special orders of the Government previously obtained in each case."

Drawing attention of all the officers to the earlier instructions respecting the punishment of mutineers, deserters and rebels and the burning of villages issued on 31 July 1857, the Commissioner issued specific instructions regarding the destruction and disposal of properties of the rebels. The policy laid down with regard to the lands and estates of the insurgents was to "bestow the estate on a faithful and loyal subject", and to resettle the unoffending inhabitant on his land in the event of his having left it either due to the pressure of rebels or fear of the troops under British officers moving about to restore law and order.[39]

Complete destruction of the forts

In the last para[40] of this Circular, the instructions were given to them that "all fortified buildings when taken should be razed as early as possible when such may be practicable and there may be no intention of occupying them with our troops." Accordingly, while suppressing the revolt in this region, the following forts were completely destroyed by the British duly pointed out earlier. The list runs as follows:

1. In the Sagar district : Rahatgarh and Garhakota
2. In the Damoh district : Khamkhera, Balakot, Hindoria and Narsinghgarh

3. In the Jabalpur district : Bilahri and Bijairaghogarh
4. In the Narsinghpur district : Heerapur
5. In the Hoshangabad district : Satwas

Besides these large forts, there were several small forts which were completely destroyed by the British.

Confiscation of the property of the rebels

The confiscation of the property of those who had fought against the British in these territories was another severe measure. No mercy was shown to anyone against whom there was the slightest suspicion of disloyalty. The work of confiscation was methodically carried on, in so thorough and sweeping a way, that almost every person of consequence suffered from its unjust operation.[41]

The Deputy Commissioners were asked to prepare a list of persons who had risen against the British authority with a view to confiscate their property. Every village was thus surveyed, and names of persons recorded whose guilt or innocence was never carefully scrutinized. In this manner, district after district was combed and the property of suspected persons was confiscated. Thus, the policy of confiscation was pushed on with great severity and the slightest excuse or suspicion was enough to bring the people under its cruel operation.[42]

In the Sagar district[43] where the Rajas of Banpur and Shahgarh had played a leading and dominant role in the revolt, their states were confiscated and both the rulers were banished from their states as already mentioned while dealing with the suppression of the revolt in this district.

In the Damoh district[44] the estate of the Mangarh was confiscated as a reprisal for the revolt of the Raja. His whole property was confiscated.

In the Jabalpur district[45] as the leading zamindars of the territories around Jabalpur had been the foremost in organizing a large force against the British, they were the worst sufferers from the confiscations. For instance all the property of Raja Shankar Shah and his son, Raghunath Shah, was confiscated, and even when the days of cruel and vengeful reprisals were over, the British authorities did not spare the innocent and helpless widow of Raghunath Shah whom they decided to be "worthy of no consideration". Similarly the ruling family of Bijairaghogarh was banished and the principality confiscated.

In the Register of Confiscated Estates in the Jabalpur district,[46] a list of the confiscated estates, dated 15 September 1858, was as follows :

"Names of rebels	Land confiscated		
	Malguzaree Area	Muafee Jumma	
1. Raja Shankar Shah	737	795	Farmed till new settlement to
2. Raja Raghunath Shah	210	540	Junurjun Purohit

Obaree (or quit rent) of 2 villages : Poaitha and Khoogaon."

In continuation of the above entries, a supplementary statement of estates[47] which would be confiscated, dated 15 September 1858, was as follows :

"Name of rebel	Name of Pargana	Name of Mouja	Jumma	Remarks
1. Bhao Singh	Bilahree	Mohuma	125	These estates are in the courts of being
2. Himmut Singh	Bilahree	Neemkheda	200	farmed for recovery
3. Raja Mehpal Singh	Koombhee Bhutgaon	Taluqa	3400	of balances due by the rebel
4. Issoredoss	Koombhee	Taluqa Khirainee	4500	defaulters."
5. Lachman Singh & Moorut Singh	Sonepur	Narainpur	834	

These estates and hundreds of even less known land holders, scattered all over the district, were also deprived of their property on the slightest suspicions. There were many who had forsaken their estates and gone into hiding to escape from the British persecutions. A prize was put on their heads and all their possessions were confiscated.[48]

In the Narsinghpur district,[49] a list of estates which had been confiscated, dated 3 April 1858, was as follows :

"Pergunna	Muhal	Proprietor	Jumma	Ground of confiscation
1. Sreenuggur	Moirpeepuran	Kishore Singh and Bholey	468	For connection with rebels
2. Chawarpatta	Dilwar (5 villages)	Narwar Singh	865	For rebellion
3. "	Muddunpore (7 villages)	Dilhun Shah	310	For rebellion
4. ".	Half village of Gungae	Shobha Singh	108	For connection with rebels
5. "	Half village of Kuttungee	Rao Bahadur Singh	570	For rebellion
6. Narsinghpur	Heerapur khas (9 villages)"	Sutkunjoo	1272	For rebellion

A statement[50] of these states by whom now held was also given as follows : "Moirpeeprun was held by Madaree Malguzar of Salewarah, Dilwar and Muddunpore were held by Dewan Nizam Shah, Gungae was held by Sawant Singh, Kuttungee was held by Rao Soorut Singh and Heerapur Khas by Ranee Gunga, mother of Oomed Kaur of Diheree."

In the Mandla district,[51] in the register of confiscated properties, dated 8 July 1858 only two names were given, Bikramjeet Lodhee of Ramgarh and Bijai Singh Lodhee of Shaipoorah.

The Shahpur *taluka* in the Betul district[52] was confiscated for complicity on the part of the *malguzar* in rebellion.

Rewards for the apprehension of rebels

In accordance with the orders of the Government of India, Major Erskine submitted[53] on 5 March 1858, a list of leaders of rebel bands in the Jabalpur Division for whose apprehension he had offered rewards of various denominations. By orders of the Government of the North-Western Provinces, he was authorized to offer rewards upto 500 rupees for the apprehension of the offenders, merely reporting the circumstances for the information of the Government when the amount exceeded 100 rupees. He reported the circumstances of the rewards accordingly. As the Sagar list had not reached him, he requested the sanction of the Government for these rewards for the remaining districts : (See : Appendix V). It included 59 names in the Jabalpur, 29 in Damoh, 5 in Narsinghpur, 42 in Hoshangabad, 15 in Mandla, 2 in the Seoni and none in the Betul districts of his division. It also included 11 names in Nagod for which rewards were offered by Lt. Osborne, Superintendent of Nagod. This long list signifies the intensity of the revolt in this region which in the long run, proved far more troublesome to suppress. The Government of India duly sanctioned[54] these rewards on 11 May 1858.

A list of rebel leaders in the Sagar district containing 95 names was duly submitted[55] on 30 March 1858 on getting the information of the Sagar authorities : (See : Appendix VI). It was duly sanctioned[56] by the Government of India on 17 May 1858.

These lists contained the names of all prominent leaders of this region who played a leading and dominant role in their respective districts.

Racial bitterness and arrogance

One of the consequences of the outbreak and its failure was to create a racial bitterness which poisoned the relationship between the Englishmen and Indians almost permanently. It generated in the minds of the British a hysterical sense of fear, which found an expression in an exhibition of racial arrogance.[57] To what absurd limits this attitude could take them is revealed in a Circular letter[58] issued by Major Erskine to the Deputy Commissioners of the districts in the Saugor and Nerbudda Territories. It is dated 11 March 1858 when according to Erskine, "the tide of rebellion seemed to be receding." The Circular is as follows:

"I shall feel obliged by your fully making known to your all Government servants that when they meet an European gentleman, whether he may be in civil employ or not, that they will be considered as disrespectful and be treated accordingly, if they do not make the customary *salaam*.

It is not necessary that policemen should make a military salute. I consider their native custom will show greater respect.

Native not in the service of Government cannot be punished for not saluting, but all well-tried and all well-inclined natives will never pass or meet a gentleman without *salaaming* and though no orders could be issued on the subject, I beg you will intimate to all, in ordinary conversation and in a kindly manner, that by their markedly showing respect to European gentlemen after their native fashion, the act will conduce much towards healing the wounds which more or less existed in most districts since the last outbreak."

The stage was thus set for a high-handed repressive rule in India. The vestiges of popular revolt, wherever they were seen, were crushed ruthlessly by wreaking vengeance upon the people indiscriminately. It would appear that the events of 1857 had knocked all sentiments out of the British character. They were filled with "the mutiny-mentality" which meant that in their thought and action there was no room for considerations of human feelings and civilised behaviour.[59]

Economic exploitation of the Saugor and Nerbudda Territories

One of the results[60] of the Government passing from the hands of the Company to the Crown by the Act of 1858 was the free play given to the private traders, planters and other commercial adventures who had formerly been prevented from entering the country, in competition with the Company. In fact, Government tacitly encouraged the large-scale migration of the Englishmen into India, in the belief that a larger European population would be a safeguard against another rising by Indians. Thus, in the sixties of the nineteenth century there was an influx of the Englishmen in the country, all of them filled with the anti-Indian sentiments which prevailed in England during the 1857-58 outbreak. These Englishmen economically exploited these territories to the extreme like the other parts of India during the later half of the nineteenth century. However, the pace was slow in the beginning but its consequences were the worst later on.

Formation of the Central Provinces in 1861

After the revolt of 1857, it was finally decided to attach these territories to the Nagpur territory which had been annexed by Lord Dalhousie in the abence of direct heirs. Several considerations[61] led to the merger of these territories to the Nagpur territory to form the Central Provinces in 1861. At the time of outbreak of the revolt, these territories were a part of the North-Western Provinces. It was considered that the linking of these territories to the North-Western Provinces was unnatural. Ever since these territories were ceded to the British, they had been shifted back and forth, between the North-Western Provinces and direct administration under the Supreme Government. The economy and administrative problems of the Narmada valley were very different from those of the Gangetic valley. It was difficult for the Government at Agra to excercise proper supervision over the administration of these territories. Therefore, the Government of India felt that if these territories were joined to the Nagpur province which was peaceful during the revolt, it would conduce to orderly life and the preservation of peace in them. This view was further supported by reasons of good communications and common economic interests between the Nagpur province and these territories.

Thus, the map of the Saugor and Nerbudda Territories, which had been the centre of violence and disturbance during 1857-58, underwent a total change. It took the shape which more or less continued till the reorganisation of states on the linguistic basis in 1956.

REFERENCES

1. Anil Baran Ganguli, *Guerilla Fighter of the First Freedom Movement* (1980), pp. 93-4.
2. Dharm Pal, *Tatya Tope : The Hero of India's First War of Independence, 1857-58* (1957), preface p. iii.
3. *Ibid.*, p. 201.
4. S.B. Choudhuri, *Civil Rebellion in the Indian Mutinies* (1957), p. 222.
5. J.D., B.C., Political Case File No. 74 of 1858 (No paging).
6. *Ibid.*, paras 4 and 6.
7. *Ibid.*, No. 58 of 1858 (No paging).
8. *The Revolt in Central India, 1857-59*, compiled in the Intelligence Branch, Army Head Quarters, India (1908), p. 217.
9. G.B. Malleson, *History of the Indian Mutiny*, Vol. III (1880), p. 343.
10. D.P. Mishra, ed., *Freedom Movement in Madhya Pradesh* (1956), pp. 87-8.
11. J.D., B.C., Foreign Case File No. 78 of 1858.
12. *Ibid.*
13. *Ibid.*, Political Case File No. 58 of 1858.
14. C.P. D.G., Hoshangabad (1908), p. 38.
15. J.D., B.C., Political Case File No. 5 of 1858.
16. C.P. D.G., Betul (1906), p. 256.
17. S.N. Sen, *Eighteen Fifty Seven* (1957), pp. xv-xvi.
18. C.P. D.G. Betul, *op. cit.*, p. 40.
19. M.P. D.G., Betul (1971), p. 62.
20. D.P. Mishra, *op. cit.*, p. 88.
21. *The Revolt in Central India, 1857-59*, *op. cit.*, p. 219.
22. D.P. Mishra, *op. cit.*, pp. 88-9.
23. S.B. Choudhuri, *op. cit.*, p. 222.
24. *The Revolt in Central India, 1857-59*, *op. cit.*, p. 235.

25. Dharm Pal, *op. cit.*, foreword.
26. Home, Public, Letter to Court, 11 December 1857, No. 144.
27. *Ibid.*, paras 3 and 11.
28. *Ibid.*, para 12.
29. *Ibid.*, para 13.
30. *Ibid.*, para 14.
31. *Ibid.*, para 15.
32. *Ibid.*, paras 16-17.
33. *Ibid.*, para 18.
34. *Ibid.*, para 19.
35. *Ibid.*, para 20.
36. D.P. Mishra, *op. cit.*, p. 93.
37. R.M. Sinha, *1857 in the Jabalpur District* (1957), pp. 22-3.
38. J.D., B.C., Judicial Case File No. 31 of 1857, Circular No. 201 of 1857.
39. *Ibid.*
40. *Ibid*, para 10.
41. D.P. Mishra, *op. cit.*, p. 103.
42. R.M. Sinha, *op. cit.*, p. 27.
43. Foreign, Political, Progs., 3 September 1858, Nos.115-30.
44. D.P. Mishra, *op. cit.*, p. 103.
45. *Ibid.*
46. J.D., B.C., Revenue Case File No. 20 of 1858, p. 16.
47. *Ibid.*, p. 18.
48. M.P. D.G., Jabalpur (1968), p. 109.
49. J.D., B.C., Revenue Case File No. 20 of 1858, p. 1.
50. *Ibid.*
51. *Ibid.*, p. 22.
52. M.P. D.G., Betul, *op. cit.*, p. 63.
53. Foreign, Secret, Supplement Cons., dated 30 December 1859, Nos. 357-58.
54. *Ibid.*, No. 359.
55. *Ibid.*, Nos.361-62.
56. *Ibid.*, No. 363, also J.D., B.C., Political Case File No. 1 of 1858, p. 331.
57. D.P. Mishra, *op. cit.*, p. 94.
58. *Ibid.*, pp. 94-5.
59. *Ibid.*, p. 96.
60. *Ibid.*, p. 96.
61. *Ibid.*, pp. 107-9.

CHAPTER 10

Conclusion

The Saugor and Nerbudda Territories were swept by the waves of revolt of 1857 only a month after it had flooded the Meerut-Delhi area in May 1857. The people here had put up a brave resistance to the mighty power of the British under the leadership of the dispossessed landlords. The beginning of it was made by the revolt of the 3rd Irregular Cavalry and the 42nd Bengal Native Infantry at Sagar on 1 July 1857 which had spread like a wild fire in the whole region. At the close of September 1857, nearly whole of these territories were in a state of revolt. Upto the end of 1857 the British could make little headway as no reinforcements could be spared for its suppression.

In early 1858 the British forces under the command of Sir Hugh Rose marched through Sagar district and reduced the forts of Rahatgarh and Garhakota and relieved Sagar. The defeat of the insurgents at the Madanpur pass on 3 March 1858 left no doubt that the British would ultimately be successful. He was followed by General Whitlock who arrived at Jabalpur in the first week of February 1858, to help in the suppression of the rebellion in this region. He was asked to march to Damoh which had been abandoned by the British in September 1857. Damoh was re-occupied by him on 4 March 1858. The victories of Rose and Whitlock broke the spell of popular resistance in the Sagar and Damoh districts. The rebellions in Jabalpur and other districts were also gradually put down and Major Erskine, the Commissioner of these territories had reported[1] to the Government of North-Western Provinces on 10 August 1858, "I can now with confidence and pleasure state that peace is restored to my division of eight districts, for although we have some leaders still at large, their followers are but few."

This theme is unfolded in this research-project in ten chapters. In the first chapter, in the history and administration of the Saugor and Nerbudda Territories, its history is traced since 1818 when these territories were acquired by the East India Company from the Marathas after the third Anglo-Maratha war. They were formed what was called 'the Saugor and Nerbudda Territories' in 1820. After the suppression of the revolt of 1857, these territories were merged in the Nagpur territory in 1861 to form the Central Provinces. Thus, these territories came into existence in 1820 and had a span of nearly 40 years till merged in 1861 in a newly created Central Provinces. The nature and consequences of the British rule in these territories led to the Bundela rebellion of 1842 and the revolt of 1857 in them.

The establishment of the British rule and administration was followed by the political, economic and social unsettlement in these territories. On the economic front, the foreign rule failed miserably and brought havoc for the agricultural community both for the feudal lords and the cultivators. It can be said that the greatest evil consequence of the British rule was its land revenue policy. The excessive assessment of revenue and the rigidity in its recovery led to disastrous results. The land revenue was assessed so high and the levy demanded was so exhorbitant that they led to rapid impoverishment of the people and retarded the progress of the country.

In the second chapter, in the Bundela rebellion of 1842 and its aftermath, we have seen how the British revenue administration was the backbone of this insurrectionary movement. The British rule had undermined the power and influence of the local chiefs and the imposition of an excessive land revenue had brought about an economic ruin of the peasantry. Hence, both joined hands to oust the British regime in 1842 and found an opportunity when the British arms suffered a severe rebuff during the debacle of the first Afghan War in 1842. This rebellion was, however, suppressed in a year or so. It was a feudal revolt against the British rule under the leadership of the dispossessed feudal chiefs.

It is noteworthy that ever since these territories were taken over from the Marathas, their administrative arrangements had been frequently changing, shifting back and forth between the North-Western Provinces and direct administration under the Supreme Government. Hence, the British could not adopt a consistent policy in the spheres of revenue assessment and matters of general policy towards the chiefs and the common people.

It is also to be noted that by the suppression of the Bundela rebellion of 1842, the spirit of the rebellion was simply scotched and not killed in these territories as is evident fifteen years later when the smouldering discontent ultimately burst into the flames of 1857. In a way this rebellion was a prelude to the revolt of 1857 in these territories as during 1857 the major centres of revolt were precisely those places which had risen against the British during 1842.

In the third chapter, in the causes of the revolt in these territories, we have seen that its causes were not different from the other parts of the country. The revolt of 1857 was, however, no sudden occurrence. It was the culmination of nearly a century of old discontent against the British rule and its imperialist policies since the battle of Plassey which exploited the country to the extreme.

The aftermath of the Bundela rebellion and the policies adopted thereafter by the British further aggravated the discontent which added fuel to the fire of the revolt of 1857 in this region. In the background of the general discontent prevailing in the entire country, the causes of the revolt in these territories were studied in detail under three major heads *viz.*, (i) grievances of the feudal class; (ii) discontent of the people, and (iii) grievances of the sepoys of the Bengal Native Army employed here. The role of the *chapaties*, the bone-dust story and the sensitive issue of the greased cartridges were also discussed in detail.

In can be said that these causes of discontent were responsible for the explosive situation in India in general and in these territories in particular. It was like a ripe volcano and only a spark was needed which was supplied by the greased cartridges.

In the fourth chapter, in the outbreak of the revolt in the Sagar district, we have seen how the waves of the revolt of 1857 had touched this district in June 1857 only a month after it had flooded the Meerut-Delhi area in May 1857. The rebellious activities of Raja Mardan Singh of Banpur and Raja Bakhat Bali of Shahgarh, the neighbouring states of the Sagar district, in this district were discussed in detail. These two Rajas were mainly responsible for the revolt in it.

The Sagar troops which were sent for the relief of Chanderi showed the first sign of mutiny on 13 June 1857. The mutiny at Malthone on 25 June led to the confinement of the Europeans at Sagar in the Sagar fort on 29 June 1857. The mutiny at Sagar on 1 July 1857 by the 3rd Irregular Cavalry and the 42nd Bengal Native Infantry was suppressed on 7 July 1857. It was the beginning of the revolt of 1857 in these territories which had spread to the other parts and the disturbances became general. The repercussions of the mutiny at Sagar were noteworthy as by the end of August 1857 the Sagar district passed into the hands of the rebels except the Sagar fort and town. It was a great landmark in the revolt of 1857 in these territories.

According to Charles Ball[2] at the close of September 1857 nearly whole of the Saugor and Nerbudda Territories were in a state of revolt. The events in all the districts of these territories upto September 1857 were, therefore, discussed in the fifth and sixth chapters to maintain uniformity in dealing with the subject. In may, however, be noted that the revolt came to a climax more slowly in this region than other parts of the north India.

In the fifth chapter, in the spread of the revolt in the Damoh district, we have seen how on the outbreak of the revolt in Sagar, there was a panic in Damoh and the Deputy Commissioner of Damoh escaped to Narsinghpur, the neighbouring district and there was anarchy in the whole district. However, this district was recovered in July 1857 by the British troops but again in August 1857 the district passed into the hands of the rebels except the Sadar station. The district was again recovered by the British forces on 29 August 1857. But on hearing of the revolt of the 50th Bengal Native Infantry at Nagod and the 52nd Bengal Native Infantry at Jabalpur, and due to the paucity of the forces, this district was abandoned on 21 September 1857 and handed over to the Panna ruler. It was another landmark in the revolt of 1857 in these territories.

In the sixth chapter, in the further progress in Jabalpur and other districts, we have seen how the situation in Jabalpur was one of more anxiety and less action. The reaction of the mutiny at Sagar led to the shelter of the Europeans in the Agency-house on 4 July 1857. There were many disturbances in the Jabalpur district. The circumstances which led to the martyrdom of Raja Shankar Shah and his son, Raghunath Shah, the last rulers of the Gond dynasty of Rani Durgavati, on 18 September were discussed in detail. Consequently, the 52nd Bengal Native Infantry at Jabalpur mutinied on the same day and marched towards Patan, Katangi and Sleemanabad.

In the Narsinghpur district in August 1857 inroads by the Bundelas and the Bhopal rebels were made into the Chawarpatha pargana, north of the Narmada river, and the town and thanna of Tendukhera was plundered. In fact, all to the north of the Narmada river, except the districts of Jabalpur and Mandla, were in a state of anarchy while all to the south of the Narmada was in perfect peace.

In the Hoshangabad district the Nemawar pargana, which is on the right bank of the Narmada river, was disturbed.

On 3 July much alarm was created by *sowars* from Indore bringing exaggerated news of the rising at Indore, to the effect that Holkar had rebelled and blown away the Resident and all the British officers with guns. Soon towns of Harda, Seoni-Malwa and Sohagpur were disturbed. In September the Mewatees of Satwas in the Nemawar pargana had risen in rebellion.

In the Mandla district, signs of rebellion were visible in early July 1857 as some Malguzars had refused to pay revenue. On 2 September the Sohagpur thanna was driven in, and the attacks on the thanna of Shahpura followed on 25 and the Ramgarh thanna, south of the Narmada river, on 26 September. The police was driven in and the government buildings were burnt. Two-thirds of the Mandla district was lost and the rebels threatened Mandla itself.

The echoes of the revolt were also heard in the remaining districts of Seoni and Betul, south of the Narmada river. It is, however, to be noted that the revolt had spread to the north of the Narmada and a few ripples travelled to the south of this river.

In the seventh chapter, in the suppression of the revolt in the Sagar and Damoh districts, we have seen how the tension in the territories to the north of the Narmada river continued for a long time due to the paucity of the British forces. After the suppression of the revolt of 1857 in the major centres of India, the counter-offensive was launched by the British to quell the uprisings in Bundelkhand and the Saugor and Nerbudda Territories.

The British force under Sir Hugh Rose arrived in Sagar district in early 1858 and occupied Rahatgarh and Garhakota and relieved Sagar. At Sagar on 3 February he emancipated the European officers and men with their families who had been confined in the fort for nearly eight months. On 3 March 1858 he defeated the rebels at Madanpur pass and with this victory ended the last vestiges of the popular revolt in the Sagar district. After sometime the Rajas of

Banpur and Shahgarh had surrendered to the British but both these Rajas had to pay the heaviest price for participating in this revolt as their states were confiscated and both were banished from their respective states.

As already referred to, the Damoh district was abandoned and handed over to the Panna ruler. It was re-occupied by the British forces under General Whitlock on 4 March 1858 nearly after six months. The most turbulent of the rebels, Thakur Kishor Singh of Hindoria, alongwith other rebels, however, surrendered before Major Erskine in December 1858 on condition that no further action would be taken against them and peace was restored in it.

In the eighth chapter, in the suppression of the revolt in the Jabalpur and other districts, in the Jabalpur district the revolt was confined to the north of the Narmada river except in one instance in the Bargi pargana which was suppressed in December 1857. It was a turning point in the rebellion in this district as not a rebel was seen to the south of the Narmada river afterwards. One of the heroic figures of this movement in this district was the young Thakur Sarju Prasad Singh of Bijairaghogarh who may be considered as one of the early martyrs in the struggle for freedom.

There were many disturbances in the remaining districts and the British Government had a great difficulty in suppressing them. In the Narsinghpur district, the Chawarpatha pargana was cleared off all the rebels in January 1858. The most formidable rebel leader, Delun Shah, was captured and executed on 16 May 1858. In this revolt, most of its chief Malguzars were either passive or actively helped the British officers. Those who helped were amply rewarded.

In the Hoshangabad district, after many encounters with the rebels, the Nemawar pargana was finally occupied in January 1858. The most prominent of the rebels, Thakur Daulat Singh of Raghogarh, however, committed suicide on 19 June 1858 and peace was restored.

In the Mandla district at the close of September 1857,

two-thirds of it was in rebellion. Later on when the situation became worse, its Deputy Commissioner escaped to Seoni, the neighbouring district, on 26 November 1857. He returned to Mandla on 15 January 1858 when the situation became normal. The fort of Ramgarh was captured on 2 April 1858 and the estate was confiscated. Shahpura was re-occupied on 24 April. Sohagpur was attacked and taken with the help of Nagpur force from Raipur and Rewa troops on 18 June and the Mandla district was settled.

As referred to earlier, the districts of Seoni and Betul, to the south of the Narmada river, were least affected. The disturbances in these districts were easily suppressed.

As already mentioned, Major W.C. Erskine, the Commissioner of these territories had reported on 10 August 1858 that peace was finally restored in his division of eight districts. The main cause of the failure of the revolt in these territories, like other parts of India, was that these rebels were acting without concert, each for his own individual interest and without sympathy with the mutinous sepoys.

In the ninth chapter, in the aftermath of the revolt, we have seen how sometime after the suppression of the revolt in these territories, alarm was again spread with the arrival of Tatya Tope. He remained here for a month from his entry in the Sagar district in the middle of October 1858 to his exit to Khargone on 19 November 1858. His arrival was too late. It was a delayed excercise. It created some ripples here and beyond this it did nothing.

The cruel reprisals in these territories like the court martial and immediate hanging of the rebels, wholesale destruction of the villages, complete destruction of the forts, confiscation of the property of the rebels, rewards for the apprehension of the rebels were discussed in detail. The economic exploitation of these territories was carried on to the extreme by the Britishers. After the revolt of 1857, it was finally decided to attach these territories to the Nagpur territory which had been annexed by Lord Dalhousie in the absence of direct heirs. Several considerations led to this merger. This became the nucleus of the Central Provinces which was formed in 1861.

Thus, the map of the Saugor and Nerbudda Territories, which had been the centre of violence and disturbance during the revolt of 1857, underwent a total change. It took the shape which was more or less continued till the reorganisation of states on the linguistic basis in 1956.

If we take the overall view of the revolt of 1857 in these territories, we find that the revolt did not affect all the districts equally. In the north of the Narmada river, the districts of Sagar, Damoh and Jabalpur were the centres of anti-British resistance which had carried on a persistant war against the British. As already referred to, the martial law was imposed in these districts. The feudal lords and the people of these districts were the worst sufferers. The intensity of the revolt in these districts was more than the other districts. However, even in these districts some of its parts were not affected at all. In the Narsinghpur, Hoshangabad and Mandla districts, the movement was not so intense as the above-mentioned districts. It was suppressed in due course of time and the feudal lords and the people in these districts also suffered to a great extent. As we have already seen, there was a general panic amongst the Britishers during the revolt and in two instances, in Damoh and in Mandla, their deputy commissioners escaped to the neighbouring districts in panic. The rebellion never went south of the Narmada river except in an attempt in the Bargi pargana in the Jabalpur district and in the Ramgarh estate in the Mandala district which was soon checked. The districts of Seoni and Betul, to the south of the Narmada river, were least affected and the disturbances in these districts were easily suppressed.

It is noteworthy that the events in these territories showed almost all the peculiarities that characterized the revolt of 1857 as a whole. In these territories as elsewhere in the country, the revolt took the forms of the sepoy revolt, the feudal resistance, popular outbreak and plundering attacks from outside the state.

As we have seen that the nature of the British rule and its consequences had antagonized both the local chiefs and the people alike in this region which was manifested in the forms of the Bundela rebellion of 1842 and the revolt of 1857. Despite their backwardness, they faced the British with courage and determination under the leadership of the dispossessed and discontented feudal chiefs.

It may, however, be concluded that the revolt of 1857 was the last bid of the feudal India to regain its lost supremacy. In the words of Jawahar Lal Nehru,[3] it "was the last flicker of the feudal India." The Saugor and Nerbudda Territories were no exception to it. As such the revolt of 1857 was the feudal revolt against the British rule in these territories like the Bundela rebellion of 1842. Under the prevailing circumstances, it was but natural as the age of the popular revolt or mass upsurge had not yet dawned in India.

In this context it is noteworthy that at the time of outbreak of revolt, there were very few Europeans in these territories. In the Appendix D[4] of his Narrative of Events Major Erskine stated the list of Europeans in the Jabalpur garrison as 68 men, 30 women and 48 children, 146 in all. Likewise in Appendix N,[5] he stated the nominal roll of Europeans, Commissioned and non-commissioned officers, buglers etc. present with the headquarters at Sagar as 173 men, 67 women and 130 children, 370 in all. In the other district headquarters there were very few Europeans as in Damoh district there was only one civilian and two military officers, who were governing it.

The total strength of the British army and the ratio of the Europeans was also very small[6] looking to the vast area of these territories. At the time of outbreak in the Sagar district, the 31st Bengal Native Infantry was composed of 9

European officers, 2 European non-commissioned officers, 15 Indian officers and 860 men. In the 42nd Bengal Native Light Infantry, there were 11 European officers, 2 European non-commissioned officers and 672 Indian non-commissioned officers and rank and file. The 3rd Irregular Cavalry was composed of 2 European officers, 7 Indian officers and 396 Indian non-commissioned officers and rank and file. In the Jabalpur district in the 52nd Bengal Native Infantry there were 12 European officers, 2 European non-commissioned officers, 8 Indian officers and 626 Indian non-commissioned officers and rank and file. Thus, there were only 41 European commissioned and non-commissioned officers in the Bengal army which had mutinied or manifested a disposition of mutiny in these territories.

It goes to the credit of the British that despite their very small number and army they managed such a vast region like the Saugor and Nerbudda Territories and successfully suppressed the revolt.

One of the consequences of the outbreak and its failure was to create a racial bitterness which poisoned the relationship of Englishmen and Indians almost permanently. It generated in the minds of the British a hysterical sense of fear, which found an expression in an exhibition of racial arrogance.

On the failure of the revolt of 1857, the stage was set for a high-handed repressive rule in India. The vestiges of popular revolt, whenever they were seen, were crushed ruthlessly by wreaking vengenance upon the people indiscriminately. It would appear that the events of 1857, had knocked out all sentiments out of the British character. They were filled with "the mutiny-mentality" which meant that in their thought and action there was no room for considerations of human feelings and civilised behaviour.

In the years that followed the great revolt while the people nursed their resentment and while the British officers and civilians were racially arrogant, India was gradually transformed. The seething discontent of the people led to the birth and enlargement of the political awakening and expressed first in the movements of religious and social reforms in these territories also like the other parts of India and then in the political movements which led to the independence of India on 15 August 1947. It may be true to say that the year 1857 marked the beginning of a new era which ended in the transfer of power in 1947.

REFERENCES

1. N.E., para 434.
2. Charles Ball, *The History of the Indian Mutiny*, Vol. II (1858), p. 150.
3. Jawahar Lal Nehru, *Glimpses of the World History*, (Reprint : 1965), p. 428.
4. N.E., Appendix D.
5. *Ibid.*, Appendix N.
6. F.P. P. , C-2449, No. 133 of 1859.

Appendix I

An officer present at the scene of the execution of Raja Shankar Shah and his son, Raghunath Shah describes some of the incidents as follows :

"I have just come back from seeing the rebel rajah and his son blown from guns. It was an awful sight; but they richly deserved a far worse fate. Fancy - it has been found out that we were all to be roasted alive when caught! *He prayed, as he was being lashed to the gun, that his surviving children might be spared to burn us!!!* We went down to where the two guns were drawn up, with a detachment of infantry and cavalry, to prevent surprise - the cavalry rushing about to keep the people back from front of the guns. Soon afterwards the prisoners arrived, looking very apathetic and nonchalant; their fetters were knocked off on the ground. I was quite close to them, as we officers were inside a circle, close to the guns, into which the crowd was not allowed to come. They were then bound to the mouths of the cannon. The way is this :- You stand with your back to a cannon mouth, which is pointed to the back of the heart : you have now a very good idea of it. The artillery officers, when all was ready, gave the command in a loud, clear voice, 'Division! ready! fire!' A boom - a thud, as of a body falling - and all was over. You know I have a very soft heart, and would most likely have fainted, or got sick at home, if I had seen the same before these massacres; but I can assure you, that although I felt the awful solemnity of two souls going, with a prayer for murder upon their lips, before their God, yet I went up afterwards, with almost gratified feelings, to look at their faces, still thinking of Cawnpore, Delhi, Meerut, Jhansie, Bareilly, Fyzabad. The old man's face was quiet and severe (he never had moved a muscle the whole time before), as was also the young one's (a man of forty). Their legs and arms fell close to the canon mouths, they being tied; the head and upper part of the body being blown about fifty yards in front. Quite untouched their faces were, and quite quiet. It is a very quick death, as they can feel no pain, the region of the heart being at once blown away. This is nearly the only form in which death has any terrors for a native. If he is hung, or shot by musketry, he knows that his friends or relatives will be allowed to claim his body, and will give him the funeral rites required by his religion; if a Hindoo, that his body will be burned with all due ceremonies; if a Mussulman, that his remains will be decently interred, as directed in the Koran. But if sentenced to death in this form, he knows that his body will be blown into a thousand pieces, and that it will be altogether impossible for his relatives, however devoted to him, to be sure of picking up all the fragments of his own particular body; and the thought that perhaps a limb of some one of a different religion to himelf might possibly be burned or buried with the remainder of his own body, is agony to him."

Appendix II

A medical officer of the Bombay presidency gives the following description of an "execution parade:" - "This first parade was a horrible sight, but the blowing away from guns is most appalling. After the explosion, the grouping of the men's remains in front of each gun was various and frightful. One man's head was perched upon his back, and he was staring round as if looking for his legs and arms. All you see at the time is a cloud like a dust-storm, composed of shreds of clothing, burning muscle, and frizzing fat, with lumps of coagulated blood. Here and there a stomach or a liver comes falling down in a stinking shower. One wretched fellow slipped from the rope by which he was tied to the gun, just before the explosion, and his arm was nearly set on fire. Whilst hanging in his agony, under the gun, a sergeant applied a pistol to his head, and three times the cap snapped, the man each time wincing from the expected shot. At last a rifle was fired into the back of his head, and the blood poured out of the nose and mouth like water from a briskly-handled pump. This was the most horrible sight of all. I have seen death in all its forms - never anything to equal this man's end."

Appendix III

In a letter to Colonel Jamieson, the Commander of the British forces at Jabalpur, the mutineers of the 52nd explained their reasons for the desertion and mutiny and announced their intentions respecting Lt. Mcgregor, whom they imprisoned at Patan. This is the translation of the letter.

"To his Excellency, The Lord of Clemency, the Bountilful of the Age, his Excellency Colonel Sahib Bahadoor : may his power be perpetual!"

"After respects, the representation is this - that Shaikh Dianuth Allee (havildar-major), and Salar Buksh (naik), and Dirguz Singh (naik) - (here follows the names of ten sepoys) - and others whose names are unknown, these sepoys, sir, send here; and this regiment the havildar-major ruined, and said that the Major Sahib and Mason Sahib told the Madras sepoys to seize all the arms of the regiment and kill the men; then you will receive thirty rupees per man as reward, and be promoted to subahdar bahadoors. This speech the havildar-major made to the havildars on duty. If he had not said this we would not have deserted and saved our lives by flight, as only from the havildar-major's speech we deserted : it is proper that these men should by some means or other be sent to us - let them be seized and sent; we have committed no injury to the government; and as for the muskets and cartridge-boxes which we brought away with us, we have left our property in lieu thereof; having sold it, take the price; each sepoy left about thirty rupees' worth of property; also send pay for one month and fifteen days. We are men of honour, and are doing government service here. Your lordship answered, that 'the Madras sepoys are not under my authority;' then, having become helpless, we came away here by your order to save our lives; and on the 19th of May, when your officers fled, then we, being faithful to our salt, did not say anything to your lordship, and at that time the Madras regiment was not present; and when the Adjutant Sahib was attacked by a sepoy with a bayonet, if we had not been true to our salt, why did we seize the sepoy and make him over to you? And your highness is our lord and master; but when we did not find any way to save our lives, we fled and came here; and we had regard to your lordship's salt; if not, at that time we might have killed you. And, if you do not let those sepoys go, then this Sahib we will not kill, but, having bound him, will take him to Delhi; and if you will send those sepoys, then we will cause the Sahib to arrive where you are. Moreover, having seized those sepoys, send them with a guard of police, and it will be well, and if life remains, we will again be present in your service; we will not run away. This letter is written on the part of all the sepoys and non-commissioned officers. All sepoys, non-commissioned and commissioned officers, send salam."

Appendix IV

In the following letter written in Hindi to the mutineers of the 52nd Colonel Jamieson replied :

"To Buldee Tewarree, subahdar, and as many non-commissioned officers and sepoys who are well-wishers of the state, this advice is given - that the acts you have committed were without reason, and your ignorance and folly were great; in fact, what has happened has happened. But there is one way for your good, which, if you pay attention to, for your whole life you will remain saying, 'Bless the Colonel Sahib, and all the officers who wish our good.' The advice is this :- You have deserted, and all know that the punishment for desertion is great; but you do one thing, and you will not be punished here by us; on the contrary, we officers will solicit the governor-general to forgive your offences. The work is this:- Having brought Mr. Macgregor with you, come here without fear, and never think that any one will practice deceit with you, because when we have once written that no harm shall come to you, it shall not come. Again, what you write to send the havildar-major, &c., such a bad thing we cannot do, or ever will do; and when we showed them your petition, they expressed their willingness to go; but we will never let them go. Understand all of you, that up to this time nothing so bad had been committed which might not be pardoned; but if Mr. Macgregor is in any way hurt, or any robbing takes place, you will not escape by our endeavours to save you. Understand, also, that you have committed a very bad action; but the Colonel Sahib believes that many men have been taken away against their will, and to these men only is this advice given; for why should good men be ruined in company with the bad characters? Understand, also, that no further communication will be held with you, and not one single letter will be written; therefore, if you intend following this advice, do so quickly, because, after a delay of one or two days, your pardon will be hopeless. Whatever you do, do on seeing this letter. Why do you strike an axe in your own feet?

"P.S. - On arrival here you must take over your muskets to the colonel; afterwards - as the order comes from the governor-general - your pardon will be seen."

Appendix V

Foreign, Secret, Supplement, Cons., 30 December 1859, No. 358
List of leaders of Rebel bands in the Jubbulpore Division, for whose apprehension Rewards have been offered

No.	*Names*	*Caste*	*Residence*		*Amount (Rs.)*	*Remarks*
			Village	*Pergunnah*		
(1)	(2)	(3)	(4)	(5)	(6)	(7)
Jubbulpore district						
1.	Debee Singh	Gond	Nunney Konda	Kuttungee Singorgurh	200	Has been long a leader of rebels, reward has been already applied for but has not yet been sanctioned.
2.	Deo Kurun	Brahmin	Juberah	"	200	He is a Putteedar of Mouzah Juberah, has been long a leader of rebels, reward has been already applied for but has not yet been sanctioned.
3.	Himmut Singh	Gond	Mohoneah	Bilhery	200	Has been long at head of rebels.
4.	Bhao Singh	Gond	Nimkhera	"	200	" " " " " " " .
5.	Nawal Singh	Unknown	Elakas	Punnah	200	Inhabitant of Punnah Elaka.
6.	Gujraj Singh	"	"	"	200	" " " "
7.	Poorun Singh	"	"	"	200	" " " "

(1)	(2)	(3)	(4)	(5)	(6)	(7)
8.	Luchman Singh Thakoor	Gond	Narainpoor	Sonapoor	200	Has committed many atrocities.
9.	Moorut Singh	"	"	"	200	Has committed many atrocities, Joint Thakoor holders of Narainpoor.
10.	Juggut Singh	"	"	"	150	Has been long known as a chiefman in a Thakoorband of rebels.
11.	Kehree Singh Thakoor	"	"	"	100	Has been long known as a chiefman in a band of rebels.
12.	Raja Gungadhur	Gond	Mangurh	-	500	Elaka Dumoh.
13.	Bhoop Singh	Rajpoot	Khana	Sehorah	100	Has been long a chief rebel.
14.	Bahadoor Singh Thakoor	Gond	Jhilmilah	"	50	Mentioned as being with Narainpoor rebels.
15.	Ghybur Singh	Gond	Narainpoor	Sonepoor	50	Mentioned as being with Narainpoor rebels.
16.	Chyn Singh	"	"	"	50	" " " " " "
17.	Randheer Singh	Gond	Narainpoor	Sonepoor	50	" " " " " "
18.	Raja Meharban Singh	Lodhee	Heerapoor	-	500	Elaka Narsinghpoor, reward offered in Narsinghpoor Elaka.
19.	Mehpal Singh	Gond	Kunoja	Koombhee	500	This man attacked our police posts - Bhutgaon Chaka and Piprode and drove the police away.
20.	Khooman Singh Thakoor	"	Morgurh Mokas	-	200	Elaka Mundlah.
21.	Akbar Singh, brother of Nurbudda Bux	"	Thundwaree	Gosulpoor	200	Supposed assassin of Captain Tottenham

(1)	(2)	(3)	(4)	(5)	(6)	(7)
22.	Ram Lall	Gond	Sindorsee	Gosulpoor	50	One of the chief men with Nurbudda Bux.
23.	Nurbudda Bux	"	Agoria	"	200	This is the chief of one of the rebel gangs which looted Gosulpoor.
24.	Gunput Singh Thakoor	"	Umgaon	"	100	Long known as rebel
25.	Raja Aman Singh	"	Bhundera	"	100	On conviction.
26.	Koondun Singh	"	Narainpoor	Sonepoor	150	This man is one of note he took an elephant from a detachment.
27.	Tumal Singh	"	Alluroea	"	150	With the above.
28.	Guggut Singh	"	Burkhera	Burghy	100	One of the chiefs of the rebels who long kept a position in Pergunnah Burghy.
29.	Bahadoor Singh Thakoor Talookdar Temur	Lodhee	Lorhee	Burghy	100	One of the chiefs of the rebels who - Piperia long kept a position in Pergunnah Burghy.
30.	Bahadoor Kotwar		"	"	50	This man's name is mentioned one of those giving troubles in Pergunna Burella.
31.	Dewan Bhoput Singh	Lodhee	Lorhee Piperia	Burghy	50	Elaka Dumoh.
32.	Buksoo Bhoee	Gond	"	"	50	Vide No.30.
33.	Moha Singh Thakoor	"	Khari Deoree	"	-	Elaka Dumoh will be settled on receipt of from Lt.Nembhard.
34.	Dheeraj Singh Thakoor	"	Dubkia	"	50	Known as a leading man amongst the rebels.

(1)	(2)	(3)	(4)	(5)	(6)	(7)
35.	Beharee Brother of Goojraj	Brahmin	Garaghat	Burghy	50	Relatives and followers of the Garaghat chiefs.
36.	Ujub Singh - son of Jowahir Singh	"	"	"	50	-
37.	Gujraj Singh Thakoor	"	"	"	200	Two chiefs of Garhaghat party who have given trouble from the first.
38.	Jowahir Singh Thakoor	"	"	"	200	-
39.	Luchmun Singh Thakoor	"	"	"	50	Relatives and accomplices of above.
40.	Dheeruj Singh Thakoor - brother of Jowahir Singh	"	"	"	50	" " " " "
41.	Odaechund Singh	Bunea	Thanah	Patun Matumpore	100	Has joined the rebels from the first.
42.	Bhopal Singh Thakoor	-	Kuddo khera	Kuttungee Singorgurh	50	Joined with the Garaghat rebels.
43.	Merdar Singh relation of Jageerdar Garaghat	Brahmin	Garaghat	Patun Matumpore	50	-

(1)	(2)	(3)	(4)	(5)	(6)	(7)
44.	Bishen Singh relation of Jageerdar Garaghat	Brahmin	Garaghat	Patun Matumpore	50	-
45.	Newaj Singh relation of Jageerdar Garaghat	"	"	"	50	-
46.	Motee son of Gujraj Singh Jageerdar	"	"	"	50	-
47.	Peearch son of Gujraj Singh Jageerdar	Brahmin	Garaghat	Patan Matampore	50	Family of Garaghat Thakoor as rebels.
48.	Jugmohun Singh son of Jowahir Singh	"	"	"	50	
49.	Mehpal Singh son of Jowahir Singh	"	"	"	50	
50.	Nundos son of Jugmohan Singh	"	"	"	50	

(1)	(2)	(3)	(4)	(5)	(6)	(7)
51.	Kaloe, son of Luchmun Singh Thakoor	Brahmin	Garaghat	Patan Matampore	25	
52.	Thobun Singh son of Ramchurun	"	"	"	25	
53.	Kirut Singh son of Gurbar Singh	"	"	"	25	
54.	Imrut Singh	-	Mesagaun	-	50	In company with Meharban Singh, noted rebel.
55.	Seo Bux	-	Soonwara	Burghy	50	Fugitive after giving trouble in Burghy
56.	Pearch Thakoor	-	Thamee	-	50	" " " " " "
57.	Pertab Singh	-	Sookha Bhurutpoor	Burghy	100	" " " " " "
58.	Murdan Singh	-	Poura	-	100	Present with rebels who killed Major Jenkins.
59.	Seam Sa	-	Bejorce	Burghy	50	One of the men of note rebels in Burghy
Mundlah district						
1.	Guroor Singh Surburakar of the Ranee of Sohagpur	-	Sohagpur	-	500	Destroyed the Govt. Thanah and Kucherry at Sohagpur.
2.	Bulbhudur Singh, Talookadar of Kothee	-	Kothee	-	500	Destroyed the Govt. Thanah and Kucherry at Sohagpur and also Thannah at Kothee Nigwanee

(1)	(2)	(3)	(4)	(5)	(6)	(7)
3.	Bharut Singh, brother of Guroor Singh	-	Sohagpur	-	250	An accomplice of Guroor Singh
4.	Bijey Singh Thakoor of Shaipoora	-	Shaipoora	-	250	Destroyed Govt. Thana and Bungalow at Shaipoora
5.	Aman Singh, son of Ramgurh Rajah	-	Ramgurh	-	300	Has personally joined the rebels who have plundered the greater part of the Mundla Perganna.
6.	Sookai Deewan Mundla Raja of Ramgurh	-	"	-	200	Principal advisor of the Ramgurh Rebels.
7.	Puharee Havildar	-	"	-	200	Leaders of the Ramgurh rebels.
8.	Seetaram Havildar	-	"	-	200	" " " " "
9.	Bukroo Bhoee	-	Mehgaon	-	200	" " " " "
10.	Baiga Bhoee	-	Lapun	-	100	" " " " "
11.	Mungto Bhoee	-	Loria	-	100	" " " " "
12.	Doorga Dewan	-	Kairee	Sohagpur	250	Leader of Sohagpoor rebels.
13.	Gopal Singh	-	Ghoogre	Mundlah	100	Joined Ramgurh rebels.
14.	Anunt Singh	-	Ramgurh	"	300	Leader of Ramgurh rebels.
15.	Nund Lall	Dheemar	Mundlah	"	50	Subordinate of Ramgurh rebels.

(1)	(2)	(3)	(4)	(5)	(6)	(7)
Narsinghpur district						
1.	Meherban Singh	Lodhee	Heerapoor	Narsinghpoor	1000	Sanction of Govt. C.P.solicited to these awards
2.	Bulbhuder Singh	Brahmin	Sahujpoor	Deoree in Saugor	1000	" " " " " " " "
3.	Narwar Singh	Raj Gond	Delwar	Chaorpatha	1000	" " " " " " " "
4.	Delhan Sa	"	Mudunpoor	"	1000	" " " " " " " "
5.	Bhoop Singh	"	Gungaee	"	500	" " " " " " " "
Baitool district						
-	-	-	-	-	-	-
Hoshangabad district						
1.	Manik Lall Police	Brahmin	Ishanabad	Korah Zilla	100	Sanction to the rewards entered in Duffadar-Cawnpoor, this statement has not been obtained, but is herewith solicited.
2.	Ramsahaye, Police	Brahmin sepoy	Nutheepoor	Busbur Zilla Lucknow	100	
3.	Saligram, Police sepoy	"	Rewaree	Zillah Futtehpore	100	
4.	Buckteur Pandey Police Naik	"	Kunouz	Furruckabad	100	
5.	Sobhan Khan, Police Sepoy	Musulman	Sohagpoor	Hoshangabad	100	Reward offered 17th July 1857.

(1)	(2)	(3)	(4)	(5)	(6)	(7)
6.	Shaik Lall, Police sepoy	Musulman	Sohagpoor	Hoshangabad	100	Nos. 4, 5, 6, 7, 8 and 9 since apprehended.
7.	Doorga, Police sepoy	Aheer	Malgaon	Kurungurh - Zillah Cawnpore	100	
8.	Bhugwandeen, Police sepcy	Brahmin	Siabanee	Zillah Futtehpoor	100	
9.	Sahib Ally, Police sepoy	Masulman	Semiree	Hoshangabad	100	
10.	Daulat Singh Police	Rajpoot	Raghogurh	Holkar's territory	1,000	Reward offered 19th October 1857
11.	Mahmud Khan, Jumadar	Mewatee	Ryepoora	Nemawar	200	" " " " "
12.	Male Khan	"	Junjal	Nemawar	200	" " " " "
13.	Utmal Jemadar	"	Dudwas	"	200	" " " " "
14.	Bhore Khan, Jemadar	"	Kubruz	Holkar's territory	200	" " " " "
15.	Bodhe Khan, Jemadar	"	"	"	200	" " " " "
16.	Nanhe Khan, Jemadar	"	Mathnee	Elaka Nema-war Holkar's	200	" " " " "
17.	Golab Khan, Jemadar	"	Kunouz	Elaka Nemawar Holkar's terr.	200	" " " " "

(1)	(2)	(3)	(4)	(5)	(6)	(7)
18.	Kumurdeen Khan	Mewatee	Ambara	Nemawar Zilla Hoshangabad	200	Reward offered 19th October 1857
19.	Suhaboodeen Khan	Fukeer	-	"	200	" " " " "
20.	Maley Khan	Mewatee	Khareea	"	200	" " " " "
21.	Peer Khan	"	Berkheree	"	100	" " " " "
22.	Kadir Khan	"	Muhey	"	100	" " " " "
23.	Khyrattee Khan	"	Dehreea	"	100	" " " " "
24.	Bagh Singh	"	Sutwas	"	100	" " " " "
25.	Shere Khan	"	"	"	100	" " " " "
26.	Jugmul	"	"	"	100	" " " " "
27.	Sindah	"	"	"	100	" " " " "
28.	Nihal	Korkoo	"	"	100	" " " " "
29.	Putua alias Bhoora	Mewatee	"	"	300	Reward offered 16th November 1857
30.	Datar Singh	Rajpoot	Pahunteela	"	50	
31.	Soojan	Brahmin	"	Hoshangabad	50	
32.	Holker	Barhye	"	"	50	
33.	Luchmun	"	"	"	50	
34.	Eswunt Rao	Pundit	Sumsabad	Hurda	100	Reward offered 6th January 1858
35.	Ramgopal	Brahmin	Timarnee	"	50	" " " " "
36.	Dhora Singh	Gond	Futtehpoor	Zilla Hoshungabad	100	Dacoity and plunder of property value Rs. _ Reward offered 25th January 1858.

(1)	(2)	(3)	(4)	(5)	(6)	(7)
37.	Seora	Gond	Futtehpoor	Zilla Hoshungabad	50	Dacoity and plunder of property value Rs. _ Reward offered 25th January 1858.
38.	Duriao	"	"	"	50	" " " " " " "
39.	Nirput Singh	"	"	"	50	" " " " " " "
40.	Deochund	"	"	"	50	" " " " " " "
41.	Munsookh	"	Nudeewora Taluka	"	50	" " " " " " "
42.	Heera Lall	"	Mirdah Mugurdha	Bhopal	50	" " " " " " "
Nagode district						
1.	Nehpal Singh Chief of Myhere	Jogee	Myhere	-	2,000	
2.	Mukoond Singh	-	Punnat	-	2,000	
3.	Surjoo Pershad, chief of Bejeyraghogurh	Jogee	Bejeyraghogurh	-	3,000	
4.	Ganeshjoo, brother of Mukoond Singh	-	"	-	300	
5.	Budhoo Singh, uncle of Mukoond Singh	-	"	-	300	

(1)	(2)	(3)	(4)	(5)	(6)	(7)
6.	Lalla Chuter Singh, brother-in-law of Mukoond Singh	-	Bejeyraghogurh	-	300	
7.	Dewan Sarda Persaud	-	"	-	200	
8.	Dewan Dalgunjan Singh	-	"	-	200	
9.	Sheolall Baree, Killadar	-	"	-	100	
10.	Bijoo Bhistee	-	"	-	100	
11.	Rampershad, Thanadar of Kailwara	-	"	-	100	
Dumoh district						
1.	Indur Singh	Ghosee	Soojneepoor	Narsingurh	500	Has long been a leader of rebels and has committed many atrocities.
2.	Kishore Singh	Lodhee	Hindoria	Dumoh	500	" " " " " " " "
3.	Kushorey Mosul	"	"	"	100	" " " " " " " "
4.	Bhose Dewan	"	"	"	50	" " " " " " " "
5.	Kanjoo Jhulukwar	Brahmin	"	"	50	" " " " " " " "

(1)	(2)	(3)	(4)	(5)	(6)	(7)
6.	Heera Lall	Lodhee	Jerut	Nursingurh	200	Has long been a leader of rebels and has committed many atrocities.
7.	Hindoopur	"	"	"	200	" " " " " " " "
8.	Deokurn	"	Kindsoh	"	200	" " " " " " " "
9.	Bissam Singh	"	"	"	200	" " " " " " " "
10.	Surneet Singh	"	Balakote	"	200	" " " " " " " "
11.	Maure Singh	"	"	"	200	" " " " " " " "
12.	Sone Singh	"	"	"	200	" " " " " " " "
13.	Sonejoo Kuttarch	Brahmin	Huttah	"	100	Sir Punches of the rebels.
14.	Newal Singh Huzaree	Rajpoot	"	"	100	Sir Punches of the rebels.
15.	Telloke Singh	Boondela	Hurpalpoor	"	100	Rebel leader.
16.	Aman Singh	Rajpoot	Kareejole	"	200	" "
17.	Mulkhun Singh	Lodhee	Ubhana	"	200	" "
18.	Tejee Singh	"	"	"	100	" "
19.	Merban Singh	"	Tuppa Sura	Tejgurh	500	" "
20.	Bhopal Singh	"	Panjee Pueraee	"	100	" "
21.	Mamu Singh	"	"	"	100	" "
22.	Hansraj	"	Kaslooa	"	50	" "
23.	Maharaj Singh	"	"	"	50	" "
24.	Pertab Singh	"	Tuppa Ramgurh	"	50	" "

(1)	(2)	(3)	(4)	(5)	(6)	(7)
25.	Luchmun Singh	"	Puraseye	Tejgurh	50	Rebel leader.
26.	Jowahir Singh	"	"	"	50	" "
27.	Aman Singh	"	Sundhye	"	50	" "
28.	Pudum Singh Rajah	"	Kharee Deoree	"	50	" "
29.	Dowlut Singh	"	Mohra	"	100	" "
Seonee district						
1.	Goolab Puttaree	Gond	Singun Poory	Lucknadown	50	This man was one of the leaders of the attack on the Kedarpoor outpost and of that on several other villages.
2.	Luchmun	"	Rangajhary	"	50	" " " "

Camp
Commissioner's Office
The 5th March 1858

Sd. W.C. Erskine
Commissioner

Appendix VI

Foreign, Secret, Supplement, Cons., 30 December 1859, No.362
List of leaders of Rebel bands for whose apprehension Rewards have been offered or should be issued

No.	Names	Caste	Residence: Village and Pergunnah	Amount (Rs.)	Circumstances
(1)	(2)	(3)	(4)	(5)	(6)
Saugor district					
1.	Khooman Singh	Lodhee	Patan Pergh Benaika	400	This man has long been at the head of rebels and a proclamation has been issued for his apprehension alive by the Deputy Commr. of Saugor with reward sanctioned by Commr. in his letter No.A dated the 19th July 1857.
2.	Sheikh Rumzan	Mahomedan	Cawnpoor	500	A Soobhadar in the 42nd Regt. N. I. who set himself up as Governor of Saugor, reward has been offered for his apprehension and sanctioned by Commr's Letter No.15, dated the 24th August 1857.
3.	Dulmeer Khan	Puthan Mahomedan	Banee Saugor	250	Moonshee of the 42nd Regt. N.I who took an active part in the mutiny, reward has been offered for his apprehension alive and sanctioned by Commissioner's letter No.15 dated 24th August 1857.

(1)	(2)	(3)	(4)	(5)	(6)
4.	Acherjoo	Gond	Kunerah Pergh.Saugor	100	This man has long been at the head of rebels and has committed many atrocities, reward has been offered by the Commr. in his letter No.124, dated 21 September 1857.
5.	Bhugwan Singh	"	"	200	" " " " " "
6.	Seo Lall	"	"	100	" " " " " "
7.	Daulut Singh	Ponwar	Bumoree Ilaka Tehreere	1,000	This man has long been at the head of rebels, reward has been offered for his apprehension and sanctioned by Govt. C.P.
8.	Rajah Murdan Singh of Banpoor	Boondela	Banpoor	8,000	This man has invaded British territory assured the Govt. and proclaimed himself ruler. He has raised large forces and opposed troops, reward has been sanctioned by Govt. for his apprehension.
9.	Raja Umer Singh	Gond	Chaka Ilaka Bhopal	1,000	He plundered the villages Singhna, Ugrah, Sullia and Semra Gopal Mun, he is the leader of large band of dacoits and has committed many atrocities.
10.	Lala Doolare Lall	Kaith	Banpoor	1,000	This man is the chief advisor of the Rebel Rajah of Banpoor and leader of his forces at Nurriaolee.
11.	Maheep Singh	Boondela	Jaklone	1,000	He is a leader of rebels, has plundered the whole country and committed atrocities.
12.	Gundrup Singh	Purdhar	Pindrooa Pergh.Malthone	500	This man is a leader of rebels, has plundered many villages and been guilty of atrocities.

(1) (2)	(3)	(4)	(5)	(6)
13. Mairwan Singh	Lodhee	Heerapoor Ilaqua Jubulpore	1,000	This man invaded the Saugor district with a - band of plunderers, opposed the troops and levied blackmail on the inhabitants.
14. Ahmud Bux, Tehseeldar of Khorye	Mahomedan Shaikh	Jubulpoor	1,000	Was Tehseeldar of Khoryee and joined the rebels of Banpoor.
15. Peer Ally, Toomundar	Mahomedan Syed	Mauza Banker Pergh - Kote kasim in Gurgaon	500	This man was Toomundar of Khorye and joined the rebels of Banpoor.
16. Juswunt Singh	Lodhee	Patun	500	This man joined with Khooman Singh son of Bisram Singh.
17. Oomrao Singh	Boondelah	Jakhlone Ilaka Lullutpore	500	Has long been at the head of rebels, plundering villages and levying blackmail.
18. Doolajoo Duffadar of Sowars	Rajpoot	Jherouta Pende-ree Pergh. - Khimlasa	300	Duffadar of Sowars has joined the rebels.
19. Luchmun Singh, Lumberdar	Dangee	Hilgun Pergh.	500	Has long been at the head of rebels, plundering villages.
20. Tarwar Singh	Gond	Gora Pergh. Bhera	200	" " " " " "
21. Kishore Singh	Aheer	Julunder Pergh. Nurriaolee	500	This man was present with the rebels when they established their thanna at Jyseenugur, and was also present with Nabab of Amapanee and Patharee when they established their thanna at Rahutgurh.

(1)	(2)	(3)	(4)	(5)	(6)
22.	Permanund Rawut	Brahmin	Mulkwan Ilaka Shahgurh	1,000	This man is one of the Rajah of Shahgurh's accomplices, has long been at the head of rebels, and plundered numerous villages.
23.	Rajdhur Rawut	"	"	1,000	" " " " " "
24.	Sheo Pershad	Lodhee	Sema Dhana Pergh. - Saugor	200	This man is a relative of Permanund Rawut. Has long been at the head of rebels and plundered many villages.
25.	Futteh Singh	Dangee	Heerapoor	100	" " " " " "
26.	Thakoor Bhugwan Singh	"	Mouzah Tonsee Pergh. Rehlee	100	" " " " " "
27.	Doorjun Aovstee	Brahmin	Sanoda Pergh. Saugor	100	" " " " " "
28.	Rao Bukhut Bully	Boondela	Narhut Pergh. - Khimlasa	1,000	Has long been at the head of rebels, and established his Thannah at Malthone and Narhut.
29.	Koour Luchmun Singh	"	"	500	Has long been at the head of rebels, is a brother of the above.
30.	Thakoor Khoob Singh	Dangee	Mooar Ilaka Pitterah	100	Aiding in plundering.
31.	Jowaher Singh	Boondela	Chandrapoor Pergh.Khorye	200	This man plundered Mouzah Sanodah.
32.	Gangadhar Lumberdar	Brahmin	Burdia Pergh.-Nariaolee	200	This man plundered Mauzah Khasrye.
33.	Nerput Singh	Dangee	Boordha Khera	200	This man with Indur Choudhree plundered Mauza Puduria.

(1) (2)	(3)	(4)	(5)	(6)
34. Bhugwunt Singh formerly Lumberdar	-	Khirola Pergh.Dhamonee	100	This man plundered Mauzah Khirolah.
35. Mohun Singh	-	Hinota	100	This man with other rebels plundered Mouzah Gidwanee.
36. Oomaro Singh	Gond	Semra	100	This man with the Rajah of Chouka plundered the grain of Moheeb Singh.
37. Oomrao Singh	"	Kunera Pergh.Saugor	100	This man with other rebels plundered Mouzah Somlah Pergh. Saugor.
38. Mohan Singh Lumberdar	-	Heerapoor	200	This man with other rebels plundered Mouzah Bussia Bansha.
39. Mohun Singh	-	Semra Panraree	100	Aided in establishing the rebels' thanna at Soorkee
40. Luchmun Singh	-	"	100	Aided in establishing their thanna at Soorkee
41. Gunesh Puthairia	Brahmin	Khemaria Pergh.Rehlee	100	Aided the rebels at Gurra kotah.
42. Ram Ruttun Pathuk	"	Khokooree Pergh.Nuriaolee	200	This man with other rebels plundered Mouzah Hinota Pergh.Nuriaolee and also Mouzah Esurwara Pergh. Nuriaolee.
43. Rama	Boondela	Banpoor	1,000	He has long been at the head of rebels and plundered many villages.
44. Bodun Dowah	Aheer	Shahgurh	1,000	He is one of the chief advisors of the Shahgurh Raja and taken possession of the Rehlee Pergunnah.
45. Balmukoond Mukhtiar of the Raja of Shahgurh	Kaith	Saugor	1,000	This man has established his thanna at Banda in the name of Rajah of Shahgurh and attacked the British force, he is a rebel leader and been guilty of many atrocities.

(1) (2)	(3)	(4)	(5)	(6)
46. Maharaj Singh Dowah	Aheer	Shahgurh	1,000	This man plundered Mauzas Oolelun and Bhanswai and also the house of Rakhun Huzaree of Patua Gunj, he is a rebel leader and been guilty of atrocities, he is one of the chief officers in the Shahgurh rebel force.
47. Deewan Khooman Singh	Dangee	Pattae Pergh.Rehlee	500	This is a rebel leader and plundered many villages.
48. Luchmun Singh	"	Mokulpoor Pergh.Saugor	500	He has long been at the head of rebels and plundered many villages.
49. Ganeshjoo	Boondela	Narhut Pergh.Khimlasa	500	This man has long been at the head of rebels, plundered many villages and established Thanas in the name of Shahgurh Rajah.
50. Indur Choudharee	Ghosee	Soojneepoor Ilaka Dumoh	1,000	He has long been at the head of rebels, plundered many villages and been guilty of many atrocities, by mutilating Hurkaras and Government servants.
51. Dewan Upperbull Singh	Boondela	Durree Pergh.Doogaha	1,000	Has long been at the head of rebels and with Rajah Shahgurh's force established a Thanah at Malthone
52. Dewan Jodhan Singh	"	Amlea Pergh.Malthone	1,000	" " " " " "
53. Rao Bhopal Singh	Lodhee	Nemone Pergh.Benaika	1,000	This man plundered Mauzah Gidwanee and Birchow, and is in open rebellion.
54. Rao Balwunt Singh	Dangee	Gurhola Pergh.Khoorye	1,000	He has long been at the head of rebels and levying blackmail.

(1)	(2)	(3)	(4)	(5)	(6)
55.	Chintaman-Mookhtyar	Brahmin	Rehlee Ranee Tobunpoor	200	This man with other rebels established his thanna at Deoree and attacked the British force at Uchulpoor, and plundered many villages.
56.	Gopal Singh	Dangee	Uchulpoor Pergh.Rehlee	500	This man has long been at the head of rebels assisting the Shahgurh Rajah.
57.	Koonor Doolajoo	Boondela	Narhut Pergh.Khiml	200	This man has long been at the head of rebels assisting the Shahgurh Rajah.
58.	Koonor Dokul Singh	"	"	200	" " " " " "
59.	Koonor Duleep Singh	"	"	200	" " " " " "
60.	Koonor Gunesh Singh	"	"	200	" " " " " "
61.	Koonor Duryao Singh	"	"	200	" " " " " "
62.	Koonor Bahadoor Singh	"	Etawa Pergh.Doogaha	200	" " " " " "
63.	Koonor Urjoon Singh	"	Gora Kishungurh Pergh.Malthone	200	" " " " " "
64.	Koonor Murdan Singh	"	"	200	" " " " " "
65.	Bholejoo	"	Dhorey Pergh.Malthone	200	" " " " " "
66.	Chatoor Singh 1st	"	Bandree Pergh.Malthone	200	" " " " " "
67.	Chatoor Singh 2nd	"	Palethee Pergh.Doogaha	200	" " " " " "
68.	Nooel Singh	"	"	200	" " " " " "

(1)	(2)	(3)	(4)	(5)	(6)
69.	Girwar Singh	Boondela	Pethoria Pergh.Malthone	200	This man has long been at the head of rebels assisting the Shahgurh Rajah.
70.	Punchum Singh	"	Gooro Pergh.Khimlasa	500	" " " " " "
71.	Bishram Singh	Dangee	Bilehra Pergh.Saugor	200	This man has long been at the head of rebels aiding the Chouka Raja and plundering many villages.
72.	Kunhy Lumberdar	"	Singra Pergh.Saugor	200	" " " " " "
73.	Humer Singh Talookdar	Lodhee	Marlee Pergh.Rehlee	500	This man has long been at the head of rebels levying blackmail and looting villages.
74.	Dewan Gumbheer Singh	Boondela	Jakhlone Ilaka Lullutpore	200	Is a leader of rebels and plundered Mouza Noma.
75.	Lala Kurun Singh	Gond	Gorickpoor Ilaka Bhopal	200	This man with other rebels stopped the Dak on the Deoree.
76.	Gunesh Singh son of Punchum Singh	Boondela	Ghosi Pergh.Khimlasa	200	This man was amongst the Raja of Banpoor's force when he established his thanah at Khorye.
77.	Kurun Singh former Lumberdar	-	Khoorye	200	" " " " " "
78.	Ruttun Singh	-	Chainpoora Pergh.Nugurda Ilaka Bhopal	200	This man is a leader and plundered many villages.

(1)	(2)	(3)	(4)	(5)	(6)
79.	Boodh Singh	Purdhor	Bailyee Pergh.Bhera	500	This man with other rebels plundered Mauzas Bandrana, Bailyee, Lemra Pergana Bherah and Jagree Pergunnah Saugor and collected the revenue of several villages.
80.	Kusoreh, former Lumberdar	Aheer	Buseea Bhountee Pergh.Nuriaolee	200	This man plundered Mouzas Munow Pergh. Nariaolee and also Mouza Bussea Bhountee.
81.	Khem Chund Lumberdar	-	Jamondhana	200	This man with other rebels plundered Mouzas Banghur and aided the Nawab of Amapani in establishing his thanna at Rahutgurh.
82.	Kumod Singh	-	Pattaee	200	This man with other rebels plundered Mouzas Burdham Belyee, Semra Pergh. Bhera and Jagree Pergh.Saugor.
83.	Pershad Singh	-	Singrawun Pergh.Benaika	200	" " " " " "
84.	Kishore Singh	-	Tora Pergh.Rahatgurh	200	This man with the Raja of Chouka plundered Moheeps grain from Duddoo Deber.
85.	Beeharee	-	Bhapel Pergh.Saugor	100	This man with other rebels plundered Mouzas Puthoria and Ledhrah.
86.	Sanmut Singh	-	"	100	" " " " " "
87.	Deewan Sarnet Singh	Dangee	Pattaee Pergh.Rehlee	200	This man aided the Raja Shahgurh in establishing his thana at Rehlee.
88.	Deewan Bhuboot Singh	"	"	200	" " " " " "

(1)	(2)	(3)	(4)	(5)	(6)
89.	Golab Singh	Lodhee	Patun Pergh.Patun	200	This man aided in establishing a rebel thana at Benaika.
90.	Anunt Singh	-	Bhapail	100	This man with other rebels plundered Mouzas Puthora and Ledhrah.
91.	Dewan Aebelal	Gond	Pathoria Pergh.Dhamonee	100	This man plundered Mauza Pipuria Allaee and aided in the plunder of Kirola Pergh. Dhamonee.
92.	Doorjun Singh	Lodhee	Mugurdha Pergh.Benaika	100	This man with other rebels plundered Beharee Dobey's 90 maunds of wheat and 15 maunds of ghee.
93.	Mahadeo	Lodhee	Anjnaia Pergh.Benaika	200	This man with other rebels plundered Mauzas Peparia, Chumosee and Tinsooa.
94.	Dheraj Singh	Dangee	Sulya	200	This man with Luchmun Singh of Hilgun and Turbur Singh of Giraree aided in plundering and committing other atrocities.
95.	Jankee Dass Misr Obareedar	Brahmin	Jairwara Pergh Narialaa	100	This man aided the rebels and levied Blackmail.

Sd. W.C.Western
Dy.Commissioner 1st Class

Glossary

Adawlut	:	A court of justice.
Ameen	:	A person employed by a court to investigate accounts connected with a suit, to prosecute local enquiries.
Amil or Aamil	:	An officer of the Government in the finance department, specially a revenue collector.
Atta	:	Powdered grain
Bania	:	A member of one of the traditional trading castes.
Batta	:	Allowance.
Bazar	:	A permanent market or a street of shops.
Burukundauze	:	An armed retainer; an armed police-man.
Chabutra	:	A paved or plastered platform.
Chaprasee	:	Peon.
Chowki	:	Mounting Guard.
Chowkidar	:	A watchman. The word is usually applied to a private watchman. In north India the village Chowkidar is the rural policeman and he is employed for watch and ward in the small town.
Coss	:	In Bundelkhand it is nearly 3 miles
Cutcherry	:	An office of administration, a court house.
Dafadar	:	Commandant of a body of horse, head of a party of police, a police officer.

Durbar	:	The executive government of a native state.
Dussehra or Dashahra	:	A Hindu festival which celebrates the victory of good over evil, as exemplified in the victory of the Lord Rama over the demon king Ravana. It generally takes place in October.
Faqir	:	Mendicant
Feringhee	:	A general term used for Europeans.
Ghat	:	A landing place, a part of descent to a river or from a mountain.
Ghee	:	Boiled butter.
Ghuri or Ghuree	:	A little fort.
Harkara	:	A messenger; a spy; a courier; an emissary.
Haveli	:	Family seat of big Malguzar.
Hoondi	:	A bill of exchange in Indian language.
Jagirdar	:	A feudal chief who holds an assignment of land from a ruler in return for military service.
Jumma	:	Land revenue.
Kamdar	:	Agent
Kamvisdar	:	Pargana officer.
Khalsa	:	State.
Khas	:	Special, particular, royal.
Khilat	:	A dress of honour presented by a superior on ceremonial occasions.
Koorseenashin	:	Peson who had the privilege of obtaining a chair.
Kotwal	:	A police officer; Superintendent of Police; native town magistrate.
Lumburdar	:	The cultivator who, either on his

		own account or as the representative of other members of the village, pays the government dues and is registered in the Collector's Roll according to his number; as the representative of the rest he may hold the office by desent or by election.
Mahajan	:	A banker and merchant.
Malguzar	:	A former revenue collector on whom the British administration conferred proprietory rights on land.
Maund	:	Standard weight in British India of 40 *sers* of 80 tolas each or rupee weights and thus the maund 82 2/7lbs. avoirdupois.
Moharrum	:	The name of the first month of the Moḥammadan lunar year. In India the term is applied to the period of fasting and public mourning observed during that month in commemoration of the death of Hasan and his brother, Hussain.
Mukhtyar	:	An authorised agent.
Munsiffs	:	'One who does justice' (insaf), a judge. In British India, it is the title of the native civil judge of the lowest grade. This office was first established in 1793.
Nazar	:	Present offered to a superior.
Nizamat Adawlut	:	The court on the criminal side termed 'Nizamat Adawlut'.
Najeeb	:	A kind of half-disciplined infantry

soldier under some of the native governments; also at one time a kind of militia under the British; receiving this honorary title as being gentlemen volunteers.

Nazir : The title of a native official in the Anglo-Indian Courts.

Pakka house : Is of burnt brick or stone with lime and generally with a terraced plaster roof.

Panchayat : A council or court of arbitration (with five members).

Pargana : An administrative unit.

Patta : A tile deed.

Patel : The headman of a village.

Patwari : Village Accountant

Pugree : Turban

Raj : Rule

Salaam : Salute

Sunnud (Sanad) : A deed of grant by the government; privilege or right.

Sowar : A cavalry solider

Serishtadar : The head ministerial office of a court, whose duty is to receive plaints and see that they are in proper form and duly stamped, and generally to attend to routine business.

Surburahkar : One who is holding all the powers of the state next to Raja.

Suttee (Sati) : The rite of widow-burning i.e. the burning of the living widow alongwith the corpse of her husband, as practised by people of certain castes among the Hindus and eminently by the Rajputs.

Subedari	:	Province
Sudder (Sadar) Ameen	:	Chief Ameen. This was the designation of the second class of Native Judge.
Sudder (Sadar) Board	:	This was the Board of Revenue of which there was one at Calcutta and one in the North Western Provinces at Allahabad.
Taluqdar	:	The holder of an estate so designated.
Thug	:	An assasin who kills people by deception.
Ubari	:	A revenue-free grant.
Ubaridar	:	Holder of a ubari state.
Walayties or Vilayties	:	Foreigners or Europeans
Zamindar	:	In some parts of India collection of land revenue was done through hereditary agents, who in their turn collected it from their tenants. These agents were called landlords or zamindars.

Bibliography

(I) Original Sources

A. Manuscript

(1) The Record Room of the Government of Madhya Pradesh, Nagpur

The following original manuscript records of the Saugor and Nerbudda Territories preserved in the Record Room of the Government of Madhya Pradesh, Nagpur, pertaining to the period of my research-project were exhaustively consulted.

(i) Juppulpore Division, Bundle Correspondence

The records of the Jubbulpore Divisional Offices in the Central Provinces have been classified under various departments, political, revenue, judicial etc. They are really 'Bundle Correspondence' as all the records are bundled together without proper indexing, as such they are not systematically arranged.

(ii) District Records

The district records of all the eight districts of the Jabalpur Division, namely, Sagar, Damoh, Jabalpur, Narsinghpur, Hoshangabad, Mandla, Seoni and Betul are preserved here.

There was a great difficulty in consulting these records as they are not indexed at all. These original records form the basis of this research-project as they contain the detailed study of the events in these territories during the revolt of 1857.

(2) The Naional Archives of India, New Delhi

The Proceedings Volumes, Original Consultations, Letters from the Court of Directors to the Governor-General of India in Council and Letters to the Court of Directors from the Governor-General in Council of the following branches of several Departments pertaining to the period of my research-project were thoroughly consulted. The proper indexing of these documents greatly facilitate the work of my research-project.

(i) Home Department
- (a) Public Branch
- (b) Judicial Branch
- (c) Revenue Branch

(ii) Foreign Department
- (a) Secret Branch
- (b) Foreign Branch
- (c) Political Branch

(iii) Military Department

The original records in the National Archives of India, pertaining to the period of my research-project are not the detailed study of the events but they are precise. Hence, the author has consulted the original records at both the places at Nagpur and New Delhi for the detailed and precise description of the events in these territories.

B. Published Records

(1) Further Parliamentary Papers

The Government of India had asked Major W.C. Erskine, Commissioner of these territories on 22 June 1857 (*vide* Jubbulpore Division, Bundle Correspondence, Political Case File No.10 of 1857, p.109) to submit immediately a connected Narrative of Events which had taken place in the Saugor and Nerbudda Territories and in future submit weekly narratives. He had duly submitted the weekly narratives till the final submission of his narrative of events on 10 August 1858. These weekly narratives formed the bulk of the Further Parliamentary Papers presented to both House of Parliament by command of Her Majesty in 1858. These papers are a very rich source of information.

(2) Narrative of Events by Major W.C. Erskine

Major W.C. Erskine was asked by the Secretary to the North-Western Provinces on 30 April 1858 (*vide* Narrative of Events, para 1) to submit an historical narrative of the events attending the mutinies and rebellion in 1857-58 in his division until the final restoration of peace. Accordingly, he submitted on 10 August 1858 'the narrative of events attending the outbreak of the disturbances and the restoration of authority in the Saugor and Nerbudda Territories in 1857-58'. This can be said the first person account of this important event in this region. It contains almost a month to month account of the incidents that happened under his eyes. He was a witness to it or he got information from men who witnessed them. As such it contains material of unique importance. It was published in 1881. In the absence of the other accounts left over by the residents of these territories, about how the sepoys and civilians confronted the situation brought about by the outbreak, this narrative of events forms the primary source of this research-project. The author has liberally drawn from it in discussing the main events of the revolt in this region. At times it tells more of the British point of view of the event and as such we have to study it carefully and impartially.

C. Reports, Miscellaneous Publications and Gazetteers

(1) Reports

(i) Reports on the Land Revenue Settlement of the Saugor district, 1889-97 and 1911-16.

(ii) Report on the Land Revenue Settlement of the Jubbulpore District, 1886-94.

(iii) Reports on the Land Revenue Settlement of the Narsinghpur District, 1885-94 and 1923-26.

(iv) Report on the Land Revenue Settlement of the Hoshangabad District, 1891-96.

(v) Final Report of the Land Revenue Settlement of the Mandla District, 1904-10.

(vi) Report on the Land Revenue Settlement of the Betul District, 1894-99.
(vii) Report on the Land Revenue Settlement of the Seoni District, 1867.
(viii) Reports on the Administration of the Central Provinces, 1861-62, 1862-63, 1892-93.
(ix) R.M. Bird : Note on the Saugar and Nerbudda Territories, 1834.

(2) Miscellaneous Publications

(i) A Handbook to the Records of the Government of India in the Imperial Records Department, 1748-1859, 1925.
(ii) Acts of the Governor-General of India in Council, 1857-58.
(iii) Bundelkhand Agency Records.
(iv) Selections from Educational Records Vols. I & II, 1920.
(v) Wilson, H.H. : Glossary of Judicial and Revenue Terms, 1855.
(vi) Yule Henry and Burnel A.C. : *Hobson Jobson* : A glossary of Anglo-Indian colloquial words and phrases, 1903.

(3) Gazetteers

(i) Central Provinces District Gazetteers :
Betul (1906), Damoh (1906), Hoshangabad (1908), Jubbulpore (1909), Mandla (1912), Narsinghpur (1906), Saugor (1905) and Seoni (1907).
(ii) The Imperial Gazetteers of India :
Vols.I, II, VIII, X, XI, XIII, XIV, XVIII, XIX and XXII.
(iii) Madhya Pradesh District Gazetteers :
Betul (1971), Damoh (1974), Hoshangabad (1979), Jabalpur (1968), Narsinghpur (1971), Sagar (1967) and Seoni (1989). The District Gazetteer of Mandla is yet to be published.
(iv) Provincial Gazetteers of India :
Central Provinces, 1908.

(II) General Works

Aitchison, C.U. : *A Collection of Treaties, Engagements and Sanads*, Vol.III (1909) and Vol.V (1933).

Aitchison, C.U. : *Land Revenue Administration in the Central Provinces of India*, 1905.

Aitchison, C.U. : *Lord Lawrence*, 1916.

Baden, Powell, B.H. : *The Land Revenue Systems of British India*, Vol. II, 1974.

Baker, D.E.U. : *Colonialism in an Indian Hinter land: The Central Provinces, 1820-1920*, 1993.

Ball, Charles : *The History of the Indian Mutiny*, Vol. I & II (1858).

Bird, R.M. : *The Indian Mutiny*, 1858.

Chatterjee, N.L. : *India's Freedom Struggle*, 1958.

Chattopadhyay, H.P. : *The Sepoy Mutiny : A Social Study and Analysis*, 1957.

Chaudhury, S.B. : *Civil Disturbances during the British Rule in India (1765-1857)*, 1955.

Chaudhury, S.B. : *Civil Rebellion in the Indian Mutinies, 1857-1859*, 1957.

Chaudhury, S.B. : *English Historical Writings on the Indian Mutiny*, 1857-59, 1979.

Chaudhury, S.B. : *Theories of the Indian Mutiny*, 1965.

Chowfin, D.E. : *Society and Economy in the Sagar-Narmada Territories, 1818-61*, (unpublished thesis) University of Jabalpur, 1991.

Colchester, Lord, *ed.* : *History of Indian Administration of Lord Ellenborough*, 1874.

Collier, Richard : *Sound of Fury : The Indian Mutiny*, 1966.

Cunningham, A. : *Descriptive List of the Mutiny Papers*, 1860-63.

Devi, Ritambhari : *Indian Mutiny : 1857 in Bihar*, 1977.

Dharm Bhanu : *History and Administration of the North-Western Provinces*, 1955.

Dharm Pal : *Tatya Tope : The Hero of India's First War of Independence*, 1957.

Dighe, V.G. : *Peshwa Baji Rao I and Maratha Expansion*, 1944.
Dodd, G.D. : *The History of the Indian Revolt and the Expedition to Persia, China and Japan*, 1859.
Dodwell, H.H. *ed.*, : *Cambridge History of India*, Vol. VI, 1932.
Duff, A. : *The Indian Rebellion*, 1858.
Dutt, Romesh Chunder : *Economic History of India in the Victorian Age*, 1906.
Dyer, J.F. : *Introduction to the Land Revenue System of the Central Provinces*, 1924.
Embree, A.T., *ed.* : *India in 1857 : The Revolt against Foreign Rule*, 1963.
Forrest, Sir George : *History of the Indian Mutiny*, 3 Vols., 1904.
Forrest, Sir George : Selections from the Letters, Despatches, and other State Papers preserved in the Military Dept. of Govt. of India (1857-58), 4 Vols., 1893-1912.
Ganguli, Anil Baran : *Guerilla Fighter of the First Freedom Movement*, 1980.
Gupta, Bhagwan Das : *Bundel Kesari Maharaja Chhatrasal* (Hindi edition), 1958.
Gupta, Pratul Chandra : *Nana Sahib and the rising at Cawnpore*, 1963.
Harris, John : *Indian Mutiny*, 1973.
Haq, Syed Moinul : *Great Revolution of 1857*, 1968.
Herbert, Christopher : *Great Mutiny, India, 1857*, 1980.
Holmes, T.R. : *A History of the Indian Mutiny*, 1885.
Hunter, W.W. : *Marquis of Dalhousie* (Reprint), 1961.
Joshi, P.C. *ed.* : *Rebellion 1857, A Symposium*, 1957.
Kaye, J.W. : *A History of the Sepoy War in India, 1857-58*, Vols. I, II & III, 1870-76.
Kaye, J.W. : *The Administration of the East India Company*, (Reprint) 1966.
Kaye's & Mallesons's : *History of the Indian Mutiny*, of 1857-58, ed. G.B. Malleson, Vols. I to VI, 1880-97.
Keena, H.G. : *British Administration during the Revolt of 1857*, 1887.

Khan, Syed Ahmad : *Asbab-e-Sarkashi-e-Hind*, (Persian) 1859.
Lowe, T. : *Central India during the Rebellion of 1857-58*, 1860.
Majumdar, R.C. : *The Sepoy Mutiny and Revolt of 1857*, 1957.
Majumdar, R.C. : *The History and Culture of the Indian People : British Paramountcy and Indian Renaissance*, Vol. IX, 1963.
Malleson, G.B. : *History of the Indian Mutiny, 1857-58*, Vols. I, II&III, 1879-80.
Malleson, G.B. : *The Indian Mutiny of 1857*, 1891.
Malleson, G.B. : *The Mutiny of the Bengal Army by one who served under Charles Napier*, (Red Pamphlet) 1857-58.
Martin, R.M. : *The Indian Empire*, Vols. I & II, 1860.
Mcmunn, George : *Indian Mutiny in Perspective*, 1931.
Mead, H. : *The Sepoy Revolt : Its causes and its consequences*, 1857.
Mehta, Ashok : *1857, The Great Rebellion*, 1946.
Michael, Edwards : *Red year : The Indian Rebellion of 1857*, 1973.
Mishra, D.P. *ed.*, : *History of the Freedom Movement in Madhya Pradesh*, 1956.
Mishra, J.P. : *The Bundela Rebellion*, 1980.
Mukherjee, Rudrangshu : *Awadh in Revolt 1857-58, A Study of Popular Resistance*, 1984.
Nehru, J.L. : *Glimpses of World History*, 1935, Reprint 1965.
Norton, John Bruce : *The Rebellion in India : How to Prevent Another* ? (Reprint) 1988.
Panikkar, K.M. : *A Survey of Indian History*, 1954.
Pogson, W.R. : *A History of the Boondelas*, 1828.
Prajapati, H.L. : *Land Revenue System and Administration* (with special reference to Sagar district), 1986.
Prasad, S.N. : *Paramountry under Dalhousie* (Reprint), 1964.
Raikes, C. : *Notes on the Revolt in the North-West Provinces in India*, 1858.
Rawding, F.W. : *Rebellion in India, 1857*, 1977. *The Revolt in Central India, 1857-59*, Compiled in the Intelligence Branch, Army Head Quarters, India, 1908.
Rizvi and Bhargava : *Freedom Struggle in Uttar Pradesh*, 5 Vols., 1957-60.

Roberts, Field Marshal : *Forty One Year in India*, 1897.
Roberts, P.E. : *History of the British India under the Company and the Crown* (Reprint), 1945.
Russel, R.V. and Rai Bahadur Hira Lal : *The Tribes and the Castes of the Central Provinces of India*, Vol. III, 1916.
Russel, W.H. : *My Diary in India in the year 1858-59*, 1860.
Sardesai, G.S. : *The New History of the Marathas*, Vol. III, 1948.
Savarkar, V.D. : *The Indian War of Independence*, 1947.
Sen, S.N. : *Eighteen Fifty Seven*, 1957.
Sen, Snigdha : *Historiography of the Indian Revolt of 1857*, 1992.
Sengupta, Kalyan Kumar : *Recent writings on the revolt of 1857, A survey*, 1975.
Sen Gupta, Sankar *ed.* : *War of Independence : Centenary Souvenir*, 1957.
Sharma, Gautam : *Indian Army Through the Ages*, 1914.
Shrivastava, M.P. : *The Indian Mutiny, 1857*, 1979.
Sil, J.N. : *The History of the Central Provinces and Berar*, 1917.
Sinha, R.M. : *Bhonslas of Nagpur*, 1967.
Sinha, R.M. : *1857 in the Jabalpur District*, 1957.
Sinha, S.N. : *Rani Laxmi Bai of Jhansi*, 1980.
Sinha, S.N. : *The Revolt of 1857 in Bundelkhand*, 1982.
Sleeman, W.H. : *Rambles and Recollections of an Indian Official*, 1915.
Stokes, Eric : *Peasant armed : The Indian Revolt of 1857*, 1986.
Tara Chand : *History of the Freedom Movement in India*, Vol. II, 1967.
Tahmankar, D.V. : *The Ranee of Jhansi*, 1958.
Thompson, Edward and Garratt, G.T. : *Rise and Fulfilment of British Rule in India*, 1934.
Warner, Lee : *Life of the Marquis of Dalhousie*, Vol. II, 1904.
Weighman, A.J. : *No Friend for Travellers*, 1956.

Index